Insights into Uganda

Kevin O'Connor
aka 'Roving Eye'

TOURGUIDE PUBLICATIONS
www.foutainpublishers.co.ug

Tourguide Publications
P.O. Box 488
Kampala
E-mail: info@tourguide-uganda.co.ug
E-mail: tourguide@foutainpublishers.co.ug
Website:www.tourguide-uganda.co.ug

An imprint of Fountain Publishers Ltd

Distributed in Europe, North America and Australia by African Books Collective Ltd (ABC), Unit 13, Kings Meadow, Ferry Hinksey Road, Oxford OX2 0DP, United Kingdom. Tel: 44(0) 1865-726686, Fax:44(0)1865-793298.E-mail: abc@africanbookscollective.com Website: www.africanbookscollective.com

© Kevin O'Connor 2016
First published 2016

All rights reserved. No part of this publication may be reprinted or reproduced or utilised in any form or by any means, electronic, mechanical or other means now known or hereafter invented, including copying and recording, or in any information storage or retrieval system, without permission in writing from the publishers.

ISBN 978-9970-637-39-3

Contents

Preface .... *xi*

1: Gender and Sexual Orientation
Let's castrate Kadokech 1
Good riddance to bad rubbish! 4
Ugandan women better than men 6
Miniskirts – Buturo requires a brain transplant 8
Obama, Zuma and polygamy 9
When is something un-African? 11
Some truths about homosexuality 13
The long and short of it 15
To bend or not to bend? 17
Why women sit the way they do on *boda-bodas* 18

2: Sex and Love
It's better to kiss in public 22
Bukenya, Nakku is a non-issue 24
Polygamous? What's your motivation? 26
Mystery Date wins Uganda "Snob of the Year" award . 29
Big Brother Africa – a case study in polygamy? 31
Kazini, Zuma and polygamy 33
Lower Uganda's age of consent to 16 years 36
Why are Ugandan bars so dark? 38
Of bums, hips and manhoods 40
"Ask Uncle Kevin" – new problem page 42

Unhappy Valentine's Days.. 44
Sex in Uganda's crowded rooms 46
When a Ugandan woman does not "produce"............... 48
Ugandans and their secrets 50
Ugandans and zero sons and daughters......................... 51
Norbert Mao will win the race 53
Chips chicken better than sex!.. 54
Let's celebrate International Childfree Day.................. 56

3: *Bazungu* (white people)
The Irish, tribes and jokes... 60
Mourning an animal corpse 62
Slow *muzungu* loves Ugandan slowness 64
Perverts, paedophiles and pencils 66
Muzungu v Ugandan eccentricity 69
Would you eat while walking?.. 72
Old *muzungu* gets dirty looks... 74
Time to say "goodbye" to the colonial suit and tie....... 76
Ugandan and *bazungu* nicknames 78
A *muzungu's* "long call" too far...................................... 79
Drinking beer from bottle, glass or straw?.................... 81
A rich *muzungu's* hair transplant 83
Things that might surprise a *muzungu* in Uganda........ 84

4: The Environment
Uganda, the pearl of bird watching................................ 88
You don't always have to behave..................................... 90
Old buildings deserve respect.. 92
The tiny difference between success and failure 94

Fish, cattle and paving stones 96
Would you put a cup of tea on the ground? 98
Drinking and dropping a "duck's soda" 101
Sir Alex Ferguson and Uganda's historic buildings 103
Where are Kampala's parks? 105
Some animal pupu issues 107
Why tarmacking roads might not be a good thing 108

5: **Religion**
"Never mock God!" Well, yes and no 112
No HIV/AIDS cures at crusades 114
Frowning upon gospel opportunists 116
Pastor Kiwewesi's disgraceful wedding 118
Pastors – why no pothole miracles? 120
Archbishop's priorities are wrong 122
Archbishop Orombi helps set world record 124
Did Christianity generate a culture of
lies in Uganda? 125
The telling of lies in Uganda – Part Two 127
How religion brainwashes us 130
Ug Sh 12 million wasted praising
Archbishop Orombi 132
Sodomy, pasta and miracles 134
Have no faith in faith 136
Execution is always wrong 138
Missionaries brought already damaged
goods to Uganda 140
The Catholic Church's funeral 142
There is no God 144
Sundays – to work or not to work? 145

6: Language

"Move over, I have diarrhoea!" 148
Unintended humour in a Kampala toilet 151
Now you wouldn't misspell 'misspell', would you? 153
Is the mobile phone destroying Uganda's greeting culture? 155
Will you laugh at my jokes? 157
Bigmen, smallmen and humour 159
The story about "storage" 161
"Apology" and "forgiveness" – more than just words 163
Keep English simple 165
Ugandan greetings made easy 167
How to find the meaning of fascinating phrases 169
Why do Ugandans say "Er?!"? 171
Ugandans' overuse of "over" 173
Enkya never comes 174
Proverbs and culture 176
Are you able to mimic? 177
"OK please" is OK 179
A book you can't put down 180
Some unusual names 182

7: Sport

Lessons from the MTN marathon 185
Why more Ugandans should support smaller Premiership teams 188
Let's kill off American sports scholarships 190
Making the right choices 193
Athletics has shown me Uganda 195
Ludo a sport? How ludicrous! 197

Pity those who don't understand sport 199
Beijing Olympics – there will be no medals for Inzikuru 202
God bless the underdog 204
FDC calls for unlimited term limits 206
Ugandan patriotism destroyed by English Premier League 208
Sitting and standing in football stadia 210
When neocolonialism won at the Cecafa Cup 213
Idi Amin's Golden Age? 215
An athletics training experience for Cranes' footballers 217
Two World Cup memories 219
Namboole Stadium – learning from the past 221
Namboole Stadium – a national disgrace 222
60th Anniversary of the 4-minute mile 224
The Margaret O'Hogartaigh Women's 5000m Memorial Race 226
Did Cheptegei "choose money over honour"? 229

8: Music

Music to soothe the soul 232
The *sagala* song hits Uganda 234
Lucky Dube's songs will never die 237
UB40 – No money to go 240
Is Juliana getting fat? 243
The late, great Lucky Dube lives on 245
What music at your funeral? 247
Disco music and much else spoils my football viewing 248

Unhappy and happy New Year's Eves 250
What music motivates you? 252

9: Education
MUK graduates, I have no money for your parties! ... 255
PLE results boredom 259
Journalistic corruption and PLE results 261
Don't send children to single sex schools 263
Oral communication skills are key to your career ... 265
"Back to school" and bullying 268
Examination worries 270
Study less for higher grades 271
Good and bad memories 273
Memories of teachers 274
Ugandans' educational concerns 276

10: Media
Truth, lies and advertising 279
The advantages of journalists' misspelling 282
USPA should right its shameful omission 284
Kevin evicts *Big Brother Africa* 285
Beware of ambiguous headlines 287
Allegations, allegations and more allegations 289
Roving Eye relaunch 291
Your newspaper – the business page meets the sports page 293
Journalists in love with photos of themselves 296
Red Pepper's Friday 13 superstitious nonsense 298
Is O'Connor a "scumbag"? 300
Phrases too loved by journalists 302

A "Kandahar" whopper 304
MPs swearing-in overkill 305
Dead but not dead! 307

11: Poverty and inequality
Sporting inequality and cars 310
Brave Mukula bathed in cold water 312
Electrocuted by a hotel's prices and fence 314
1920s UK and 2009 Uganda – some similarities 316
How much would you need to be paid to ....?.... 319
137 years to earn what Ronaldo gets in a day 321
Of economic and social inequality 322
A British dog causes surprise in Kampala! 324
Jamwa – more guilty than of being fat? 326
Akright should sack its ad agency 327
Too poor to buy a newspaper 329
Why are you not rich? 331

12: Health and death
Grey hairs all over the Queen's land 335
Burn me when I die! 337
Making use of a digital weighing scale 339
Obituaries – lies and more lies 341
Would you shake hands with Jim Muhwezi? 344
Antiretroviral drug money "eaten" 346
Budget should increase tobacco taxes 348
When you should use the "F-word" 350
The man who saved my life 353
Unseasonal thoughts on death 355

Could tobacco play a part in Uganda's population control?........358
The dangers of alcohol........360
Pet insurance – whatever next........362
Do you pick your nose?........364
All good wishes to Mr Gureme........366
Shortages and corruption in the health sector........367

13: *Katogo* (mixture)
Hurdles in telling humour........370
In trouble for speaking out........372
To comb or not to comb – that is the question........375
Bus passengers must be more outspoken........378
Kevin meets a seer........380
Gadaffi renames Uganda........382
Resignation – not the Ugandan way........384
Getting on top of your problems........386
How I pity corporate managers of 2009........389
Children, church and carnage........392
A small lie told in Kampala........394
The importance of the 50th anniversary........395
O'Connor and hand movements........397
Learning something new........399
Construction ignorance........400
Five, not four, jokers in a pack........402
Nabbed by the traffic cops........403
Spam, spam and spam........405
Why I fear driving........406

Glossary........409

Preface

Insights into Uganda is a selection of my *Roving Eye* newspaper articles published in the *Sunday Monitor* mainly in the 2007 – 2011 period, plus new articles written in 2015, specifically for this book.

Many topics are covered, but I have steered clear of politics – both because my knowledge is not that great, and because I feel that this is a subject for Ugandans, rather than a foreigner, to address.

I must give special thanks to my parents – my late father Pat and my mother Betty - who ensured I received the education that they never had the opportunity to enjoy. If I had been required to leave school at 14 years, like they and most children of manual workers were in the 1930's, my life would surely have been very different.

I would like to thank Charles Bichachi of the *Monitor* and Joseph Bugabo of *Tourguide Publications* for their support and encouragement. I am similarly indebted to Bernard Atuhaire.

My gratitude goes out to the many Ugandans whose comments and views have found their way into the articles. For reasons of anonymity I have often changed your names, but I have always tried to stay true to the accuracy of what you told me. Similarly, many of your quotes are the words as spoken, and have not been changed for grammatical reasons.

As I said in the preface to my first book *Ugandan Society Observed*, I must thank Uganda. As I walk slowly and languidly around, it strikes me that, (with the exception of driving vehicles), your character and my character share much in common; and, Uganda, you gave me chances to flourish, in journalism and athletics coaching, which would never have come my middle-aged way in my country of birth.

And finally, the greatest thanks of all are reserved for my wife, Sue. She provided the ideas for many articles and proofread most. She, to use the words of a man I greatly admire, Professor Richard Dawkins, "coaxed me through all my hesitations and self-doubts." Throughout the 34 years we have known each other, Sue has encouraged me on to higher levels of achievement that I could not possibly have attained by myself.

Kampala
December 2015

1

Gender and Sexual Orientation

Let's castrate Kadokech
(8 April 2007)

Very, very occasionally, one reads a newspaper article that is so, so foolish and so, so stupid that one wonders if the male writer has had their brain removed by Masculine Intellectual Mutilation (or MIM) before they put pen to paper. For such an article ("Female circumcision is a cultural right," *The New Vision*, 22 March 2007, p11) was written by Mr. S. Kadokech (Director, Budaka Community Development Initiative).

FGM's dangers

Kadokech argued that female circumcision – more commonly know as female genital mutilation (FGM) – was part of the Ugandan/African cultural heritage and, therefore, should be preserved (while being made medically more safe).

The article has fortunately generated many articles and letters condemning Kadokech's nonsense (e.g. "Female genital mutilation more gross than you thought" by Irene Mulyagonja, *The New Vision*, March 30 2007, p10). These articles have rightly highlighted the many medical dangers, sometimes fatal, of FGM during circumcision and during childbirth. So, I will not repeat these dangers here.

Sexual pleasure

However, FGM involves the removal of the clitoris which means that *the woman cannot then experience an orgasm during sex*.

Kadokech is, therefore, totally wrong when he writes:

> "Female circumcision can be compared to the Islamic and Jewish practices of male circumcision, which even Jesus Christ consented to."

Unlike FGM, male circumcision does **NOT** result in a loss of orgasmic/sexual pleasure.

The correct male comparison with FGM is not circumcision, but castration, where a man's testicles are removed.

Kadokech should only support FGM, if he is prepared to undergo castration. I do not foresee any prospect of a testicleless Kadokech, so he is not only wrong in his views, he is also a hypocrite.

FGM and culture

How do the Kadokechs of this world get it so wrong? It is that they don't recognise that every culture in the world has its good points and its bad points. The good points, one seeks to preserve and the bad points, one seeks to change.

Thus the defilement of housegirls by male members of the household (often the husbands, fathers or uncles who employ them) is undoubtedly a part of Ugandan culture, for it has existed as long as anyone can remember. But, would Kadokech argue that we should seek to preserve such defilement as it is part of the culture? Of course not. It is right we should change the culture by providing the maximum protection to the exploited, underage housegirl.

The same reasoning applies to the efforts of the many Ugandans who have sought to end FGM in this country. Thus, as Phillip Briggs writes ("Uganda – The Bradt Travel Guide" p439), when the Sabiny Elders Association was formed in 1992, it "aimed to protect the Sabiny culture by preserving songs, dances and other positive customs, but also wanted to eliminate more harmful traditions, most notably FGM."

If female genital mutilation is what Kadokech calls circumcision, then male genital mutilation (MGM) is castration. One cannot support FGM without supporting MGM. So, hurry up Kadokech, show us your testicles – we want to cut them off!

Good riddance to bad rubbish!

(11 November 2007)

A recent *Roving Eye* told the story of Mary, whose boyfriend David, without telling her, removed the condom during a sex session, as he wanted her "to produce".

Mary is not a goat, but a 21-year old Ugandan woman, who has many plans and ambitions over the next 5 years, and whose salary pays for her siblings' school fees. She, therefore, did not wish to get pregnant until her mid to late twenties.

The good news is that Mary was neither impregnated, nor infected with HIV and speedily ended the relationship. But Mary's story begs the following question:

- What is it about Ugandan men or the country's culture, or stage of socioeconomic development, which made David behave in such a nastily selfish way?

I turned to some Ugandan women friends for an answer to these questions.

Choice of words can say much about the attitude and values of the speaker, and it was David's choice of words that was picked up by Dorothy, a 40-year-old school manager. She observed:

> "*Produce*, meaning to have a baby, just shows the still predominant belief amongst Ugandan men that women are baby machines."

Similarly, Irene, a 34-year-old senior sports official, saw men such as David as:

> "Regarding women as tools of production for manufacturing human beings, irrespective of the needs and responsibilities of the woman to her siblings and parents."

So, indeed, David did regard Mary a bit of a goat, and whether he used the same sexual position as used by goats, I have no idea. And if "goat" is too harsh, implying that David thought of Mary as a sub-species, there is no doubt that his behaviour was fuelled by gender inequality. Back to Dorothy:

> "Relationships in Uganda are still very much a man calling the shots. Many women would be flattered if their boyfriend is trying to get them pregnant. So, a man can take it upon himself to think she would be thrilled if he said 'I want you to produce.'"

And Irene added:

> "Women are expected to be submissive and many men believe what can 'tie' a woman to a man is having children. A woman, especially a traditional one, will always find it difficult to leave a man once she has a child with him as society considers her 'second-hand' property. Selfish and insecure men try all means to put a woman in a situation that benefits them, including impregnation. This could be the case with David, who wants to tame Mary!"

When Mary told me her story, my overwhelming feeling was that 'you will never be able to trust that man again' whether it be in love, in money or in whatever. We can try appreciate the societal factors that have shaped David's attitudes, but when he removed that condom without informing Mary, his behaviour was absolutely despicable. He could have ruined her life, her dreams. If, when she red-carded David, Mary had shouted at him "Good riddance to bad rubbish", her words would have been more than justified.

Ugandan women better than men
(23 March 2008)

As I am an author, journalist and volunteer athletics coach, I hope nobody thinks I am an idler. There is a group, sometimes groups, of idlers in every trading centre in Uganda. They may be idle, but they are often smart, for as Carol Natukunda explains in her recent article, "Idling as a way of life" (*Sunday Vision*, March 16 2008):

> "It doesn't cost that much to acquire a corporate image; just get hold of an old newspaper and a file folder, put on your designer clothes and shoes bought at a fraction of their value in Owino Market, and you can hang out anywhere in the city without causing too much suspicion."

But Natukunda did seem to miss one key point about idlers – they are almost always ...... men.

Now, there are many wonderful, hardworking and high-achieving men in Uganda. But, while one should always be wary of generalisations, if we talk averages, then the average Ugandan woman is significantly more impressive than the average Ugandan man. The late, great Lucky Dube, sings "God Bless the Women" and in Uganda one rarely sees a woman doing nothing.

So why do males have almost a monopoly of idling. David, an assistant in a Kampala shop, said, "It is because ladies stay in their homes. Men go out and look for money. But some end up idling on the street."

Sarah is 35 years old and sells vegetables from a small stall. She observed:

> "Yes, idlers are all men not women. They are lazy. Women are accustomed to working. They are not idlers."

In my local trading centre, there is a group of men who sit in a shaded area just outside a lodge. I have seen them drinking crude *waragi* as early as 7.30 in the morning. A man, who lives next to the shaded area, told me:

> "These men are self-employed businessmen who work at night or are landlords who own the houses next to the shaded area."

When I repeated these comments to Sarah, she forcibly stated:

> "That man is lying, and is probably an idler himself. The landlords do not stay there. Those drinkers are idlers."

While David added:

> "The ones who take *waragi* are not responsible men. Some are even kids, sometimes from rich homes. Those men do not work at night. For if they did, they would not booze in the morning, but in the afternoon. He was definitely lying to you – those men are idlers."

It would take me about 5 *Roving Eye* columns, or possibly a PhD, to do a thorough gender analysis of Ugandan men and idling. So let me leave the final words to one man who definitely was not an idler – Lucky Dube:

> "We, praise heroes everyday
> But there are those that we forget to praise
> The women of this world.
> They don't run from anything
> They stand and fight for what's right......
> God bless the women."

Miniskirts – Buturo requires a brain transplant

(28 September 2008)

It is not yet October, but Ethics and Integrity Minister, Nsaba Buturo, may have already won *Roving Eye*'s annual nonsense prize.

Buturo said (and I assume he was not joking) that miniskirts should be banned – because women wearing them distract drivers and cause traffic accidents!! And, dear reader, I am afraid it gets worse, for he went on to say that wearing a miniskirt was like walking naked in the street!!

Can you imagine a naked Mr Buturo walking along Kampala Road, manhood dangling and all of that? Well, you should try, because I assume he sometimes wears shorts, and the male equivalent of his comments is that Buturo wearing shorts is like Buturo walking naked in the street.

But the worst part of the Buturo nonsense is their implicit demeaning of Uganda's road carnage. My wife and I drove last week from Kapchorwa to Kampala and there was all the normal overspeeding, overtaking on bends etc. by hundreds of cars, *matatu*s and lorries. And do you know something? I did not see one woman wearing a miniskirt to hold responsible for such bad driving.

The number of road accidents caused by a male driver looking at a miniskirted woman (or, dare one add Mr Buturo, a woman driver looking at a man who nicely fills his trousers, in the way that perhaps you do) must be such a tiny fraction of one percent, that they are not worth worrying about.

Mr Buturo is a representative of a patriarchal society where men have been dominant historically, and remain so into the present. Throughout the world, the large percentage of sexual attacks are performed by men on women, not vice versa. And when it comes to kids being raped, the huge majority of the victims are female. A primary schoolgirl or a housegirl, rarely has to wear a miniskirt to provoke male aggression.

And the same male aggression results in aggressive driving on the roads. Almost all the "overspeeders" are male – driving fast is their vehicular way of saying "look at my big thrusting manhood". In contrast, most of the slow, careful drivers are female.

One of the results of men dominating a society for centuries is that they shape its value system so that women take the blame. So, who is to blame for road accidents? – women in miniskirts; to blame for sexual attacks? – women in tight pants; to blame for prostitution? – female prostitutes, not their male clients. And it goes on and on. So, lo and behold, when a couple do not "produce", who is to blame? It is, of course, the woman, automatically assumed to be "barren".

The ban should not be on miniskirts but on men mouthing meaningless nonsense.

Obama, Zuma and polygamy
(1 February 2009)

Barak Obama Senior abandoned his son and was married to 3 women at the same time. Jacob Zuma has, at the last estimate, 5 wives and 18 children.

What do these facts tell us? They tell us about the difficulty that polygamous penises have in staying inside their polygamous pants.

They also tell us about some of the disadvantages of polygamy.

Let's start with Zuma. I have no idea whether he is, or is not, guilty of corruption (of spending government funds on his own home, for example). But if he is guilty, then one of the reasons widely put forward for him taking money that was not his, is the need to financially support his huge family.

And as regards Obama Senior, the polygamous disadvantage is that it is not he, but the mother, who has been recognised to have shaped President Obama. So, while the media go on and on and on in boring fashion about the new President of the United States being partly Kenyan or East African, the reality is that like so many African children born of polygamous relationships, Obama Junior was brought up by his mother. Indeed, so shaped was he by his mother and his maternal grandparents, the new President is about as African American as Tom Cruise or Brad Pitt.

John, 22, is an assistant in a Kampala shop and a part-time Makerere University Business School student. He observed:

> "Obama Senior was a typical African man. Most men here, they get money and they marry as much as they can. Some marry as many as 20 wives. The US President's father generally had money and he married more than one woman. Such behaviours is what we African men do. At the very least, you add a concubine."

> "However," continued John, "to be fair to Obama Senior, it was more than just his African background. For a black

then to be married to a *muzungu* was very unusual in the USA at that time. He experienced racism. If it was not for that racism, he would surely have spent more time with his son."

Is it not rather sad how Africa has tried to cling to the supposed "Africaness" of President Obama? As well as being polygamous, the President's father was a drunkard. In other words, he was like a lot of other African men who everyday one sees at a Ugandan local trading centre. And he deserves about as much respect as they do i.e. zero. It is a pity that Obama Senior did not take as much interest in his son as he did in his booze.

Polygamous penises, if they can't stay inside their pants, should at least put condoms on. The world would be a better and less over-populated place, if they did.

When is something un-African?

(15 February 2009)

The phrase "XXXX is un-African" is used widely in Uganda, and with good reason. The cultural and economic domination of the First World over the Third World, whether it be the colonialism of the past, or the neo-colonialism (especially in the media) of today, means that Africans are naturally keen to hang on to their cultural heritage and roots.

But sometimes I think the term "XXXX is un-African" can provide an excuse for Africans to disengage their brains from their hearts.

For example, how often do we hear, "homosexuality is un-African"? Yet, as Njoroge wa Kamau pointed out in a letter to *The East African* newspaper, "the proposition that male homosexual relationships are alien to African culture is refuted by ample anthropological evidence ...... from Sudan to Zululand."

And as regards Uganda, let us consider the 1880's, and use a quote about homosexual realities from none other than Pastor Martin Ssempa (*The New Vision*, June 3 2005, Page 8).

> "Kabaka Mwanga's homosexuality is an issue we tiptoed about for fear of offending the Buganda monarchy, which abhors homosexuality. But all historical accounts agree that Mwanga was a deviant homosexual who used his demigod status to appease his voracious appetite for sodomy by engaging in these unmentionable acts with his pages at court."

In the 1880's, there was no internet, no foreign films or magazines, and some, but not yet huge, influences on Uganda from outside Africa. So what was responsible for Kabaka Mwanga's homosexuality other than himself and his own (African) culture?

Turning to religion, every Sunday I get asked *ad nauseam* by Ugandans – have you prayed today? Have you been to church? Yet, Christianity did not arrive in Uganda until the late nineteenth century. So, therefore, is Christianity African or un-African?

Christianity has achieved much in schooling and health in Uganda. But, as this column has frequently argued, given widespread dishonesty and tribalism, Christianity has been an abject failure in persuading Ugandans to "treat their neighbours as themselves."

Found in different Ugandan languages is the expression "whatever happens in the house must stay in the house," or its equivalent. Perhaps there should be a new expression –

"whatever happens in the church must stay inside the church." For dishonest behaviour Monday to Saturday seems to remain majestically untouched by Uganda's widespread Sunday churchgoing.

I am not African. But I have lived in Africa for approaching 20 years. So, as a believer of the much greater influence of "nurture" over "nature", I am presumably not now fully un-African.

I cannot, though, become tribalistic, since I find it virtually impossible to recognise anybody's tribe from their features or their speech!

But perhaps I should change my name to Kevin O'Corruption. I could then demand bribes for attacking (or not attacking) somebody or something in the *Roving Eye* column. This could be a big income generator for me, so please email me the money (in US dollars, not shillings, as I am not that African yet).

Some truths about homosexuality
(26 April 2009)

At last a newspaper article has been written by a Ugandan which discusses homosexuality in a sensible way. In "When Christians condemn God's children during the Easter season" (*Saturday Monitor* April 11 2009), Bernard Tabaire draws attention to the unchristian behaviour of nasty gay-haters such as Stephen Langa of the Family Life Network and Pastor Martin Ssempa of the Makerere Community Church.

Christianity and homosexuality
As regards homosexuality, to this list of Satan's sinners, can be added Dr James Nsaba Buturo, Minister of (supposedly)

Ethics and Integrity, who recently labelled homosexuals as, "abnormal, unhealthy and unnatural."

To the Langas, Ssempas and Buturos of this world, we must ask two questions:
- Where is your "treat your neighbour as yourself"?
- Where is your recognition of the truth that, the world over, somewhere between one in ten and one in twenty human beings are born genetically homosexual?

I ask these questions not as a homosexual myself, but as a heterosexual. Yes, I like the ladies, and whether you are a black, brown, yellow or a white female, the more beautiful you are, the more sexually attracted to you I will be. And not only that, I have a particular taste in women i.e. I especially like tall, slim ladies!

School gayness - normal
The only time I have ever felt sexual feelings towards other males was as a teenager. Most human beings start developing sexual desires when they are too young to have access to the opposite sex. So there is often some sexual experimentation with friends of the same sex. This is a normal and natural part of adolescence and a standard part of heterosexuality. So much of the noise about gay and lesbian behaviour in Ugandan schools is nonsense. Most of these youngsters are just experimenting, and will become heterosexuals as soon as they grow older and their society allows them sexual access to the opposite sex.

Neighbourliness
In today's Uganda, a percentage of the Ugandans who are nasty gay-haters, and make the most outspoken attacks against

homosexuals, are homosexuals themselves. In order to repress and disguise their own natural homosexual inclinations, they feel it important to be seen in public criticising and insulting homosexuals.

When the truth comes out about such people, let us hope they receive more "treat your neighbour as yourself" behaviour from heterosexuals than they themselves were earlier able to give to homosexuals.

The long and short of it
(16 May 2010)

I listened recently to a speech by Jim, a Ugandan lawyer. There were around half a dozen people on the stage with him. Jim, is both intellectually brilliant and a good speaker. Rather than launch into a legalistic speech, he just started by saying, "I am the only person on this stage who is vertically challenged" (i.e. small in height). It certainly was not what the laughing audience was expecting at the beginning of a formal speech!

Jim's reference to his size begs the question - Would you rather be taller or shorter than you are? My height is 5 feet 11½ inches. For part of my life, I wanted to be half an inch taller, just so I could say that I was a six-footer. No doubt I thought I could then boast to ladies that I was 6 feet tall.

I asked the same question to 15-year-old Dorothy, who is in S2. She replied:

> "I would prefer to be shorter. Because if I had a boyfriend I could put on high heels and still remain shorter than him. It looks funny if you are taller than your boyfriend or husband. Shorter people also find it cheaper to buy clothes."

In contrast, Brenda, a 23-year-old accounts assistant, wanted to be taller. Like Dorothy, she also wanted a taller husband than herself, as she felt confident that then her future children would be taller than she had been.

My desire to be a 6-footer, and the size of partner desired by the 2 ladies above, links into some university research. Thus, Nick Neave, a lecturer in psychology at Northumbria University in the UK, has argued that:

> "Tallness is very important for men. Females prefer males who are taller than them, and very small men have problems getting mates."

However, this makes little sense. Around the world in ancient times, it may be that taller men could better defend the family unit against physical attacks from other humans or from animals. But in today's world, much economic activity is characterised by mental rather than physical effort. The size of brain is more important than the size of body!

The supposed women's preference for taller men is illogical for another reason. In the long run, love continues and prospers between a couple less for physical reasons and more for mental compatibility. Companionship replaces raw sex as the driving force of togetherness.

And, if you are worried about being small, it is always worth remembering that some of highest achievers in history were small, such as Napoleon, Julius Caesar, and Gandhi.

To bend or not to bend?

(17 April 2011)

Today's article is about women bending over, or not bending over, as the case may be.

So, where to start? OK, let's say there is some mess on the kitchen floor. It has to be wiped up with a cloth. A Ugandan woman will almost always bend over from the waist to wipe the floor (or to wash her clothes in a bowl, or to light the *sigri* etc. etc.)

In contrast, *bazungu* women generally squat to perform the same action.

No doubt, Desmond Morris, drawing on his masterpiece "Peoplewatching, the Guide to Body Language" would have much to say about this behavioural difference between Ugandan/African and *bazungu* women. But I am not Desmond Morris and I neither have his phone number nor his email address.

So, I turned not to Desmond, but to Mathew, a 27-year-old shop assistant in a Kampala suburb for an explanation. He said:

> "African ladies they are stronger than white ladies. It is not so common for African ladies to squat. Instead of squatting, she just kneels down."

I don't want to confuse matters by examining kneeling. But it does also provide an interesting cultural difference between Uganda and *Bazunguland*. Women kneeling in front of other human beings, as a sign of respect, is very much part of the culture here. But in my country of birth, the same behaviour would be associated with subservience and a master/servant relationship.

And for a final word on female squatting, would I be right in thinking that Ugandan women, especially when out in the bush, most typically squat when they go to the toilet? But what Ugandan women get up to out in the bush is really a matter for them. Should I spy on them then, even if genuinely motivated by journalistic research? I could well find myself in Luzira Prison, discussing such interesting topics with the former National Social Security Fund (NSSF) boss, Mr Jamwa. Luzira Prison might be good for the diet that Jamwa surely needs to go on, but, dear readers, I would prefer to stay out of it, if at all possible.

Why women sit the way they do on *boda-bodas*

(26 September 2015)

It was a hot, humid early afternoon and I was trapped in a Kampala traffic jam near Wandegeya. The only vehicles that were moving were the *boda-bodas*. Some zipped along on the inside or outside, while others weaved in and out of the cars and lorries.

Lacking any other activity except wiping the sweat off my brow, I studied the passengers on the *bodas*, and I regret to inform you that I especially studied the women passengers. They were all shapes and sizes, nationalities, ages and probably tribes, but since when it comes to tribal recognition I have an IQ of around zero (and that's being generous to myself), I can only assume they were of different tribes.

Sidesaddle - *kikazzi*

But what particularly caught my attention was that some of the female passengers sat facing the driver's back, with one knee to the left of him and one knee to the right of him.

Other ladies, however, sat at 90 degrees to his back, with both legs together, pointing towards the side. In the UK we call this position "sidesaddle", which term has roots in mainly bygone times when many people rode horses and sat on saddles, with women normally on sidesaddles. But even today, Queen Elizabeth II rides sidesaddle at ceremonial events like "Trooping the Colour."

Jackson, 40, told me that he had been working in "the *boda-boda* industry" for 10 years, and that the Luganda word for sidesaddle is *kikazzi*. He continued:

> "During the day, most women sit *kikazzi*. But at night they sit like men. The reason is about culture. Most women in Buganda, they don't want to be seen sitting at the back of a man with their private parts close to his body."

Falling off

Patrick runs a computer repair centre in a Kampala suburb. He shares the same age as Jackson, of 40, but did not share the same insights into the position chosen by women on the back of *bodas*. He started by saying:

> "I can't really tell you anything about that. It just depends on how the woman wants to sit. Some women are comfortable when they sit like men, others are not, and they sit like women."

However, Patrick, became more interesting when he shifted the discussion to road safety:

> "Let me tell you a story, Kevin. One day, I was riding a motorbike. My sister was on the back. The wind blew off her cap, and she tried to catch it. Because she was riding *kikazzi*, she fell off the motorbike and damaged herself. But if she had been riding like a man, she would have been OK."

Women respond

I started to think that there should be a Women's MP for *boda-boda* passengers. But if that is a step (or saddle) too far, in an article that is about female choice, I surely needed to interview some women.

So, I spoke to Fatima, 20, who told me that she would be "joining campus" later this year. She will be studying for a Bachelor's degree in Adult and Community Education at Kyambogo University.

She certainly added to my "adult education" by helpfully replying to several questions. She told me she often uses *boda-bodas*. Fatima continued:

> "I feel comfortable riding *kikazzi*, and always when wearing a dress. But when putting on a trouser, I sit behind the *boda-boda* driver."

Finally, not wishing to leave our *bazungu* brothers and sisters out of the debate, I turned to Deborah, a 55-year-old *muzungu*. She told me:

> "I don't like using *boda-bodas*. They are involved in so many accidents because they drive recklessly. As I usually wear trousers, if I do use a *boda*, I would sit behind the driver, facing his back."

Kevin needlessly interrupted with:

> "You mean you would sit behind the driver's behind? A sort of double whammy or double bummy?"

Deborah, ignoring Kevin's rude and rather schoolboyish interruption, concluded:

> "*Bodas* are so dangerous anyway, I would never, *never*, sit sidesaddle."

So there you have it, my friends. May be a Women's MP for *boda-boda* passengers would not be such a bad idea?

2
Sex and Love

It's better to kiss in public
(28 January 2007)

He thrust his tongue into her inviting mouth. Taste of mutual saliva fuelled the exciting yet rhythmic dance of their tongues. The dilation of her pupils reflected the early signs of sexual arousal that she would satisfy lustfully, cheerfully assisted by a condom, later that afternoon.

"Swapping saliva" (meaning kissing) is a phrase I had not come across until I lived in Uganda.

So that I am not misunderstood, let me point out that there had been times when I had memorably "swapped saliva" in my earlier life, but had just used different words (e.g. the British colloquialism "snog" to describe my action with a lucky, or possibly unlucky, female).

The couple described "swapping saliva" in the opening paragraph could have been walking along Kampala Road, but even in these rapidly changing times in Uganda, it is likely to have been in a more private place.

Nevertheless, the extent that Ugandan couples display affection to each other in public is receiving increasing attention in the media.

Thus, in an excellent recent article, Emma Wafula writes:

> "....a section of older Christians get angry whenever the youth hug and kiss at church.....[they feel that] hugging and kissing can be saved for later, for their sake." (*The Sunday Vision*, 21 January 2007).

The implications of much that I have read is that public displays of affection were frowned upon, sometimes regarded as taboo, in traditional Ugandan society.

Two Ugandan vernacular sayings provide clues as to why this should be the case:
- Luganda - "*Ebyomunju tebitotolwa*" (meaning whatever happens in the home should never be told to outsiders).
- Runyankore - "*amaka gamanywa embeba*" (it is only the rats that should know what is happening in the house, nobody else).

Readers will know far more about Ugandan culture than me, but my conclusion from these sayings would be that sex, and the actions that lead into it, should take place in the house and not on Kampala Road!

But matters are complicated by the history of kissing in Uganda. Thus, Wafula writes:

> "In high school, we were told that kissing is a bad habit that was brought by the *bazungu*."

She then quotes Church of Uganda Archbishop Henry Luke Orombi:

"Kissing is a foreign culture and so many would be offended if it is done in public," with 'public' meaning in the presence of one or more other people.

"Even the idea of 'Kiss the bride,'" Orombi continues, "is foreign and would not be understood by elderly relatives attending a wedding."

The weakness of this position, and indeed more generally of the taboos attached to public displays of affection by traditional culture, is that some of these elderly relatives would be polygamous, while others may have merrily defiled their housegirls. This anti-social behaviour is possible precisely because it was expected only to take place 'in the house'.

If on Kampala Road the housegirl was kissed by the head of the household in their run-up to sex, then at least the rest of us would know something of her exploitation before it was too late to do anything about it.

Bukenya, Nakku is a non-issue

(15 April 2007)

The huge amount of newspaper space that has been devoted to Vice President Bukenya and his friend (or girlfriend? Or second wife?) Nakku, has been so massive that many trees in a forest must have been cut down in order to manufacture the paper on which to print this boringly repetitive story.

Now, I know I am a stupid *muzungu*, but why all the fuss? Is not Bukenya just behaving according to his country's culture? For Uganda is a mainly polygamous society, not just amongst its Moslem, but also amongst its Christian, communities.

Polygamy

Every Ugandan family that I have got to know really well has, at some stage, gone polygamous i.e. the husband, after making babies with the "official wife", then made babies with another woman.

In one case, the Dad fathered a child with his neighbour's housegirl (despite he and his children being members of Kampala Pentacostal Church, and who never tired of endlessly telling everybody about how "saved" they were).

In another case, the wife was a hugely impressive educationalist who had provided her husband with 10 children. Nevertheless, that did not stop him from impregnating one of his wife's students.

In a third case, there was the married senior banker who was having an affair with a young barmaid who worked in a pub adjacent to his bank. At first, they used condoms, but then in bed one night, he told her "I need more sons." So, the sex became live, and the result was indeed a son, though at the expense of him infecting the barmaid with HIV/AIDS.

And lastly, there was our friend who generated income in short trips overseas so her children could attend better schools in Kampala. Unfortunately, "when the cat's away, the mice will play" and her husband fathered a child with another woman, before he eventually died of HIV/AIDS.

Public knowledge

And so the list goes on. It is public knowledge that many well-known Ugandans are polygamous. For as Henry Ssali wrote in this magazine on April 1 2007:

> "Right from many of our cabinet ministers, to our honourable MPs, to other dignified people around town, they are in two or even more relationships."

And, therefore, as Ssali points out, "it looks like very few Ugandan men qualify to rebuke Bukenya."

There will, of course, be monogamous exceptions, but is this not the case of the monogamous exceptions proving the polygamous rule?

Polygamous? What's your motivation?

(13 May 2007)

What percentage of Ugandan men are polygamous? I have no idea. And a sample survey is hardly likely to produce a truthful answer to the question, "are you polygamous?"

But as David, 55, a former stadium manager told me:

"The number of polygamous men in Uganda has definitely decreased owing to their fear of catching HIV/AIDS."

Or as John, a 30-year-old engineer, observed:

"Polygamy was generally accepted in our setting until the deadly disease of HIV/AIDS knocked on the door."

Male motivation

Of course, people are having extramarital affairs in all countries and cultures. But the motivation for men having extramarital affairs in, say, the UK, is the thrill of sex with someone new and different. Whereas, my perception of the motivation in Uganda is that it is to produce more kids, especially sons. But when I put this point to Ugandan friends, they greatly disagreed. Thus, Peter, a 45-year-old priest, responded:

"Men want more kids; hence polygamy? No, Kevin, that's not right in today's Uganda. In the past certainly - the more children the better, for various reasons. But not really any more. Children only come largely because both men and women are slack as far as use of contraception is concerned."

Mary, a 32-year-old lawyer, observed:

"I do not agree that the motivation for polygamy for Ugandan men is to have more children (sons). I would say that for a certain category of men, it is still the thrill of having sex with someone new and different - younger than the wife and therefore more exciting."

Mary then provided some examples:

"Take the case of the businessman in Kampala who makes a beeline for Makerere University every beginning of the new academic year to get a fresher; or one who has an affair with each of his secretaries and dismisses them when he tires of them. The motivation to have more sons is increasingly becoming rural, though it continues among a few urban men in Uganda."

Lies

To what extent does polygamy result in the telling of lies? At some stage during a marriage/relationship, a polygamous man must tell a woman a lie e.g. he tells her that he is at a meeting with work colleagues, when, in fact, he is in a lodge with his girlfriend. Jimmy, 28, a senior journalist commented:

> "Obviously one lie leads to another, so to be consistent you keep telling lies. You need to keep lying about where you have been. You need to lie to create time for the other woman i.e. going for a business meeting etc. You need to lie even about money, because usually you have to spend on the other woman, too. Some men even build their other women homes and buy them cars. So lies have to come in."

Thus, lies about "the other woman" appear to lead to lies in other aspects of a relationship, especially money. But Mary put forward a very different view:

> "I do not think that lies in a relationship involving money result from polygamy. Lies about money and other resources are due to the general subordination of women in marriage - the woman is inferior to the man in every way, and the man must have control of all resources in the family including money, time, sex etc. The lies exist even before the man starts to practice polygamy because the woman has little or no information about the man's earnings."

Conclusion

The coming of monogamous Christianity to polygamous Africa was a disaster for truthfulness. Africa would today be a far more truthful place had the missionaries stayed at home.

Mystery Date wins Uganda "Snob of the Year" award

(19 August 2007)

Ambassador Ssali (25) and Jeniffer Namugera (23) were a recent *Mystery Date* in the *Saturday Vision*. Two single people are brought together for a meal at an expensive restaurant, and while Ssali lived up to his name as a reasonable ambassador of the human race, Namugera showed herself to be an awful snob.

A snob is defined as:

> "A person who sets too much value on social standing, wishing to be associated with the upper class and their lifestyle, and treating those viewed as inferior with condescension and contempt."

Thus, Namugera said of Ssali:

> "I expected to see a tall, dark, smart guy, but he wasn't. He was dressed casually – in the middle of the week! I wanted him to wear a decent shirt and an ordinary pair of trousers not a T-shirt, red coat and a necklace."

Well, in the photos of them, Ssali looked pretty smart to me. And should he ever wish to be the starter at an athletics meeting, the red coat would come in handy.

I doubt if Namugera and I would survive a mystery date, or any other type of date for that matter, as:

- My favourite attire, Monday to Sunday, is casual shirt, jeans and training shoes.
- Her hairstyle reminded me of the mop used by my late father when cleaning the floor of the bank in London where he was the caretaker.
- A snob is not likely to fall in love with the son of manual workers.

But Namugera got worse. She observed:

> "When I arrived ... he looked at me and said, 'Ogamba ki. Gyebale.' He kept communicating in Luganda in spite of my insistence on English. I know Luganda very well, but when I go for a date, I do not speak Luganda, moreover at an executive restaurant!" (!! – Yes she really did say this).

So, according to Namugera, it is not acceptable to speak in a local language at an up-market restaurant. My friends, we are not just dealing with a snob here, but a snob of the highest order, a genuine Premier League Snob.

Namugera continued:

> "When I asked him about his education background, I expected something else, not the primary and secondary schools he attended."

So, move over *Universary Primary Education*, *Universal Secondary Education*, *one nation* and all of that. What matters to the Jeniffer Namugeras of this world is which elite school you attended.

And does Namugera appreciate that her views on Ssali told us far more about her character and personality than about Ssali's?

So, Mr Ambassador Ssali, *Hallelujah Praise the Lord* – you had a lucky escape from Uganda's "Snob of the Year".

Big Brother Africa – a case study in polygamy?

(2 December 2007)

My advice to potential viewers of *Big Brother Africa* (BBA) is to "get a life" and turn off the TV. However, the fallout between winner Richard of Tanzania and his Canadian wife Ricki provides an interesting case study for those interested in monogamy and polygamy in Africa, and in cross-cultural human relationships in general.

According to *The Red Pepper* (November 24 2007, Page 25) Richard's father and siblings have criticised Ricki for "betraying and not supporting" Richard during his 98 days on BBA.

From a monogamous angle, these comments are bizarre. Richard fell in love with Tatiana, introduced his whopper to her kandahar (vagina), and also had sexual contact with Nigerian Ofunneka. So, what was Ricki supposed to do – jump up and down with joy and celebrate? Monogamy would say that it was Richard who "betrayed" Ricki, not vice versa.

From the polygamous cultural standpoint, however, things look very different. Tatiana can be viewed as a potential "co-wife", whose contribution to Richard's happiness Ricki should recognise and appreciate.

When (not at all beautiful) Ricki married (extremely handsome) Richard – and what were looks being traded for in this marriage contract? – I wonder how much Ricki knew, if anything, about polygamy in Africa?

Ricki's situation reminds me of the observations, a few years ago, of Mary, a 29-year-old Ugandan professional, who holds a senior job in a health NGO. Her father is polygamous. She told me:

> "I do worry about some of my *bazungu* girlfriends. They fall in love with Ugandan men without knowing what they may be letting themselves in for; and without understanding the culture that has shaped these men and may eventually shape a husband's future behaviour."

And certainly, when I meet a Ugandan woman in love with a *muzungu* man, I have more confidence in the longevity of their relationship, than when it is *muzungu* woman in love with a Ugandan man.

Don't get me wrong. I am not saying that the monogamous culture of my country of birth is superior. With a divorce rate of around 40% and extramarital affairs aplenty, it is hardly a success story. But what I would say is that when the missionaries arrived in Uganda and overlaid African polygamy with Christian monogamy, the result was deception in human relations of disastrous proportions. What was previously done openly, was now done secretly in a lodge or wherever. And often the first "the official wife" knows about it is when the "co's" turn up with their children at the husband's funeral. At least Ricki had the advantage of openly watching her husband's behaviour unfold on television!

They say that "travel is an education." We can certainly agree that Ricki's travels to Tanzania have been an education for her.

Kazini, Zuma and polygamy

(9 March 2008)

Polygamy – now there's a subject and a half. It is rarely out of the news, in one form or the other, in Uganda. Thus last week we had the fisticuffs (fight) between the former Army Commander, Major General James Kazini, and Dr Robert Kagoda of the JBK Medical Centre in Buziga.

Now, I suppose a doctor is a good person to have a fight with, since if you need medical treatment afterwards, you don't have to go far to find a doctor. But as, according to Dr Kadoga, Kazini "hit him with a gun on the head" (*The New Vision*, March 3), it may have been more of a case of, "Physican, heal thyself" (*Luke 4:23* – King James Version).

So, what were the two men fighting about? According to the front page story of *The New Vision* (March 4), Maj. Gen. Kazini had said that "the Kampala doctor with whom he exchanged blows on Sunday was 'hiding' his (Kazini's) junior wife, Ms Winnie Kente" with whom he (Kazini) has a two-year-old daughter.

Roving Eye does not claim to be a world expert on polygamy, though it is true that before my aged cat, Kitty, died last year, he was the senior cat ("The Official Cat") among our pets, while young Lucky was the junior cat. However, since both cats had been castrated/neutered/spayed (an operation which Mr Jacob Zuma – see below - may wish to consider) there were no problems of the children of the junior cat turning up unexpectedly at the senior cat's funeral.

However, my understanding of polygamy was increased by an article by fellow columnist, Nicholas Sengoba ("Zuma's growing stock of wives and the burden of Christianity" *Daily Monitor* 4 March).

I knew that before the coming of Christianity, Africa was polygamous. But, as Sengoba explains:

> "When the European missionaries landed in Africa with the new religion, the greatest hurdle for most of the converts was giving up polygamy...."

In order to take advantage of the education and vocational skills provided by the church and its schools:

> "Most natives took to practicing Christianity during 'broad daylight' before reverting to the old ways in 'the night', in the absence of the prying eyes of the society – what is known as being 'Anglican by day and African by night'".

Sengoba argues that the tremendous interest of the African public in Zuma is precisely because he is not 'Anglican by day and African by night' i.e. he does not try to hide his polygamy and is open and relaxed about it.

It seems that Zuma has innumerable wives and girlfriends and has had "the disputed figure of 18 children" with them.

Jacob Gedleyihlekisa Zuma, President of the African National Congress, and quite likely the next President of South Africa, is a most terrible role model for his country and for the continent of Africa.

Leaving aside the allegations of corruption and rape, what does it say about the brain cells of a man who, during his rape trial, said that after having live sex, he thought he could prevent himself getting HIV/AIDS by *bathing*. Hopefully, even Ugandan schoolchildren who read *Straight Talk*, let alone adults and potential Presidents, are aware that while bathing may remove sexual fluids, it does not stop the spread of HIV/AIDS.

And then there are the economic effects on Africa of large polygamous families, like that of Zuma's and their counterparts in Uganda.

At 3.4%, Uganda's annual population growth rate is the third highest in the world. Before any readers send me nasty emails (or even pleasant ones), please remember that the following was not written by *Roving Eye*, but was the editorial of Uganda's government-owned newspaper:

> "If Uganda's population continues to grow at this rate, economic growth will not result in substantially increased per capita incomes."
>
> "It is wrong to believe that a large population will bring prosperity. Look at Ethiopia or Bangladesh, countries with populations of over 100 million yet stuck in abject poverty."
>
> "Government needs to do more to bring Uganda's population growth rate down to a manageable level. If it does not, Uganda's infrastructure for education, health, power and communication will get progressively overloaded and more Ugandans will drift into poverty."
>
> (*The New Vision* November 12 2003)

For all the above reasons, South Africa, as well as Africa, need a Jacob Zuma Presidency like they need a hole in the head.

Lower Uganda's age of consent to 16 years
(16 March 2008)

The age of consent in Uganda is 18 years i.e. the law states that it is illegal for a Ugandan under 18 years to have sexual intercourse with a member of the opposite sex.

According to Mr Bumble, in Charles Dickens's *Oliver Twist*, 'The law is an ass – an idiot.' Consideration, on whether Ugandan law on the age of consent is idiotic, should be undertaken in the light of the following statistics: "64% of {Ugandan} women said they had started sex before age 18; 50% of the males had started sex by that age." These figures are from a report entitled *Protecting the next generation in Uganda: New evidence on adolescent sexual and reproductive health needs* (The Guttmacher Institute). They are based on two national surveys conducted between 2004 and 2006, involving more than 16000 males and females aged 12-49, and were brought to my attention by Richard M. Kavuma's article in *The Weekly Observer* (March 6 2008).

The 64% (female) and 50% (male) figures relate to the answers provided by 20 to 24-year-olds. Given the emphasis placed on abstinence in Uganda's HIV/AIDS campaigns, I suspect that in reality, the percentages are even higher i.e. some respondents would have said they had not had sex before age 18, when, in fact, they had.

But even taking the figures as they are, one must ask the question, "What is the use of a law which is broken by two-thirds of women and one-half of men?" Uganda's law on the age of consent is indeed "an ass". It does not capture the reality of Ugandans' sexual behaviour, and has many negative effects. For example:

- Uganda's already overstretched policing and judicial systems are stretched even further and, therefore, provide less protection to the acutely vulnerable i.e. girls aged 10 to 15 years.
- Presumably, there are men in the country's overcrowded prisons for having consensual sex with 16 and 17-year-old girls. Do they need to be there?

In *Roving Eye*'s view, Uganda's age of consent should be reduced to 16 years, the age that it is in many other countries.

I spoke to two knowledgeable Ugandans who believe that the country's age of consent should remain at 18 years.

Gilbert Awekofua (39) is studying for a Master's degree in public health leadership and is an editor and counsellor at the Straight Talk Foundation. He emphasised that he was speaking to me in a personal and not an official capacity:

> "I work with young people and read their letters every day. A woman's body is only mature enough to have a baby after 21. Indeed their pelvic bones can still be growing at 25 years. The highest percentage of maternal deaths is amongst teenage mothers because their bodies are not fully prepared. Lowering the age of consent to 16 would make a bad situation, worse."

Mary Kavuma, 45, is a lawyer who specialises in gender issues:

> "There are two reasons why the age of consent should not be reduced from 18 to 16 years. Firstly, educational – more young women would think it is their right to have sex and get married. Therefore, fewer young girls would get an education. The second reason is medical – even fewer young women would use contraception, thus exposing themselves more to pregnancy and HIV/AIDS, as well as all the other risks associated with early

pregnancy. The law does not reflect the reality, but it is trying to set up standards."

This is where Mary and I part company. The law cannot stick its head in the sand. It has, to a considerable extent, to link itself to the reality of a society. We may want zero, or only one-fifteenth of, Ugandan women under-18 years to have had sex, but the stark reality it that two-thirds do.

I once knew a Ugandan girl who became pregnant at 13 years. The considerably older man who impregnated her was never brought to justice. If Ugandan police and lawyers spent less time chasing the "defilers" of 17-year-olds, they would have more time to chase the defilers of 13-year-olds. And that wretched man might well now be in prison instead of leading a comfortable life. The age of consent in Uganda should be reduced to 16.

Why are Ugandan bars so dark?

(20 June 2008)

It is late evening, and a *muzungu* visitor to Uganda sits at a table outside a bar. Feeling hungry, she picks up the menu, and then turns to my wife and exclaims, "It's so dark here, I can't read the menu!"

Why are Ugandan bars at night, if not dark, so dimly lit? Are the owners trying to reduce electricity costs? Thinking that this was not the answer, I turned to a few friends in my local trading centre for assistance on understanding Uganda's badly lit bars.

Julian, 29, owns a small shop. He increased my understanding by zero per cent, as his reply was, "I am a saved man. I don't go to bars."

Thanks for nothing, Julian! But his assistant, Alex, 23, threw much light on bars' little light. Dressed in a long white coat, and mending an electrical wall socket in the *duuka* next door to Julian's shop, Alex explained:

> "People don't want to be seen taking booze. Also, old married guys go out with other ladies and don't want to be observed. That's why you often find that light is dim."

Abdullah, a 21-year-old butcher, agreed with Alex. He said:

> "It is dark in bars because no-one wants to be seen. I might want to take a certain girl there while my wife is at home. I don't want rumour or people researching and disorganising my life."

So, it could well be that polygamy reduces the wattage of the light bulbs used by bar-owners.

But, what about a young, non-polygamous courting couple – why would they prefer bars to be dark? It has been said that Uganda is a sexually conservative society (though housegirls might not necessarily agree with that). For example, a Ugandan friend told me about her first sexual encounters. Her boyfriend always insisted on them having sex in the dark. Also, he would never let her see his penis. Interested to know what his manhood looked like, she waited for him to go to sleep, and then put the light on to have a look at it.

Now, it is often in a bar that the first steps towards the sexual act are made – the fingers touch, the knees brush under the table, a hand caresses etc. etc. If destination sexual act is done in the dark, perhaps this early part of the journey towards it requires something approaching darkness?

So what does all this mean for *Roving Eye*? Well, when I am at a bar, whereas really exciting things may be happening at (or under) the tables of nearby courting couples, at my table the excitement is regretfully limited to reading the newspapers. But the darkness means I can only see the newsprint with the aid of a torch. I hate to think how many batteries I have used up in dimly lit Ugandan bars – could the fake teetotallers, the polygamists and the courting couples reimburse my battery costs, please?

Of bums, hips and manhoods
(17 August 2008)

"FOR MANHOOD ENLARGEMENT", scream the A4 notices plastered around the streets of central Kampala, "NO SIDE EFFECT – 0775 557755".

Let me start by saying that 0775 557755 is not my phone number i.e. I am not trying to promote my own business, or that of anybody I know, so please, I don't want any desperate manhood enlargers demanding immediate treatment, thinking they are phoning me.

Whoever is the owner of this business has a similar one. For, also scattered around Kampala, are notices offering to increase the size of "bums".

Now modesty does not permit me to discuss whether my manhood requires, or does not require, enlarging. Nor do I wish to discuss this subject by email (though, if you happen to be the recently crowned "Miss Uganda", I may be persuaded to change my mind).

But, when it comes to "bums", many Ugandans would question whether I have a bum at all, given its very small nature. In other words, don't blink, or you will miss it. So, with no bum, no chin and a big nose, I doubt whether my current job application (to become a male model) stands much chance of success.

The virtual absence of a bum has never bothered me too much. So what is it about "bums" and bum size in Uganda that has generated so many posters around Kampala? I turned for an answer to my friend Michael who is 38, lives in a Kampala suburb and whose bum size I did not notice, possibly because both he and I are heterosexuals.

Michael told me that the bum posters were targeting women, not men. The reason being, explained Michael that "us men, we want women with bum – not too big, but quite big."

"So, why is that, Michael?" I asked.

"Actually, I don't know" was his reply, a reply whose usefulness was similar to the size of my bum i.e. almost zero.

Now, dear reader, you may not have realised it before, but if you rearrange the letters in the word "bums", you get "mubs", and it was this realisation that prompted my next question:

> "What would a MUBS (Makerere University Business School) babe think of my tiny bum size?"

Michael's sexist answer would enrage many university departments of gender studies, but at the same time would be an interesting topic for a PhD thesis. He said:

> "There's no need for a man having big bums. According to me, it is not important for a man, but it is important for a woman."

All complainants should contact Michael please, not me.

A third body area for the Kampala A4 poster is "hips". But whether it be size of hips, size of bums or size of manhood, one thing is definitely true. The human condition is such that we are rarely satisfied with what God gave us, but want something different and "better". But whether it is actually "better", of course, is highly debatable. For example, a woman's sexual pleasure has very little do with the size of a guy's manhood, as most women do not orgasm as the result of penetrative sex (however big the manhood), but require additional clitoral stimulation from their lover.

So my advice to all you potential manhood enlargers, you bum expanders and you hip wideners out there, is to save your money, by not telephoning 0775 557755.

"Ask Uncle Kevin" – new problem page
(9 November 2008)

Dear Uncle,
I graduated, got a job and married about a year ago. Two weeks ago, my wife finished checking her emails and did not sign out. When I sat to look for the emails I had sent her before the marriage, I was surprised to find an email from a man, a partner of her workplace's company. He wanted to make love with her, requesting for her phone number. My wife replied with her phone number, apologising for the delay. I was devastated. This was one month before our marriage.......

What can I do? I am in a dilemma.
George

Dear George,
Although your problem first appeared in the *Saturday Vision*, the *Sunday Monitor*'s new problem page will show you how much better our products are to those of a State-run newspaper, by providing below some very easy answers to your difficulty.

Look on bright side
Think how much worse the emails could have been. They might have been from 3 different men, all saying how much they enjoyed sex with your wife. She might have replied how wonderful the live sex was with them, especially when compared to sex with her husband, whose whopper is so tiny that she must wear glasses to see it. Yes, George, my dear friend, those emails could have been much worse, so you need to look on the bright side.

Manchester United
As you are a Man U fan, I advise you to instead think about their victory over Chelsea in the 2007 Champions League Final, in order to cheer yourself up. Also, at least you did not discover the problem with your wife on the same day as Man U's biggest match of the English Premier League season (against Fulham). Those emails would have distracted you from more important things in life.

Prayer
Go to Kampala's Miracle Centre and pray for healing, that is, the healing of your wife's computer. It may be that a virus brought those emails to her computer. There are many strange viruses out on the internet that could mean that those emails were not real emails. Your wife's computer needs to get saved.

Repent your sins
You looked at your wife's emails without her permission. So it gives you a good opportunity to repent this and other sins. For example, tell her of the time you looked at yourself in a full-length mirror while wearing her underwear. Also, when you pocketed in a *matatu* thinking, not of her, but of *Miss Uganda*.

Corruption

If all else fails, and as Uganda is so corrupt, I suggest you blackmail your wife while also asking for a bribe. Tell her that you require a certain number of Ugandan shillings to compensate for your hurt pride. If you do not receive this payment by the next Man U home game, that you will inform the following people about the emails: her workmate's wife; her mother; your mother. That will wake her up – hook, line and singlet – to the fact that she is married to a real man who can do more than read her emails.

Well, George, I hope one, or all of the above solutions, will help you with your little problem.

Yours sincerely,
Kevin O'Counsellor
Uncle Kevin is not a professional counsellor

Unhappy Valentine's Days

(14 February 2010)

Today is Valentine's Day and it is supposed to be a time of happiness for lovers, young and old, around the world. But for many people, the reverse is true. Mr A or Ms B might not have a lover to spend time with!

Possibly even worse, the love of their life may be a dim and distant memory. For example, I have a female friend in the UK who, after a failed marriage, fell deeply in love with a younger man. After 10 blissful years together, he had an affair with their next-door neighbour and the relationship came to an end. Every Valentine's Day since then (i.e. six of them), this wonderful woman has been alone and unhappy, with only memories of 'what might have been' to get her through a tough 24 hours.

Another sad Valentine's Day story is Daudi's. He is 25, and works for the Ugandan Red Cross. When we spoke, he was wearing a nicely ironed blue shirt and a striking brown check tie.

> "Last year," Daudi lamented, "I was with my lover who disappointed me. I arranged to meet her in a big hotel – the *Mbale Resort Hotel*. She was there with friends of hers who were not people I knew. I asked her who they were and she replied that I should 'mind my own business'! There was one particular man who she said was her brother, but I am sure he was her lover. I lost my temper with her and we had to break our relationship. It was the worst Valentine's Day of my life which I will never forget to my death."

In contrast, Jim, a 25-year-old shop assistant, has only pleasant Valentine memories which he thought was due to his youth. He said:

> "I always celebrate Valentine's Day so much. Since I've only had girlfriends in recent years, I've not celebrated that many. That is why I am not yet disappointed."

My own unhappy Valentine memory is from over a quarter a century ago. I had not seen the girl I was madly in love with for a year as she was spending a long period living and working in Australia. So, it was a deeply depressed Kevin who went by himself to see a film in London, at one of those large complexes that have many small cinemas within the same building.

So, let me start with the bad news of February 14, 1983. Halfway through the film, I went out for a "short call". After urinal relief, I resumed watching the film. A few seconds later, I realised that it was a different film from the one I had been watching! Yes, you've guessed it – Roving Eye had been so deep in his depressed thoughts that he had gone back into the wrong cinema hall!

The good news of Valentine's Day 1983 is that the young lady did return from Australia later that year, to eventually become my wife. And, although I am on my 83rd yellow card, I am pleased to say that she still is my wife, and that we have enjoyed many happy Valentine's Days together in Uganda.

Sex in Uganda's crowded rooms
(7 March 2010)

Last week, the World Bank highlighted Uganda's worrying population explosion. In other words, there is a lot of sex going on in Uganda and a lot of babies being born into already large families.

But where is all this sex taking place? And how is parents' lovemaking affected by there being many children sleeping/living in the same room/house?

No shouting
"They have to put on silencers" was Geoffrey's answer to this second question.

Geoffrey is the 31-year-old owner of a small business in Kampala. And until this conversation with him, I always thought that a silencer was something that an American gangster put on the end of a pistol so that nobody could hear the murderous gunshot.

But back to sex:

"That means," continued Geoffrey, "that the parents have got to have a low voice. That is no shouting. You can whisper. If they shouted they would wake up the children."

My next question to Geoffrey was, "Who makes the most noise – the man or the woman?"

"Actually it's the women" he replied.

Bad *muzungu*

Well, you could have fooled me Geoffrey. Most women do not reach orgasm through penetrative sex and their partners are too unknowing or too selfish to provide the additional clitoral stimulation required for them to achieve climax.

Being a bad *muzungu*, I then asked Geoffrey another tough question. "When you reach an orgasm, have you ever disturbed the neighbours?"

"No, never!" was his brief reply.

> "And Geoffrey, have you ever put a pillow in your mouth to stop the noise?"
>
> "No, don't ask me that, Kevin" a shocked Geoffrey exclaimed. And then taking the conversation in a different direction, he continued, "It's different in the village, but in Kampala you can even find a family of eight living in one room."
>
> "It is embarrassing," interrupted Daudi, Geoffrey's 27-year-old assistant, "that some people have to sleep with their many children in a single room in Uganda..... When it comes to sex, you really wonder how it's done in a 'silent' way so that children may not hear. To me it suggests sex in a crowded room is not so much of fun."

Sunday school

And what better person to provide a final comment on these issues than my almost 96-year-old aunt, Norah Jesse Beasleigh nee Dacey. She grew up in a poor family in South London. There were 7 sisters and one brother, and she told me over the phone:

> "I think my parents used to have a Sunday afternoon romp. I remember we used to be going off to Sunday school and my father would say to my mother, 'Come on Amy, come and have a lay down'. We children knew nothing about sex, and we did not think or dream of our parents having sex."

And as for me, *Roving Eye*, when I have sex the only other member of the household I have to worry about disturbing with my orgasmic noise pollution is ………the cat.

When a Ugandan woman does not "produce"
(11 April 2010)

They had lived together as man and wife for 2 years. But she had not "produced". So, he gave her a red card.

This is a too common story in Uganda. Leaving aside the automatic assumption that the "fault" for the absence of children lies with the woman and not with male impotency, it captures the basic nature of a Third World country like Uganda, where the average number of births per woman is approaching 7, compared to a First World country, where it is frequently under 2.

The result is that there is much more emphasis on "baby production" in all aspects of Ugandan society – from the number of articles on pregnancy, childbearing and kids in a newspaper like this one, through to the harsh realities for the woman described above (never mind her intellect, personality or job – the only thing that matters is whether she can "produce" or not. The distinction between human beings on the one hand, and dogs, goats and cows, on the other, becomes invisible.)

The woman's experience has nothing to do with being African and everything to do with Uganda's level of economic development. The situation was the same in the USA or UK in bygone eras.

When poverty rules, there is nobody (and no pension nor welfare state) to safeguard you in old age. So, you have a lot of children who can look after you when you get old. But as the society (and yourself) grows richer, this need reduces, so you have fewer children, and in a virtuous circle, the result is that the society grows richer, so that future generations have fewer children still.

And the story that started this article had a wonderful ending. When the man gave the woman a red card, he did not realise that she was already pregnant, and not only that, pregnant with his son. After she gave birth, he, being a typical man, wanted her back. But she had seen the truth i.e. that he valued her not on the basis of love, but on the basis of her production ability, as if she was no more than a cow or a goat. Now, it was her turn to give him a red card, and what a wonderful, and wonderfully deserved red card it was too.

Ugandans and their secrets

(10 October 2010)

An interesting Luganda phrase, or should that be proverb, considered earlier in this chapter, is *ebyomunju tebitotolwa* i.e. what happens in the house should never be told to outsiders. When I asked Brian, a 23-year-old butcher, for his understanding, his reply was, "Not good to tell your secrets to anybody."

So I asked Brian to provide me with an example. In between cutting up small pieces of meat for – and I hate to admit this, given all the poor Ugandans for whom meat is an infrequent luxury – my cat, Brian thought deeply and then said:

> "Maybe I have an obstacle with my wife. Maybe I caught my wife playing sex with another guy. It would not be good for me to talk to somebody about it."

An example provided by Philip, a 34-year-old Ugandan friend, also used sex to illustrate the proverb:

> "Let me say your wife has refused playing sex with you for some good days. You need to go and tell people about it? No, you have to solve it yourself."

This preference for personal secrecy over openness is found with other Ugandan tribes. For example, as we found previously, there is the Runyankore saying *amaka gamanywa embeba* (it's only the rats which should know what is happening in the house, nobody else). And this preference can have interesting results when Ugandan culture meets *bazungu* culture. For instance, I often find that in a conversation with a Ugandan, they will learn far more about me than I will learn about them.

You may say that this is just because Kevin is up his own ****. And didn't he, in last week's *Roving Eye*, argue that Mr Gureme enjoyed talking about himself at great length?

So let me provide another example in which I have greater confidence given that both Brian and Philip illustrated the Luganda proverb by drawing on love/sex.

Two different *bazungu* women (one Polish, the other Dutch) had male Ugandan lovers. They both told me that their relationships ran into severe difficulties because of their tendency to open out e.g. to discuss problems within the relationship with friends. This would greatly upset their partner and shows that what is acceptable in one culture can be unacceptable in another.

Ugandans and zero sons and daughters
(5 December 2010)

It is important in life to recognise, and to admit to, one's mistakes and misjudgements. Almost exactly 11 years ago, I wrote the following in a *Roving Eye* column, and with the benefit of hindsight, I can see that I made a mega-misjudgement about Stephen.

> "In 1998, two young Ugandan lovers, Stephen and Mary (names changed) had HIV/AIDS tests. He tested positive; she tested negative. Eighteen months later, they are still together, still in love, and enjoying safe sex using condoms."
>
> "Mary told me, 'I realise I will never be able to have a family, have children. But I want to stay with Stephen for the rest of my life. I love him.'"

It was not long after this that Mary admitted to my wife that Stephen was insisting on having "live" sex. He then gave Mary, who like him, had been educated at Nkumba University, a "red card", before cohabiting with a village girl.

For Mary asked him too many questions, while the compliant, soon to be impregnated, village girl happily obeyed his every instruction.

To make matters worse, Stephen "ate" the money we gave him to buy the then hugely expensive ARV drugs at Mildmay Hospital, and which we had raised from our friends and relatives. He even lied to us, saying that he was going on 4 months overseas training, so that he could get a big advance of the money, which he then no doubt spent on mobile phones and much else.

Both Mildmay and ourselves having failed, I told Stephen's sister about his condition, thinking that it was only his family that might knock some sense into his head. This resulted in an obscene letter, in which he threatened to shoot me, for telling them.

Stephen died 2 weeks ago. The fact that he lived so long must have meant that his family succeeded in getting him to take ARVs.

But how did my newspaper article get it so wrong about Stephen? One reason was that I had not fully appreciated the effects of Uganda's childcentric, Third World, socio-economic culture. On average, Ugandan women have 7 babies each. Most Ugandans cannot imagine a happily married couple who do not have children (something that is common in the First World). So, telling Stephen that he could not have "live" sex was, for him, like receiving a death sentence.

Author's Note
In 2015, I learnt that if ARVs lower the viral load of the infected partner to a very low level, then having "live sex" is less likely to result in the infected partner infecting the unifected one or any resulting babies. But I did not have this information when I was advising Stephen.

Norbert Mao will win the race
(30 January 2011)

So, I hope the headline above has attracted you to yet another article by the *muzungu* with a big nose, no chin and no bum.

And to which race am I referring? Is it the Presidential race? The Democratic Party candidate race? An egg & spoon race? A 3000 metres steeplechase race?

No, it is none of these. If there was a race whose winner would be the most outrageously over-publicised lover, then Gold Medal would certainly go to Mr Norbert Mao.

It was back in December 1999 when *Roving Eye* proclaimed:

> "If I read one more article about how much Norbert Mao and Naomi Achieng love each other, I will be sick."

> "'I will be sick' might have been read as 'I will be ill'. So, to have avoided such misunderstanding, I should have written, 'I will vomit all over my clean training shoes.'"

My *brilliant* (well, you know how modest I am not) article continued:

> "Week after week, month after month, our newspapers have been full of Norbert and Naomi {love} stories as if their relationship was a matter of global importance."

The couple basked in self-publicity, and they and their friends in the media seemed to imply that their relationship was in some sense extraordinary. But as one young Ugandan said to me at the time, "Do they think they are the first two people to fall in love?"

Worse than that, they are also from the same tribe (Acholi) and same social group, so that they should meet and fall in love was boringly predictable, and certainly highly ordinary.

Extraordinary love breaks accepted barriers. For example, in the Indian context, it would be when a Moslem and a Hindu fall in love and get married. In the Ugandan context it would be when a Bantu falls in love with someone from a Nilotic or other non-Bantu tribe, and despite objections from parents, family and elders, marries them. And if one was a Nilotic Moslem, and the other a Bantu Christian (or vice versa), that would indeed be truly "extraordinary" love.

So, eleven years later, how has the Mao's *supposedly* "extraordinary" love translated into married life i.e. what is the state of the Mao's marriage? I have no idea. And we are not likely to find out the truth. For the Acholi expression capturing the secrecy of what takes place in the home is *ma time kany gik kany* (what happens here, stops here).

Chips chicken better than sex!

(24 April 2011)

In Uganda, we all know that a guy's idea of a good evening is to buy a girl chips, chicken and *Bellos*, then take her to a lodge.

Here are the reasons why women feel that they would prefer to go home after eating the chips chicken, and forget about sex in a lodge.

- Chicken satisfies longer than sex.
- Chicken can be tough, but never as tough as bad sex.
- Chicken smells better than most men.
- Chickens have no tribe.
- Chickens don't answer back.
- Chickens don't rape and defile.
- Chickens don't fart (or if they do, they don't pretend they haven't).
- Chickens' kids don't require school fees.
- You can pack chicken, take it home and have it when you want.
- Have live sex and you are dead; have dead chicken and you live.
- Men only want to give you their penis; but with chicken you have choice – leg, thigh, breast, gizzard, liver etc.
- Buying chicken is cheaper than buying sex.
- Fat chickens are delicious, while fat men are just fat.
- Chickens don't need condoms.
- Chickens don't give you AIDS.
- Chips chicken does not wake you up in the middle of the night demanding things.
- You don't have to eat chicken when you don't want to.
- When you eat chicken you don't have to pretend you are having an orgasm.
- Eating chicken is less messy than having sex.
- After chicken, you only have to wipe your mouth with a cloth, not a man's penis and stomach.
- Evangelical pastors' views on chicken make more sense than their views on sex.
- You never meet an evangelical chicken.

- At a Christmas party, the chicken comes before the sex.
- Co-chickens are less of a problem than co-wives.
- You can watch your Mum and Dad having chicken, but you can't watch them having sex.
- You don't have to kneel in front of a chicken.
- (According to at least one Ugandan woman) chickens are better at sex than most Ugandan men.

So, what does all this mean? Ugandan society, like all societies, has been shaped by men according to what they want and what they think is important.

So, last week, I spoke to a 35-year-old, unmarried Ugandan woman who, in her search for a husband, has had around six sexual partners. She told me:

> "Eventually, you get tired, fed up with it. It's just a game. You have to pretend that what the man is offering is what you want. And it's not. His idea of a fashion statement is to get his head shaved, wear a blue shirt and undo a button on it! It's pathetic! His idea of romance is buying you *Bellos* and chicken, and then a room in a lodge. If that's all Ugandan men can do before they get their penises out, give me soft chicken anytime!"

So guys, remember when you buy your *kyana* chips chicken, and think it's the beginning of something wonderful, for the lady the chips chicken are probably the best part of the evening.

Let's celebrate International Childfree Day
(2015)

Today, August 1, is International Childfree Day. It celebrates childfree men and women around the World.

This Day would not be celebrated, and probably not even understood, by many Ugandans. In "Ugandans and zero sons and daughters", which appears earlier in this chapter, I observed, "On average, Ugandan women have 7 babies each. Most Ugandans cannot imagine a happily married couple who do not have children (something that is common in the First World)."

So, how common is "childfreeness" (a term much preferred to "childlessness" by those of us who have no children) in the First World? The UK's Office for National Statistics estimates that one quarter of women of childbearing age will never have a baby. The proportion of women without children has almost doubled since the 1990's, with one in five 45-year-olds yet to start a family. In the USA, one in five women in their early forties is childfree, rising to one in three in Germany and Japan.

Famous childfree women

These statistics were in an article about the famous British actress, Helen Mirren ("Mirren confronts the final female taboo" *Daily Telegraph,* February 2013). She is just one of very many famous childfree women. Others include the American talk show host, Oprah Winfrey; former Australian Prime Minister, Julia Gillard, and the most powerful woman in the World, German Chancellor, Angela Merkel. All three women are in happy long-term relationships with men. Thus Winfrey says of Stedman Graham, her partner since 1986:

> "Stedman and I have a great relationship that allows me to be me in the fullest sense, with no expectations of wifedom and all that would mean." (*Daily Monitor,* 29 September 2003).

Uganda – are attitudes changing?

As a 62-year-old childfree man who has lived in Uganda for 21 years, this "issue" (sorry for the ambiguity) of having no children is about the only area of my enjoyable life here where I do occasionally need access to my own British culture to show me that my wife and I are not freaks for not reproducing. I am constantly asked, "How many children do you have?" Even, given my grey hair, "How many grandchildren do you have?" I get so fed up with these questions, and people's failure to understand my explanation, that very, very occasionally, on long hot days, I am rude and reply in Luganda, *"Sirina akasolo"* (I don't have a manhood).

But attitudes in Uganda are slowly changing, especially amongst its educated elite. Thus, Mike Ssegawa ("Who said children are a must-have in marriage" *Daily Monitor*, September 4 2014) forcefully states:

> "If you are the kind who wants no children, ignore the naysayers. Do the same to those in-laws who call you names like sterile or barren. Live your life the way you want to."

Bebe Cool and *Fatboy*

James Onen (AKA *Fatboy*), the 40-year-old presenter at *Sanyu FM*, recently got into an argument with musician Bebe Cool, initially over Nigerian versus local music, but which moved on to childfreeness. Bebe was not so "Cool" and, according to the *Kampala Sun* (June 19 2015) screamed at Onen:

> "You are there, already in your 40's, and you do not have kids yet. Yet you call yourself a man."

Onen's response was far more thoughtful and stinging:

"For a lot of people it seems having children is the true sign that you are a man. But this doesn't impress me because rats and cockroaches have children – in fact, several times more children than any human being will ever produce. Does this therefore make them superior to Bebe Cool (probably, *hahahahaha*)."

And Bebe Cool, when not performing on stage, is performing to type in bed. For we learn from the *Daily Monitor* (10 July 2015) that his wife, Zuena Kirema, has flown to the USA to give birth to their 4th baby. Their choice of location for the birth is worth an article in itself. But let us just observe that at this rate the couple will soon be reaching Uganda's average of 7 babies per woman, rather than using their brains and bring down the country's frighteningly fast population growth rate of 3% per annum. This rate means that Uganda's population (34.9 million in 2014) is doubling every 20 years. Hence the country's impressive economic growth is only partly converted to increased GDP per head (Source – National Planning Authority).

Francis Bacon

As we celebrate International Childfree Day, let me leave the final word to English philosopher and statesman, Francis Bacon, who, 400 years ago, wrote:

"The perpetuity by generation is common to beasts; but memory, merit and works are proper to men. And surely a man shall see the noblest works and foundations have proceeded from childless men, which have sought to express the images of their minds ......So the care of posterity is most in them who have no posterity."

3

Bazungu (white people)

The Irish, tribes and jokes
(10 June 2007)

An Irish (Aer Lingus) plane is approaching London Airport. The control tower asks the pilot for his height and position. He replies:

"5 feet 11inches and sitting at the front."

This old joke has an interesting basis. In the UK (certainly during my growing-up years) it was often suggested that Irish people were not intelligent and even plain stupid. This, of course, is nonsense.

Irish men and women have provided some of the finest thinking and writing to have illuminated the human race. Oscar Wilde is a classic example. Nevertheless, many jokes were made at the expense of the Irish, and I can safely repeat the one above, because my own name – Kevin Patrick O'Connor – is about as Irish as you can get. And my great great great grandfather emigrated from southern Ireland to England in the 1820's.

Mary, 26, is a heavily pregnant accountant, and a Samia by tribe. I can confirm I am not the father to Mary's forthcoming baby (at least I don't think I am, but who knows what can happen after too many *Nilos*).

But I did ask Mary if there were any tribes or communities in Uganda who are the butt of jokes in the same way as the Irish are in the UK:

> "That is not the case here Kevin," she replied. "One tribe will tell jokes about another tribe, but there is not one particular tribe that everyone tells jokes about."

Ugandans overseas

Ugandans living overseas, reading the *Sunday Monitor* on the internet, may be able to provide examples of communities in their country of residence who are the Irish equivalent in having jokes made about them.

Ethnicity and community can provide the basis for both kind and unkind jokes. But much humour is unrelated to these, and sometimes the very best jokes are simple quips that are retained in the mind for decades. I recalled one of my favourites while I was attending an athletics competition last Sunday at Mandela National Stadium.

There was a bulge in my trousers, caused by a mobile phone stuffed in one of the pockets. At the same time, the race starter was having problems with his starter gun, which was firing more blanks than a castrated eunuch.

All this reminded me what the American actress, Mae West, famously asked when approached by a policeman in Los Angeles in February 1936:

> "Is that a gun in your pocket, or are you just pleased to see me?"

Anyway, I can confirm that no beautiful women said to me at Mandela National Stadium Namboole:

> "Kevin, is that a mobile phone in your pocket, or are you just pleased to see me?"

Mourning an animal corpse

(5 August 2007)

Our cat, Kitty, died last weekend. It would be difficult for many Ugandans to understand the huge feelings of loss and grief that my wife and I have experienced. Why is this?

Differences, and differences in expectation and behaviour, between rich and poor countries, are often explained by economics.

Economics, especially the grim economics of poverty, explains much in life.

To a poor Ugandan, the idea of a pampered pet is incredible.

For, a pet in a rich country, typically a dog or cat, is kept for no other purpose than company and friendship. It will be well fed, often on meat twice per day, and will sometimes be overweight.

So for a Ugandan – struggling to meet human family needs like school fees, medical expenses etc. and enjoying meat only on big occasions – it is not sensible to own a pet, or indeed any animal, which does not have an obvious purpose.

Thus, pigs in Uganda are kept for their pork; cows for their milk and meat and dogs, generally, for security reasons.

But I am not a Ugandan, and certainly not a poor Ugandan. On our very first day in Uganda in 1994, we first met Kitty, who was already 2 years old. He was a friend and companion over the next 13 years, and when he died it was very much like losing a close relative or friend.

But there is more than just economics in how Ugandans respond to the notion of an animal as a pet. Thus, Gertrude, a teacher from Busoga, told me:

> "The idea that a dog is dirty is ingrained in the African mind. You will rarely find an African with a dog in their car – let alone hugging or kissing a dog, as you often see Europeans do. And in Luganda, if you want to insult somebody, you just tell them, '*Oli ng'embwa*' (You are like a dog)."

After Kitty died, we buried him in our compound, and then planted a rose bush on top of the grave.

Burying a pet, also raises interesting cultural differences. Thus, George, an Iteso, once told me:

> "Burying animals is thought to be very bad. It is almost as if you are putting a curse on clan members. If you find an animal buried near your door it would be regarded as juju performed by somebody wishing you dead."

And Kalungi, a Muganda, observed:

> "We would throw a dead dog near a Jjrikiti tree. We would never bury a dead dog or cat, no matter how much it was loved."

Similarly, Loretta, a Mufumbira from Kabale, had a family dog for 15 years, to which she was greatly attached. But when it died, it was still thrown in the garbage pit.

> "Burying that dog," observed Loretta, "would have been regarded as wasted time, energy, money and land."

Loretta, however, identified some changes in Ugandan attitudes:

"My children have buried pets. They even had a little ceremony and placed a cross on the grave. The younger generation's attitude is changing and becoming more westernised."

Kitty has gone, but he is not forgotten for, days later, I am still feeling sadness at his passing. A combination of economics and culture explains the depth of my grief, and it has been a helpful part of the mourning process to write this article.

Slow *muzungu* loves Ugandan slowness
(9 December 2007)

In his "How to be a Ugandan," Joachim Buwembo refers to the:

> "Famous American journalist and author, David Lamb, who said in his book *The Africans* that the only time that an African is in a hurry is when he is behind a wheel. The Ugandan is no exception."

The implication is that in other areas of life, Ugandans are slow. Beware generalisations! But it is the case that, for example, one often sees Ugandans walking slowly, languidly, along a street.

Perhaps, this helps to explain why I feel so at home in Uganda, or, as I wrote in the preface of my recently published book ("Ugandan Society Observed"):

> "I must thank Uganda. Your character and my character seem to share certain similarities".

Walking and running

For, I am also by nature, slow. And, I too walk slowly along streets, often deep in thought, "my head in the clouds."

Where I differ from Ugandans, and certainly many Ugandan men, is that I drive slowly.

Slowness invades most areas of my life. My *Outlook* task list is full of undone tasks. And while I enjoy slowly writing one *Roving Eye* article per week, the grind of tight daily journalist deadlines, and the speed required to meet them, would quickly send me to nervous breakdown land.

During the competitive running career of my youth, I often got outsprinted at the end of races.

And talking of running, there is an expression in Luganda – *aduka mpola mpola atuuka wala* (he who runs slowly, reaches further). This has similarities to the proverb in English, "Slow but sure wins the race."

Sex

There are areas of life where, indeed, slowness is an advantage. For example, ladies, if you had a romantic encounter with me in bed, you would surely not want it to be over faster than you can say "Pastor Benny Sinn". Much more preferable would be a slow passionate build-up, lingering climaxes, multiple orgasms, and all these things experienced even before I've taken off my trousers!

Speed in sex, and certainly self-interested male speed, can be hugely disadvantageous for the female. When I was researching a *Roving Eye* article ("Ugandans discover the vibrator" *Sunday Monitor* November 14 1999) Rebecca, a 31-year-old professional from eastern Uganda, told me:

"When it comes to sex, most men here just jump on top of you, and mechanically thrust away until they ejaculate, and then roll off you satisfied."

"They assume orgasm for them means satisfaction for you. They are blissfully ignorant that I am lying there unfulfilled, still only at the very early stages of sexual enjoyment."

"In contrast, some of my most intense sexual experiences have been with a vibrator, and certainly this is the only time I have enjoyed a multiple orgasm."

The Bible

So let's leave the last word to the Bible. James 1:19–20 goes *something* like this, and certainly *something* like this if you have had a long day in the office, or drunk too many *Nile Specials* – let every human being be quick to hear, slow to speak and slow to become angry. In this way, things will turn out nicely.

Conclusion

So whether it be walking, running, driving, sex, speech or anger, slowness has its advantages. Well, that's my story, and I'm sticking to it.

Perverts, paedophiles and pencils

(8 June 2008)

So, there I was, about 3 years ago, walking along a road in an eastern part of London. As is often the case when I am walking, I was deep in thought.

A boy, about 9-years-old, came out of a grocery shop, crossing my path 2 metres in front of me. I looked up, momentarily smiled, and walked on.

Half a second later, his mother, who had followed him out of the shop, screamed at me, "Don't smile at my son, you pervert!"

A pervert is a person with very unusual/abnormal/deviant sexual desires. So, I was extremely shocked and upset. Though, I was reassured later that day, when my niece (who teaches in a school in London) told me, that even by British standards, the mother's reaction was extreme.

I was reminded of this incident by Dismas Nkunda's article in *The Weekly Observer* (29 May 2008, p8). He was flying from New York to London and was allocated a seat next to a 12-year-old boy of Kenyan extraction. They struck up a conversation. A little later, there was an announcement over the loudspeaker for Mr Nkunda to go to the back of the plane. There, a flight attendant told him that the boy was unaccompanied and that he must not sit next to either a male or female adult, but to a kid of around the same age {or, I presume, to sit next to nobody at all, and be looked after by the flight crew}. They would therefore move Nkunda elsewhere in the plane. Nkunda got back to his seat and began to pick up his luggage. In his article, he described the boy's reaction:

> "He said he had no problem with someone whom he had struck up a conversation about Kenya....he asked the stewardess whether I was a cannibal."

Nkunda explained to the boy that the airline was just trying to protect him from strangers who misuse youngsters by saying or doing bad things.

> "The boy protested again, saying that whenever he is in Kenya, he moves with any person and nothing wrong has ever happened to him. I left him in tears."

I understand the boy's reaction. As I walk around Kampala, every day I have kids who I do not know, running up to talk to me, sometimes wanting to hold my hand. This, of course, happens a lot because they are interested to make contact with a *muzungu*. But, I have lived 16 years of my life in Africa, so I often smile and chat because I appreciate that African culture means I can behave in this friendly way.

However, I have also lived 35 years of my life in the UK (plus 5 in India), so I know that young British kids are taught never to talk to adult strangers. (In reality, to *male* strangers, since the vast majority of cases of adult sexual abuse of children is by men. My Mum frequently told me when I was of primary school age, "if you get lost, or have a problem, always go and ask a woman for help").

So, what is at the heart of Nkunda's article, and today's *Roving Eye*, is the acute fear of paedophiles (people who want to have sex with young children) in countries like UK and USA.

This fear of perverts and paedophiles is so strong, that the results in other areas of life will surprise many Ugandans. Here are three examples drawn from my training as a UK Athletics qualified coach.

In the UK, if I want to video a young athlete running, so I can analyse their running action on the video in order to correct faults, I must first obtain the permission of the parents. This is just in case I might be a paedophile who gets sexual pleasure from watching the video and/or sending it out on the internet to other perverts.

Secondly, I was taught on the UK Athletics courses that I must never touch the body of any athlete (young or old; male or female). For example, if a runner tells me they have a pain in their leg (thigh, calf, foot etc.) and I need to find the exact spot, I must not use my fingers, but another object (I normally use a pencil) to touch their body. I have coached many different Ugandan athletes over the last 14 years. When I touch them with a pencil, their first reaction is surprise. But when I explain the reasons why I use a pencil and not my hands, they laugh and they laugh and they laugh.

Lastly, to hold a UK Athletics coaching license at all, every 3 years I must undergo a "criminal records check" to make sure I am not a pervert or any other sort of bad person.

This has been a serious article about very different behaviour between Africa and elsewhere in the World. But let's finish it on a humorous note. As I walk through Kampala tomorrow, I do not want any "beautiful brown babe" shouting across the street at me:

"Kevin, please come and touch me with your pencil!"

Muzungu v Ugandan eccentricity
(20 July 2008)

"Otafire overspeaks," observed Isaac Wasswa. "He is eccentric. He speaks words of high voltage that can anger people."

Isaac runs a small grocery shop in my local trading centre and is a good friend. We had been discussing eccentricity. An eccentric is someone who is a bit odd or unconventional. Their behaviour departs from the norm – it is unusual.

I had asked Isaac to name a Ugandan eccentric. His reply was "Kahinda Otafire."

In a recent newspaper interview, a journalist asked me, "Do you think you are weird?" I replied:

> "Well, I know I am eccentric......it's difference that makes human beings interesting. Perhaps that's what makes people think I'm interesting, because I am a bit different."

So, what makes me a bit different? What is my claim to eccentricity? Appearance, possibly. My nose is unusually big, even by *bazungu* standards. And as the word "unusual" is found in most dictionary definitions of "eccentricity", let me add that my hair is unusually long for a fifty-something man and, because of my age, is increasingly white. So, I do stick out in a crowd, and it was no surprise when recently, at the Mandela National Stadium, the President of the Uganda Athletics Federation told me that he was easily able to spot me amongst a crowd of spectators on the distant side of the track. When I remarked to him that "nobody looks like me in Uganda", his reply was:

> "Kevin, nobody looks like you, even in England!"

While some might have felt insulted, I took his comment as a compliment to my eccentricity.

But eccentricity, rather like a disease, can be infectious. For, back in my local trading centre, Isaac Wasswa suddenly said to me, "I, too, want to be eccentric."

Isaac is not the first person I would associate with eccentricity. He is a conservative, conventional man who works extremely hard in his small shop – 15 hours per day, 7 days per week. All my efforts to get him to take a little leisure and do something different, for example, "let's go out and have a cheap Ethiopian meal next Sunday" always meet with the failure of his standard reply, "I can't go, I've gotta work."

So, before taking on the challenge of suggesting appropriate eccentricities, I said to Isaac:

> "Are you sure you want to be eccentric? Why, exactly, do you want to be eccentric?"
>
> "People will want to look at me," he retorted. "Everyone will want to look at me."

But, to make Isaac eccentric, is a tough challenge. One answer would be for him to walk through Kampala without trousers and underpants, since then, indeed "everyone will want to look." However, as Isaac's next destination would then either be Luzira Prison or Butabika National Referral Mental Hospital (Butabika Hospital, as it is known to most Ugandans), such a one-way ticket to eccentricity would not be sensible.

There then followed much conversation between Isaac and me as to his best eccentric option. Eventually we agreed that for him, also, it lay with his hair, and was captured by his comment:

> "It is not normal, in 2008, for a man to have a big Afro hairstyle. It will make people look at me and I would like that."

So, 5 weeks ago, Isaac started growing his hair. To my ageing eyes, he doesn't yet look much different, and I think it could well be Christmas before he has his "big Afro". When that day arrives, I should surely drag him from the prison of his shop, and we celebrate his achievement at an excitingly eccentric Ethiopian eatery.

Would you eat while walking?

(28 July 2008)

Walking home along the pavement of London's busy Edgware Road, while eating fish and chips wrapped in newspaper, is an early childhood memory. Today, Londoners will often be seen walking while eating and drinking. It may be a sandwich, or a burger, or a cup of coffee or a soda, or any variety of snacks and drink. Sometimes, they will even be rushing e.g. walking fast along a crowded pavement, while they are chewing and swallowing the food.

At the International Court in The Hague, I would have to plead guilty to having lived in Uganda for many years before realising that Ugandans generally do not share such "*bazungu*" behaviour. For as Albert, a 27-year-old Nebbi-born newsvendor told me:

> "It is not right to eat while walking. I would always find a specific place like a restaurant."

So, why this Ugandan dislike of feeding footing feasters? For an answer, I turned to Ben, 30, who has a shop in Kampala. He started his answer with, "I am a Muganda....." At which point I rudely interrupted and said:

> "I am also a Muganda. I belong to a new clan called the *enfuudu* (tortoise) clan as my wife tells me I am slow at everything I do."

Ben smiled his patient, gentle smile, put down his soldering iron with which he had been repairing the inside of a television, and said:

> "Now, Kevin, please listen to me. I am a Muganda. In Kiganda culture, it is shameful for someone to walk while

eating when he is mature. So when we were growing up, they taught us not to eat while walking. We should buy something and then sit and eat. Standing and eating is OK, but *never* to walk and eat. It doesn't show manners to walk and eat. That's the way the Baganda bring up their children. I can't speak for other tribes."

Fearing that if I ended the article there, my computer inbox, which is already overflowing with unanswered emails, would be swamped by a flood from non-Baganda, I approached Aggrey, 26, for a view. Our discussion, though, started on an unhappy note. Aggrey was upset, not about gorging, gulping, guzzling pedestrians, but about having had his mobile phone stolen. His mood, though, was improving, as he had just got some "inside information" from a friend who works in a major phone company that they would shortly be reducing the price of one of their phones from 45,000 to 35,000 or even 29,000 Ugandan shillings. Fortunately, I was not having to use up any airtime to listen to this, and at last I got him on to the main topic of masticating marchers. Taking a sharp look in the direction of Ben across the street, Aggrey emphasised:

"It is not just the Baganda. The majority of tribes, possibly all of them, would not walk and eat at the same time."

Thinking that I could now put the issue to bed, it was unfortunate that I still needed to buy some meat, as the apparent Ugandan unity on "walking and eating" was disturbed by an entirely different view. Geoffrey, a 23-year-old butcher, lifted up his huge knife to cut both small pieces of cow's meat, and certainty from my mind, when he said:

"I would eat because if I am hungry I want to satisfy myself. It is not bad to eat in a street when walking."

So, a very different opinion from Geoffrey. But Albert, Ben and Aggrey had told me enough to make me think long and hard before walking along Kampala Road eating chips, in the same way as I had done on London's Edgware Road, all those years before.

Old *muzungu* gets dirty looks

(24 May 2009)

The Regulation of Interception of Communication Bill (2007) – more commonly known as the Phone Tapping Bill – is causing much controversy and stress amongst the political classes. I swear that the hair of my fellow non-inker, Amama Mbabazi, is a bit whiter than it was a few weeks ago.

I wonder if there are any phone calls that you make where a phone tapper could jump to the wrong conclusions concerning what you are talking about?

I make around 20 telephone calls a week to a 21-year-old Ugandan woman. Our typical phone conversation is, "Please be ready in 10 minutes. I will pick you up in my car and we will go to the hotel."

I am sure that many Ugandans hearing such a telephone call from an old *muzungu* man to a much younger woman would automatically think "sugardaddy" or "polygamy".

However, I coach the young woman, not at sex, but at athletics. And the actual reason we would be going to the hotel is for her to do a tough weight-training session in its excellent gym. Our other telephone calls would be more readily understandable to the phone tapper. They would be specifically about training (e.g. 10 x 400 metres at Mandela National Stadium), big races coming up, recovery from injury etc. But who knows which particular conversation the phone tapper listened to and on which their conclusions are based?

A similar situation arises when I have taken the athlete to the *Game* superstore to buy items like ankle weights or weight-training gloves. The "dirty looks" I receive from some other shoppers are a "sight to behold".

But the worst "dirty looks" are aimed at me at the hotel. For, after training, around 11am, we pass out of the hotel's main entrance together, both of us carrying bags!

The joke between me and the several Ugandan female athletes I have coached is that I should wear a badge which says, "I AM AN ATHLETICS COACH, NOT A SUGARDADDY". And when we approach a possible "dirty looks" situation, such as when getting into a *matatu*, the athletes have sometimes jokingly shouted at me, "Coach where's your badge!?"

It is interesting that it took me quite a long time to understand Ugandan culture and actually see the "dirty looks". Over a decade ago, I was coaching the All-African Games 800m bronze medallist, the great Grace Birungi. But I was still fairly new to Uganda, and on the very many occasions that I used to walk through Kampala with Grace – perhaps on the way to an Embassy to collect her entry visa to compete in a big international race – I was not aware of anybody looking at us strangely. But undoubtedly some were.

So, phone tappers beware if you tap my phone. All may not be what it first appears.

Time to say "goodbye" to the colonial suit and tie

(8 November 2009)

Once, I was a prisoner of a suit and tie, but circumstances have permitted, that for the last 13 years, I have been able to dress casually. So *"Roving Eye"* now generally is found wearing training shoes, jeans and T-shirt. Nowadays, I can just about remember how to tie a tie knot. And when I had to attend a formal occasion recently, my tie felt so strange, it was almost like having a circular lifebuoy or a mongrel dog around my neck! The tie also made me feel hot, even though I was only wearing a cotton shirt with no jacket.

Every single reader of today's column will be carrying prejudices of one type or another in their heads. I must admit that in 2009, I am prejudiced against formal clothes, and no doubt sometimes to their wearers. But I should be careful, as over the centuries and millennia, few areas in life have given us more warning words than the danger of judging people by their clothes.

As long ago as the sixth century before Christ, the Greek writer, Aesop told us:

> "It is not only fine feathers that make birds."

And, more worrying for prejudiced me, 200 years ago, the British writer William Hazlitt came up with these wonderfully striking words:

> "Those who make their dress a principal part of themselves will in general become of no more value than their dress."

Nevertheless, my preference (or call it prejudice if you like) for informal clothes continues. In politics, Nelson Mandela's trademark informal shirts set him apart from other male presidents and politicians. Their boring uniforms of sober suit and tie would rightfully earn them the title of "grey men in grey suits." Since when has a politician wearing the required suit and tie uniform protected us from their bent ways? They are but "wolves in sheep's clothing."

And the added irony is that suits and ties are the uniforms of the conservative status quo bequeathed to Ugandans by the colonialists. And they were not even the uniforms of all the Britons of that period - not of its miners, its cleaners, its agricultural workers – they were the uniform of Britain's colonial service, extremely posh and exclusive at the top.

Putting colonialist and sociological concerns to one side, a basic functionality should also apply to clothes. For instance, do they keep you warm (when it's cold) or cool (when the weather is hot)? Uganda is often hot, but not as hot as many African countries which do not enjoy its cooling altitude. There seems little sense in wearing a suit and a tie, however "hot" fashion-wise, in a hot African climate.

This article has been full of prejudices, both my own and other people's. But, as climate change tweaks Africa's temperatures to even more upward extremes, is it not time for Uganda to consign its "suit and tie" culture to history?

Ugandan and *bazungu* nicknames
(13 March 2011)

You have a name, but you may also have a nickname, which is used humourously or affectionately, and occasionally nastily, by others, instead of your real name.

Bosco is a 48-year-old unemployed Ugandan. He told me that when he was in his early twenties, his nickname was "Stallion". So, I said, "Dear Bosco, why on earth was your nickname 'Stallion'?" His reply was:

> "I was in a student hostel and I had a habit of changing girls, that is bedmates, as often as I changed clothes. So, my friends called me 'Stallion', a he-horse made for mating."

A few minutes earlier, Daniel, a 28-year-old technician, had confessed that his nickname was "Kapit".

Now, I have heard of "Kaput" as in "My television has gone "Kaput", but "Kapit" was a word I had never heard before.

> "When I was 6 years old", Daniel explained, "I used to have a rabbit. A young rabbit. But that rabbit got lost. I was so upset that I started to cry. Instead of saying 'my rabbit', I mispronounced it and said 'my kapit.' My oldest brother started calling me 'Kapit', and every time I cried he would say, 'Kapit, don't cry'. That's how I got my nickname."

At secondary school, *Roving Eye* had several nicknames. There was "Bones" because I was so thin. And "Diamond Head", because, presumably, I have a pointed head. And let's face it, pointed heads are not unknown to Ugandan cartoonists when they caricature their politicians.

And my third nickname, not entirely inappropriate as we enter the final stages of the Cricket World Cup, was "Mr Attack".

Now, sarcasm is an especially British form of humour. Needless to say, my most frequently used cricketing batting strokes were not attack ones, but defence ones, such as the forward defence. But, in order to poke fun at me, my fellow schoolboys sarcastically nicknamed me not "Mr Defence", but "Mr Attack".

However, as I like:
- Attacking pastors.
- Attacking fat politicians, traffic policemen, indeed anybody fat.
- Attacking all football fans that do not support Fulham F.C.

Perhaps, "Mr Attack" is not a bad nickname for me after all?

A *muzungu*'s "long call" too far
(27 March 2011)

She is not my co-wife, but, on this very page, she is most certainly *Roving Eye*'s co-columnist. I am talking about none other than that distinguished lady, *Woman About Town*.

Now anything *Woman About Town* can do, *Roving Eye* can do. She may think she has a monopoly of diarrhoea (see her "Pride comes before a fall and a really bad joke" *Sunday Monitor*, 13 March 2011) in which she describes a road trip where she had to rush out of a car, only to "long call" in somebody's innocent vegetable patch. But *Muzungu Bignose* can match her every inch (or should that be every fluid ounce) of her brown torrent way.

So, there I was, before athletics coaching, slowly jogging along the beautifully scenic wooded winding paths that lie just beyond Kampala's Kyambogo Cricket Oval. "Life is great" I thought to myself. Then, without warning, like a gush out of the blue, the *ekiddukano* (diarrhoea) struck. "Oh my Gawd!" I cursed, then I rushed into the bushes before belatedly lowering my shorts and underpants. Carrying no TP, I used some big brown leaves to partially clean my bum, which were even browner by the time I had finished.

And, with only my cut away running shorts covering my manhood, I walked back along the winding paths, then tiptoed along the edge of the running track, hoping that none of the athletes would see the incriminating underpants evidence that I was trying to conceal in my right hand.

When I recounted this story in my local trading centre, Joseph, 27, commented:

> "Kevin, *bikokoma* is the name of the leaves of the jackfruit tree. Those leaves are particularly good if I don't have toilet paper in the bush. In those local places, in the villages, they use *bikokoma*, even in the latrines."

Being an ignorant urban boy, I have no idea what leaves I used that morning near the Kyambogo Oval, but I was sure glad that they were there.

Regretfully, my life in Uganda has been (and my underpants have been) marked by an overabundance of *ekiddukano*. When I stand for the Kampala Mayorship during Obote 3, perhaps I should make this part of my manifesto? Imagine all those posters throughout our capital city which would boldly shout:

> **O'CONNOR KEVIN**
>
> **VOTE LONDA** ✓
>
> **FOR POVERTY, CORRUPTION AND DIARRHOEA**

Drinking beer from bottle, glass or straw?
(3 April 2011)

It is almost 17 years since my dainty feet first touched Ugandan soil.

OK, I agree, that this length of time does not exactly make me a Speke, Hannington or Lourdel. But, nevertheless, my arrival at Entebbe remains an important event in my little life.

So, you may ask, 17 years later is there anything that I particularly remember, that took me by surprise, during my first few days in Uganda? Was it that:
- My nose was bigger than anybody else's?
- My *akasolo* (manhood) and *kabina* (bum) were smaller than anybody else's?

Or was it something else?

Yes, it was something else. So, what was it? It was seeing people drink beer with a straw.

Previously, I had lived for:
- Two and a half years in northern Nigeria.
- Five years in India.
- Too many years in the UK.

But I had never seen anybody drinking beer with a straw until I arrived in Uganda.

So, why do some Ugandans drink beer using a straw?

Is there any link between sucking beer through a straw and the traditional practice of sucking *malwa* from a communal pot using a long reed?

Or, is it that the straw acts to increase the alcoholic impact of the beer?

Tom, a 25-year-old self-employed businessman, gave me a rather different explanation. He said:

> "I normally drink beer directly from a bottle. But, Kevin, I do sometimes drink it with a straw. The advantage of using a straw is that you don't finish the beer quickly – it takes longer to drink. You get better value for money. In

other words, we don't have money and that is why we use a straw."

My fellow Ugandans, you may ask, how does *Roving Eye* like to take his beer? The answer to that question is different from the answer to the question, how do I like to take my coffee? For, I like my coffee like my women – hot, sweet and black.

I enjoy my beer very cold, and because my behaviour has been shaped by many years of socialisation outside Uganda, I generally drink it from a glass. But, I do sometimes use a straw, which all goes to show that, indeed, "we are all Ugandans now".

A rich *muzungu*'s hair transplant
(19 June 2011)

The Manchester United footballer, Wayne Rooney, is going bald at the young age of 25. So, he has had a hair transplant and the estimated cost has varied from £7000 (around Ug Sh 28m) through to a whopping £30,000 (around Ug Sh 120m)!

To get a take on Rooney's decision on the Ugandan streets, I interviewed Timothy, a 28-year-old shop assistant in a Kampala trading centre. He told me:

> "If I went bald at 28, I would feel shame. I could not get a girl of my choice and age....23 to 25 years old. She may even think I am 40 years and above. There is a local doctor I could go to and get herbal medicines to cure the baldness. But they would charge you much. If I was rich I would go there."

Timothy, therefore, had no doubt that if he had Rooney's wealth he would have the hugely more expensive hair transplant.

If *Roving Eye* was in Rooney's position, would he have a hair transplant? I would like to say the answer would be "no". That I would just accept that I was going bald and continue with my life.

But I can't be at all sure about this. And the reason is because of my reaction when my hair started to turn from brown to white in the early 1990's. Did I "just accept" the change in my hair colour and "continue with my life"? No, I did not! I bought a product called *Grecian 2000* which was supposed to restore my greying hair to its original colour – no doubt I thought this would make me look younger. It was only when a good friend told me that my hair looked very odd and was turning "a funny kind of yellow" that I threw away the *Grecian 2000* and finally said goodbye to my brown hair.

So, if I had been tempted to restore my hair colour almost two decades ago when I was 40 years with a full head of hair, then I can certainly appreciate the possibility that I would have been in a hair transplant clinic at 25 years of age, if I had Rooney's money and high football profile.

Thus, in answer to the question, "If you were Wayne Rooney, would you have had a hair transplant", Timothy voted "Yes" and Kevin voted "Possibly" – but I always do like a fence to sit on!

Things that might surprise a *muzungu* in Uganda

(2015)

I have lived in Uganda for 21 years, and for 7 years in other developing countries. Therefore, I now barely notice many marked differences between Uganda and the country I was brought up in (the UK). Uganda is my home. It is the norm.

But my wife and I do sometimes ponder what might surprise a friend or relative (who has not been out of the UK, or at least not out of Europe) should they visit Uganda.

To start with, such a *muzungu* would be startled to find goats, cows, chickens, ducks, turkeys etc. strolling around Kampala's suburbs. The only animals to be seen on the streets of London (if we ignore Chelsea supporters…………..) are dogs and cats. And as regards the former, there is another difference. Dogs in Kampala, whose owners are wealthy enough for them to have a collar and lead, are rarely walked by the owner. They will be walked by an employee of the owner, or by a professional dog walker.

Moving from four legs to two wheels, motorcycle taxis just don't exist where the *muzungu* comes from. The *boda-boda* will be a new phenomenon for them. And they will be astounded that there can be sometimes up to four passengers (including children) on a *boda*, normally with nobody (including the driver) wearing a crash helmet. When there are no passengers, all sorts of things are carried on the back. For example: incredibly wide loads like poles; beds; corrugated iron roofing sheets; coffins (hopefully empty); livestock (including pigs, goats and chicken).

Any pedestrian in Kampala knows they have to be careful where to put their feet. Of course, there is the animal *pupu*, but much worse than that are the open manholes, which people can fall into. The covers have been stolen and sold off as scrap metal. Kampala City Council has taken to covering the manholes with huge ceramic flowerpots, which are too heavy to lift. Some even have flowers in. But those that don't, frequently get filled with rubbish.

From pedestrian to pedlar, and these two words do have the same Latin root (*pes, pedis* – foot). Many hawkers are seen moving around on foot, selling everything from clothes, handbags, shoes right through to bootleg CDs and DVDs. In December, they carry Christmas trees, with Christmas decorations hanging off themselves.

A different type of small businessman is the knife sharpener. I regularly see them outside butchers, where they sharpen knives, using the revolving wheel of a bicycle turned upside down.

In contrast to the First World (where there is great fear of paedophiles and other perverts), many young children are found playing in the streets. Worryingly, though, this can be sometimes next to very busy roads.

On a Sunday, noisy churches pollute the airwaves, with shouting, screeching evangelical preachers being particular sinners. Every day of the week, maniacal street preachers are found standing at the side of the road, normally positioned at traffic junctions.

Open trucks can be seen, ferrying manual workers, who are herded into the back, many hanging on the edges. The word "herd" is appropriate, because there is a similarity to cattle crammed into such trucks, on their way to the slaughterhouse, and whose final journey, overcrowdedly wedged together, provides a persuasive advert for vegetarianism.

An Irish friend on a recent visit to Kampala was struck (I think worried) by the number of security guards carrying guns, including those off duty, on their way home. The only people

I have seen with guns in public places in the UK are the police. And then it is only a small minority of police, like at London Airport, where there may be a terrorism threat.

These are just a handful of the differences that a *muzungu* might notice between Uganda and their home country. My apologies that they have tended towards the negative, for the spontaneous warmth and friendliness of Ugandans, is the greatest difference of all.

4

The Environment

Uganda, the pearl of bird watching
(18 March 2007)

As well as describing the feathered creatures that fly in the sky, the word "bird" has, at least in the UK, an entirely different slang meaning i.e. girl or girlfriend.

So, it is "bird-brained" O'Connor who would like to point out that the slang version of "bird" brings an interesting interpretation to the proverb:

"A bird in the hand is worth two in the bush."

To the relief of readers, *Roving Eye* will now focus on "birds" in the traditional rather than the slang sense.

Winston Churchill called Uganda "the pearl of Africa." You may, or may not, agree with that statement, but Uganda is certainly "the pearl of birdwatching". For as travel writer Phillip Briggs explains in his *Bradt Travel Guide of Uganda*:

"Uganda is arguably the most attractive country in Africa to birdwatchers. Its remarkable avian diversity – 1008 species recorded in an area similar to that of Great Britain – can be attributed to its location at a transitional point between the East African savannah, the West African rain forest, and the semi-desert of the North."

This diversity of bird species was apparent during my visit to the Ugandan Wildlife Education Centre (UWEC) in Entebbe.

For example, semi-tame and freely roaming within the Centre were a pair of Crested Cranes. It is wonderful that this bird's distinctive image forms part of our country's flag.

Then, coexisting with otters, near a manmade pool with a sandy beach, were the Hamerkop. What stood out were their hammer-shaped heads and huge, untidy nests. Necks extended, they happily flew in and out of the Centre.

I can look ancient in the morning, especially after a late night out, but am never quite as prehistoric in appearance as the Shoebill Stork housed within UWEC's large wetland aviary. And I do have a big nose, but it can't match the Saddlebill Stork's massive black, red and yellow bill.

And hanging from beneath its nest, within the same aviary, was the busy, noisy Weaver Bird. I loved the way these birds darted in and out of the aviary, through the netting.

Many times I have seen the African Fish Eagle fly and swoop over Lake Victoria. As Williams and Arlott point out in their "Birds of East Africa", the Fish Eagle is:

> "Easily recognised by its distinctive colour pattern, white head, chest, back and tail; chestnut belly, shoulders and black wings." And then there is its eery cry – "the far-carrying, wild, almost gull-like call, which is one of the characteristic sounds of the African wilds. When calling, the bird throws its head backwards, even in flight."

After viewing so many African Fish Eagle from a distance, it was stunning to see one close-up, in its UWEC aviary.

But the bird that interested me the most during my marvellous few hours at UWEC, was the African Grey Parrot. Unfortunately, despite UWEC's good work, it is probably the single most endangered animal in Uganda today. Trapping and deforestation have already made it extinct in Kenya and its numbers in Uganda are rapidly reducing. Many are illegally transported to China, where it distinctive red tail feathers are thought to have medicinal properties.

And so my brief flirtation with birds is coming to an end. Only to add that *avis* is the Latin word for "bird", and it is from this root that we get English words like "aviary", "aviator," "aviation" etc.

And what with birds both of the feathered kind and of the long-legged beautiful girl type, could it be said that *Roving Eye* has today:

"Killed two birds with one stone"?!

You don't always have to behave

(29 July 2007)

There was a noise and the earth began to shake. At first, I thought that my wife had passed gas and I waited for the bad smell to reach my nose. But the smell never came. Then, I realised that there had not been an earthquake in my wife's stomach, but a real, genuine earthquake.

It had originated in the Lake Natron area of northern Tanzania, and it made me think that just as there is a Richter Scale for earthquakes, there should also be Richter Scale (possibly Shichter Scale) for passing gas, more commonly known as farting.

It is not socially acceptable to pass gas in a public place. So, understandably it took a long time for farting to occur in a movie film – indeed, it was not until 1974 that the cowboy comedy western, "Blazing Saddles," hit the smellwaves. As one film reviewer put it:

> "In the film's most notorious, vulgar and well-remembered scene, gassed-up, wind-breaking cowboys, sit around the night's campfire eating beans - burping and farting incessantly."

Passing gas is just one of many activities that are taboo in public places.

Others include scratching one's private parts or bum.

Even the poor old nose is not immune, for it is not thought good to pick the said nose in public. Indeed, even if you were extremely hungry, picking the contents of your nose would still be frowned upon.

The word "bogey" has many meanings. One slang usage is a piece of nasal mucus.

You might think that if you were able to extract a bogey from each nostril, you could enjoy the real feast of a double bogey.

But, unfortunately, people would prefer you to eat beans in public rather than a bogey, even though the former can result in you passing gas.

And certainly, do not try to impress anybody with a "double bogey" if you are a golf player. For under the rules of golf, a double bogey is a score of two above par for any hole – the word "bogey" deriving from the mythical nineteenth century golfer, Colonel Bogey.

Many golfers seen on expensive Ugandan golf courses are businessmen with big stomachs. They would surely, therefore, score high on the "Shichter Scale," and thus would do well at an audition should "Blazing Saddles" ever be performed at Kampala's National Theatre.

The presence of the famous farting scene will mean that it will be the only time in the history of theatre that it will cost less to sit in the front row than in the back row, and that the back row will be inhabited by the Chief Guest - Gas, Gushing, General, Sir Farty F*** Face.

Old buildings deserve respect

(28 September 2007)

Call me Kevin O'Conservation if you like, but the destruction of Uganda's historic buildings is a cultural crime. For, as the United Nations Educational Scientific and Cultural Organisation (UNESCO) points out:

> "Heritage is our legacy from the past, what we live with today, and what we pass on to future generations. Our cultural and natural heritage are both irreplaceable sources of life and inspiration."

David, 35, is not an overpaid UNESCO consultant - he just has a tiny shop in a Kampala suburb. But he argues his case as well as UNESCO:

> "The knocking down of old buildings is not good. Kids who are being produced now, need to see what architecture was being built in those days. Furthermore, we should be conserving them as a tourist attraction."

The Historic Buildings Conservation Trust of Uganda (HBCT) has listed 60 buildings in Kampala for preservation. As

Bamutaraki Musinguzi observes in a superb article ("Kampala's old charm, beauty, ravaged by new buildings" *The East African*, September 10 2007):

> "Of these {60 buildings}, 12 are known to be at risk, and 8 have already been demolished. One such demolished building, *Drapers*, was the oldest shop in Kampala."

Recent wanton destruction of Uganda's architectural heritage has also resulted from the "construction" of the *Hilton Hotel* by the Sudanese Aya brothers. Two walls of Nakasero Fort have been demolished as well as the Uganda Broadcasting Corporation studios, formerly the European and Asian Hospital. Even with these former hospital buildings, stinking as they do of colonial apartheid, who is to say that they would not have been of interest to future generations of Ugandans, as they looked back on their country's history?

And the irony is whether the fort's walls and the old hospital may have been destroyed for nothing. According to *Red Pepper* (September 28, 2007 p3):

> "After incurring numerous debts...AYA (U) Ltd was put under receivership effective 20th September 2007... construction of the hotel stalled at the first floor and the investors have since vanished into thin air."

During an early morning jog in Jinja, I will unfailingly stop outside the Nile View Mansion on Grant Road and, for a few moments, just marvel at its beauty. It was constructed many decades ago by an Asian trader or industrialist. This mansion, taken together with the other historical buildings mentioned in today's *Roving Eye*, serve to highlight a point made by Vivian Craddock Williams in his "Good old city buildings" (*Sunday Vision*, June 13 1999, p25):

"All historic buildings in Uganda, with the sole exception of the tribal tombs, are architectural imports. Their designs come from both East and West, and many are intriguing hybrids of great eclectic beauty."

Even when buildings date from the colonial period, they are still part of the country's history. So let us preserve and conserve Uganda's architectural heritage. Ugandans show great respect to their old people, and may need to show similar respect to their old buildings.

The tiny difference between success and failure
(13 January 2008)

It is often the case that the margin between achieving success and failure is small, but that the consequences are huge. Let me take two examples from very difficult aspects of life. The second had huge worldwide importance with massive consequences, including for Ugandans.

Football
A few weeks ago, the Premier League football team I support (Fulham) were drawing 0-0 with Newcastle. Right at the end of the match, with only a few seconds of added time remaining, Newcastle got a penalty and won the game 1-0. The Fulham manager (Lawrie Sanchez) was sacked later that week. However, had the referee blown his whistle a few seconds earlier, Fulham would have drawn, Mr Sanchez would have remained manager, and with a little good fortune in subsequent matches would still be manager today. So, the last few seconds of that game

had huge consequences for Mr Sanchez, but was of little importance to most human beings.

American politics

The second example could not be more different. The 2000 American presidential election was the closest in that country's history. After all the expenditure, speeches, debates, adverts and lost nervous energy, just over a thousand votes in the state of Florida decided the outcome – and Florida had six million voters.

So, it was President George W. Bush, and not President Al Gore.

The margin of victory may have been tiny, but the consequences were earth-shattering, possibly literally so.

Would there have been an Iraq war with all its death and devastation, under a President Al Gore? The war was surely prompted by Bush wishing to complete his father's unfinished (Gulf War) business.

There are now many Ugandans working in Iraq, but it is in another American policy area where a small number of votes in Florida have had, and will have, a much bigger impact on Uganda. The world would have made much more progress on combating climate change and global warming had Gore, and not Bush, been president.

In the last few months in Uganda, we have seen some awful flooding and some unusually high temperatures, quite probably caused by climate change. And these weather conditions will get worse in the coming years and decades.

The English language

Over the centuries, the English language has developed many metaphors to describe such "close run" situations as the Fulham vs Newcastle football match and the 2000 American presidential elections. For example: "by a hair's breadth," "on a knife's edge," and "on a razors edge."

Bush and Gore, and Newcastle and Fulham, were certainly "neck and neck" with both Bush and Newcastle, "winning by a whisker."

But let us leave the last word to the Duke of Wellington, who nearly two hundred years ago, when speaking after defeating Napoleon at the Battle of Waterloo, exclaimed:

> "It has been a damned nice thing – the nearest run thing you ever saw in your life."

Such can be the difference between success and failure.

Fish, cattle and paving stones

(10 August 2008)

There is the Third World. And there is the First World. Happenings in one can surprise people in the other. But having spent more than a third of my life in the Third World, I think (or I would like to think) that these surprises occur less often to me.

But occur they do, as when recently watching the early Brad Pitt film, "A River Runs through it", on DVD. Set in America, the film includes many scenes where the Pitt character, and his father and brother, are fishing with rods and imitation flies. Sometimes they catch fish. So, what is surprising about this, and marks out a difference between First and Third Worlds?

Well, it came right at the end of the film, almost hidden amongst the many credits which rolled up my TV screen. The simple sentence was:

"No fish were harmed in the making of this film".

It is times like these that I wonder what a typical Ugandan, struggling to find school fees and meet all the very many challenges that life throws at them, would make of the comment, "No fish were harmed in the making of this film".

Surely, a society must have had considerable success in meeting its human needs, before starting to worry about whether fish are hurt, or not hurt, when they are caught?

In Uganda, there is worry about overfishing, but not, as far as I know, whether the fish suffer, when the fishermen pull in their nets.

Moving from fish to cows, last week, on the road from Masaka to Kampala, I saw cattle so tightly packed into the back of a lorry that I tried not to look at the animals' pained faces when our car overtook. But therein lies the danger of my values, shaped predominantly in the First World, when applied to Uganda, for the very next lorry we overtook was filled with human beings, packed almost as tightly as the cattle.

The vehicular crowding of the cattle would not be acceptable in the First World. But in the same First World, nearly all people travel the roads (and the railways) in complete comfort. In contrast, Third World people will be packed "like cattle" in vehicles, or on the backs of them, and sometimes three people, occasionally four, squeezed on a motorbike. It is such human discomfort that makes it difficult to feel sorry for the cattle, let alone the fish!

Similarly, there are those "problems" that people get so upset about in the First World – a broken paving stone, for example, can generate many letters of complaint in local newspapers from pedestrians who fear they, or a loved one, may trip over. But these are the problems, rather like a hurt fish, that Ugandans would not recognise as problems at all. Indeed, most Ugandans would be overjoyed if there was actually some pavement to walk on. There is the Third World. And there is the First World.

Would you put a cup of tea on the ground?
(2 November 2008)

Even if I lived for another one hundred years (and died in 2108 AD, at the age of 156), there would still be much about Ugandan culture that I did not know. After 14 years here, it was only last week that I became aware of the marked difference between Ugandan and my own culture when holding (or rather not holding) a cup of tea.

Earlier this year I learnt that Ugandans generally do not walk when eating or drinking. So, when on Tuesday, in my local trading centre, I bought a large plastic cup of steaming African Tea for Ug Sh 200, and then walked along sipping it, I knew I had already crossed a cultural frontier. I reached shop attendant friends, sat down on a bench outside their store for a chat, and because I wanted to show them something in the newspapers, I put my cup on the ground. A momentary look of great surprise crossed their eyes.

My UK-resident memories sometimes fade with time, age and heat. But even so, I still remember most people there would put a cup of tea/coffee down on the ground without second thoughts. And that would be on any type of ground e.g. pavement, tarmac, earth, sand, grass etc. After all, one drinks from the top of a cup, not from its bottom.

So why this big difference in Uganda, where tea-drinkers almost never put their cup on the ground?

Frank, 17, is a butcher who left school after S4. He told me:

> "There are germs on the ground you can't see with your eyes. They get into the tea. You would get some disease such as cholera. You don't put a cup on the ground because you want to stay healthy."

Mary, 32, is the mother of four children and has never been to school. She was more emphatic than Frank, and in a loud voice said:

> "It is wrong. I would never do it. You would get dust from the ground and from passing vehicles. Even flies could fall into it."
>
> "But, Mary," I interrupted, "if I was holding the cup in my hand, surely flies could still fall in it?"
>
> "Not very much," she replied, "they don't have enough chance. And, you are more likely to see them falling in the cup."

Nick, 25, is a Liverpool fan. Before we talked tea, we talked football. To say that Nick was happy would be a bigger understatement than to say that NSSF has problems:

> "Last Sunday," he shrieked, "we ashamed Chelsea who had gone 4 years unbeaten at home. We are now top of the Premier League, and we intend to stay there."

Back to the subject of the cup, and that's not the F.A. Cup, but the cup of tea. Nick remarked:

> "People move on the ground. It's very dirty. Also, someone may kick your cup. And we say in Luganda, *oba ng'oyozzeza noyanika mutaka*. This means that it would be like washing and drying the clothes on the ground, that is, in the dust."

The above discussions relate to differences in culture between countries. Typically, these differences, are neither right nor wrong, just different. But as a non-Ugandan, should I be walking a few hundred metres along a Kampala street with my cup of tea and then putting it on the ground? Should I not remember St Ambrose's advice to St Augustine over 1600 years ago, "When in Rome, live as the Romans do"?

Ben, 26, is a shop assistant during the day, while studying in the evenings for a Diploma in Computer Science at MUBS

(Makerere University Business School). He did not agree with St Ambrose's advice as applied to tea, saying I should be flexible, so people like him could become aware of international cultural differences. But he did tell me of a Luganda saying, that appears very similar to the "When in Rome" one i.e. *bwogenda ebulyambwa nawe olya mbwa*, which Ben translated as, "even though you don't eat dog's meat, when you go to a region where it is eaten, you must eat it."

That, one cup of African tea should generate so much discussion, backs up the *Roving Eye* catchphrase, "For the observer of human behaviour, every scene has its interest."

Drinking and dropping a "duck's soda"
(7 December 2008)

The little plastic bag, containing around 300mls of cold water, is knotted at the top. Just below the knot, the plastic is pierced by a small straw, which the *duuka*-attendant later told me was half of a normal straw she had cut into two.

The young Ugandan man, having bought the water for Ug Sh 100, turns away from the *duuka*, takes another long sip, and somewhere into his second stride, drops the still-partly-filled plastic bag onto the ground, before he disappears off into a busy Kampala trading centre.

I look at the sad looking bag, and the sad looking bag, now dirtied by murram dust and with straw pointing in my direction, looks at me. I pick up the bag, and as the last air ebbs out of its body, and with the remaining water running like tears down its sides, I say to it:

> "Don't look so sad little bag, as next Sunday I will make you the star of *Roving Eye*. Your heart has been knifed by

the straw, but I will do my best to make sure you have not died in vain."

Wealth and poverty

In the First World, I have never seen water sold in plastic bags. For First Worlders have money, and to the extent they need to buy water, it will be in bottles and the water can be of many different types (carbonated, still, flavoured etc.). But people there have no need to buy cold boiled water at all - they have refrigerators in their homes, and tap water is of such a high quality, that it does not need to be boiled.

But Uganda is a poor Third World country in which poverty shapes behaviour. Isa Lubowa, 30, described himself to me as a "butcherman" and said:

> "People buy this water {in plastic bags} because it is the cheapest. Only 100 Ugandan Shillings, and it is 'cooked'. It is meant for the local people – the poorer people. The rich Ugandan will not use this one. He will get mineral water at 500 {for a bottle}."

A duck's soda

Larry, a 24-year-old Manchester United supporter, interrupted Isa:

> "Do you know what we call that water in plastic bags in our local language, Kevin? We call it *soda wambata*, which means 'a duck's soda'. You see, most of the time a duck drinks dirty water. So, if it could drink clean water, it would be like it was drinking soda!"

> "But Larry," I replied, "how do you know that the water is clean? Dishonesty in Uganda might mean that, to increase profits, the shop has not bothered to boil it."

"I can't buy it from just anyone," Larry exclaimed. "I only buy it from Rose. You see," he continued, while pointing at a steaming saucepan on a *sigri* outside a *duuka* further down the road, "she is boiling it right now."

Dirty environment

The man who had bought, then dropped, the 'duck's soda' did it from a shop where 14-year-old Paul was working as an attendant during the school holidays. He has just finished S1, enjoys maths and has the ambition of becoming an accountant. When I asked him about the man throwing the plastic bag on to the ground, he replied:

> "That was uncivilised. When he had finished he should have taken it to the rubbish pit or dustbin. Now the environment becomes dirty. And it will be our duty to remove it."

Thinking of others

If, before we throw rubbish on the ground, we stop and think about the people who must clear it up after us, and if we try harder to "treat our neighbours as ourselves" (as it is unlikely that any of us would want rubbish thrown down outside our own homes), then it will be the case that last Tuesday in a Kampala suburb, a sad tearful little plastic bag, did not die in vain.

Sir Alex Ferguson and Uganda's historic buildings

(17 May 2009)

Sir Alex Ferguson may not appear to have much in common with Uganda's historical monuments and buildings, though if he continues as Manchester United manager for much longer, he will soon be a historical monument himself!

However, some recent comments by Ferguson about Premier League dressing rooms reminded me of the delicate balance that must be achieved between preserving the past and building for the future. In Uganda, this is similarly highlighted by the rapid and virtually uncontrolled growth of Kampala, resulting in the destruction of many colonial, Asian and other historical buildings.

Ferguson claims that many Premier League dressing rooms are too cramped for the modern era. He singles out for criticism those in Fulham's historic Craven Cottage. He said of the away dressing room in the Cottage:

> "It is smaller than my office. The stadium is very traditional and is one of my favourite away grounds. But when you have 18 players stripping down, plus coaches, physios and kit men, it is ridiculous really."

Ferguson might have added, "Fulham's dressing rooms are so small, there is not even space for my hairdryer," but that would not be the Man U supremo, but *Roving Eye*, speaking.

Craven Cottage was completed in 1906, and was constructed by the famous stadia architect, Archibald Leitch. Yes, there is actually a cottage in one corner of the ground, and it houses the changing rooms plus a balcony overlooking the field of play.

As Wikipedia states:

> "Both the Johnny Haynes {formerly Stevenage Road} Stand and Cottage remain among the finest examples of Archibald Leitch football architecture to remain in

existence and this has been recognised with both being designated as Grade II listed buildings."

Now only a lunatic would suggest that Craven Cottage should be demolished so that "Their Highnesses" of Manchester United can change in the size of dressing rooms that they are used to at Old Trafford. But this is implicitly what Ferguson was saying.

There is indeed a delicate balance that must be achieved between preserving the past and making improvements for the future. When it comes to historic buildings, it is a balance that both Sir Alex Ferguson, and those responsible for the development of Kampala, have got wrong.

Where are Kampala's parks?

(19 September 2010)

I grew up in London, only "a stone's throw" away from its magnificent Hyde Park. My friends, my father and I would play football and cricket in its wide open green spaces, run on its "Rotten Row" (a sandy track generally used for riding horses) and even fish in its artificial lake (the Serpentine).

London has many other famous parks such as Regent's Park, Green Park and St James Park. It is not surprising, therefore, that the British should make parks a feature of the capital cities of their colonial empire.

Thus, in India's New Delhi, where I had the good fortune to live for 5 years, I enjoyed running in Lodhi Gardens, Nehru Park, the Deer Park and on the Delhi Ridge.

It surprised me greatly, therefore, to find so few parks in Kampala. Indeed, is there actually a park in Kampala? Centenary

Park was hardly a park even before it became parcelled out as restaurant space to serve the rich and privileged.

The construction of Garden City and the Game/Shoprite complex destroyed part of Kampala's little remaining green space. And there is worse still. Mr Richard Byiringiro, Chairman of Naguru Sports Club, has recently expressed his:

> "Dismay at the manner in which our community sports grounds seem to have been clandestinely leased out to yet unknown people. We have come to learn that the Naguru Sports Club ground, adjacent to Uganda Manufacturers Association (UMA), has purportedly been allocated to an investor other than UMA or the Naguru Sports Club."

> "I hereby call upon all those in authority," Byiringiro continued, "to intervene and take corrective action against government and any official involved in leasing or sub-leasing or selling of sports infrastructure. Sportsmen and women should make this an example by vehemently opposing any alteration to sports facilities that isn't meant to benefit sports. We need more facilities, not less! I suggest that officials involved in selling, leasing or donating sports infrastructure in the country be prosecuted in courts of law to serve as a deterrent to others."

As a youngster, I had London's Hyde Park to play in. In 2010, what similar green spaces do Kampala boys and girls have?

Some animal pupu issues

(31 July 2011)

Readers may be surprised to learn that in the UK there are around 7 million dogs. Most of these are kept as pets by their owners. One statistic I have seen is that these dogs produce about 1000 tonnes of excrement each day. Dog fouling in public places (including on pavements) has therefore become quite a big issue in the UK. Owners who do not clear up their dogs' pupu can be taken to court and fined up to £1000 (approximately Ug Sh 4m).

To assist owners in clearing up their pets' pupu, many public places, such as parks and recreation areas, have designated "dog bins" in which to place it. These days, many owners, while walking their dogs, carry with them a "pooper-scooper" (a small shovel-like device) and plastic bags with which to pick up the faeces and dispose of it hygienically in the dog bins.

One recognises that the situation in a developing country such as Uganda (with fewer resources) is far more challenging. Furthermore, I have never seen any goats or cattle wandering around London suburban streets, but many are found doing so in Kampala's suburbs. These goats and cattle, together with local dogs, of course, produce substantial excrement, and clearing all of this away would be a monumental task.

Doreen, a 40-year-old Ugandan professional, told me that she hates the amount of animal pupu that is found on the roads of Kampala. She said that the quicker both the animals and the pupu are removed, the better!

I got a very different view from Michael, a 32-year-old dog walker.

"This animal pupu is not a problem. It is a normal thing as we are a community with animals. Generally people don't mind, it is part of us."

"I am aware that KCC (Kampala City Council) is trying to clear the city of animals for hygiene reasons. I would not regard cow pupu itself, in front of my house, as dangerous. It is only when flies land on it that bothers me because they can spread germs."

And as for stepping in it? Michael said that goat and cow pupu smelt like grass, and that it was far worse stepping in dog pupu which was unpleasantly smelly. And as a dog walker, he should know! He also believed that dog pupu carried more germs than that of cows and goats.

Whether that is correct or not, in Kampala, there is definitely one thing worse than animal pupu in which to put one's foot – a manhole with its cover missing!

Why tarmacking roads might not be a good thing

(4 October 2015)

The road outside my house (previously murram), and those in the immediate neighbourhood, have recently been tarmacked.

For me, tarmac (which until researching this article I did not realise was an abbreviation for tarmacadam, but don't ask me about tarmaceve) was a backward step. The immediate effect was that vehicles began to travel much faster, sometimes dangerously fast. Only a few weeks after the tarmac was laid, two primary schoolchildren were killed in an accident on the junction about 40 metres from my home.

In another accident, a car hit a sign, and then ploughed into the area where *boda-boda* motorcyclists would have been, had it not been the middle of the night.

And when I walk to my local trading centre, I no longer take the direct route along the newly tarmacked road, because I fear the speeding vehicles. Instead, I take a circuitous alley, where all I meet coming in the opposite direction are chickens and ducks.

When I conducted some interviews near to my house, it soon became clear that my preference for murram roads over tarmac put me in a minority of one. The interviews were, of course, conducted in English. But I did learn that the Luganda for murram road is *oluguudo lw'ettaka*, and for tarmac road is *oluguudo lwa kolasi*.

Juma, 18, is a *boda-boda* man. Who knows, had the second accident described above have taken place during the daytime, he might have been killed. Thinking I was a potential customer, he stopped next to me. But he only found a strange *muzungu*, with a notebook and pencil, asking some even stranger questions. Juma was brief and direct:

> "I like it like this," he exclaimed, pointing to the tarmac.
> "It's not bad. It's good."

Abdul, 15, is a student who has just started S1. And unlike a lot of Ugandans at school, his favourite subject is maths. His career ambitions are a strange combination – he wants to be either a lawyer or join the army. He said:

> "It is tarmac {that is better}. Before when it was murram, it was tough. There were holes, dust and funny-funny things. There were accidents."

In my local *dduuka* I met Ronald, 24, who is unemployed. While I was with him, Ronald bought a single stick of *Sportsman* cigarettes, and promptly blew smoke all over me (Kevin was a victim of passive smoking!). Interestingly, neither Ronald, nor the owner of the *dduuka*, Jackie, were aware that with the recent passing of the Tobacco Control Bill, it will soon be illegal to sell cigarettes by the stick – they will have to be sold by the packet. However, the enforcement of this provision looks mightily difficult.

Ronald observed:

> "I prefer the tarmac road over murram. Because it is much better. When you travel in a car it is much more comfortable. When they fixed the tarmac road they put in good drainage to take away the water."

I asked whether "overspeeding" was a problem on tarmac, and Ronald responded:

> "No, they can put humps to regulate the speed."

However, on the road to my local trading centre, the distance between the speed bumps and the centre's junction is too great. After crossing the bumps, vehicles accelerate towards the junction, which is always busy, and also adjoins a primary school.

Jackie was forthright:

> "I like the tarmac road as it is bringing development. Before, cars, especially *matatus*, they did not pass my shop. Even more people now walk past. It has helped my business. I sell more goods, more sodas, more *waragi*. There are some disadvantages like overspeeding. But overall, there are more advantages than disadvantages. Murram is not good, especially during rain."

By the end of these discussions I felt like a politician who had just heavily lost an election. Outvoted, and possibly even outargued.

5

Religion

"Never mock God!" Well, yes and no
(21 January 2007)

They are religious spam – unsolicited email, with a religious content, that appear unrequested and unwanted in my computer inbox. Towards their end, they normally include a sentence asking the recipient to forward the email to all the names in their computer's address book!

To be fair to my many Islamic friends - and to my many friends of other, or of no, religion - all such emails I have received have been Christian in content, with the senders normally being "born again".

Such emails end up speedily and unceremoniously in my junk/trash bin. The senders should remember the fundamentally secular nature of our society.

Religions have their appropriate place, and people have the right to promote them. But religious spam are no more the right avenue for promoting religion, than spam promoting pornography or advertising *Nomi* washing powder.

A recent example of religious spam did catch my eye, but only because it was so flawed, weak and illogical in its content.

Its subject header was "NEVER MOCK GOD", followed by an introductory sentence drawn from the Bible:

> "Be not deceived; God is not mocked: for whatsoever a man soweth, that shall he also reap" (Galatians 6:7).

The email then listed some men and women who, it claimed, had mocked God and, therefore, supposedly suffered premature and unhappy deaths. The list included:

- Chris Murungaru (former Kenyan Minister of Internal Security).
- John Lennon (pop star).
- Tancredo Neves (former President of Brazil).
- Cazuza (bisexual Brazilian composer, singer and poet).
- "The Man Who Built the Titanic".
- Marilyn Monroe.
- Bon Scott (rock musician).

Don't get me wrong, the purpose of this article is not to mock God. My intention is merely to highlight the weak nature of the email and its hugely flawed logic. Most especially, the sender should remember that:

- Many people who have mocked God, or questioned the existence of a God, have not prematurely died.
- Whereas many millions of people who have not mocked God, indeed have praised and worshipped him, have experienced sad, premature deaths in earthquakes, massacres etc.

The Rwandan genocide provides an example of the latter. Many of those slaughtered were Christians, and some were actually murdered in churches i.e. in the House of God.

It would be wrong to hurt the feelings of Christians, Moslems, Hindus, Sikhs, Buddhists etc. by mocking their God or gods. But do let us mock the senders of these religious spam. Such emails should, like the Titanic, sink, sink and sink without trace.

No HIV/AIDS cures at crusades

(20 May 2007)

I did not attend Benny Hinn's crusade, this weekend, as the claims of such pastors to heal and perform miracles are nonsense.

However, I did go to a Morris Cerullo crusade in Kampala in the late 1990s. I was disgusted at the suggestion that a person could be cured of HIV/AIDS. And, even worse, in order to be healed, they first had to give money to the pastor.

None of these "miracle" claims ever stand up to rigorous scientific testing. At the current time, there is no cure for HIV/AIDS. Though the taking of antiretroviral drugs greatly reduces the level of the virus in the body, and can mean the person has a life expectancy of normal length.

Money

Furthermore, to suggest that the power of prayer, combined with monetary donations, can cure AIDS is highly irresponsible. If people are told they can be cured, and they believe it, they may no longer practice safe sex.

Thus, the likes of Benny Hinn (or should that be Benny Sinn?) are working against the admirable efforts of organisations such as TASO and the *Straight Talk Foundation* who have made such huge contributions in the fightback against the AIDS epidemic.

The giving of money forms an integral part of most crusades. Is it any coincidence that many of the big pastors are extremely wealthy men and women? And who should be the next American pastor to visit Kampala, but the appropriately named Pastor Dollar. As *Business Week* magazine has pointed out, Creflo A. Dollar:

> "Has been dubbed by critics as 'Pass the Dollar' and 'Cashflow Dollar' for his ostentatious displays of wealth. He owns two Roll-Royce cars and flies around America in a Gulfstream-3 private jet."

Kayanja
Pastor Dollar is no doubt a role model for our own Pastor Robert Kayanja. Kayanja similarly oozes and drips wealth. According to the *Red Pepper* he owns:
- Rubaga Miracle Cathedral.
- Highway Holiness International, an NGO with many American links.
- Robert Kayanja Ministries, an NGO with over 1000 branches in Uganda and the USA.
- A house in Chicago.
- Businesses in the USA.
- Innumerable Mercedes Benz and land cruisers.
- A private jet.
- A magnificent house at Ggaba on the shores of Lake Victoria.

Cerullo and tax
Money is obviously very important to these pastors. Perhaps this explains why WCNC USA reports that Morris Cerullo is facing federal charges of tax evasion which include that:

> "Cerullo lied on his income tax returns, omitting more than US $ 500,000."

"The federal prosecutor said that the money in question came from offerings at breakthrough rallies and speaking fees. The feds tells us Cerullo used that money as his own............ If convicted, Cerullo could spend up to nine years in prison and pay hundreds of thousands of dollars in fines."

Conclusion

Religion certainly can play an important role in providing support to people suffering from HIV/AIDS, other ailments and the very many harsh challenges that life can throw at human beings. But it should not be used to provide false hope. To repeat, there is no known cure for HIV/AIDS, and one certainly won't be found at a religious crusade in the Mandela National Stadium.

Frowning upon gospel opportunists

(3 June 2007)

So, Pastor Benny Sinn has come and gone, and now Kampala awaits Pastor Dollar. If my language ("No HIV Cures at Crusades" *Sunday Monitor* 20 May 2007) criticising money-grabbing pastors from America was hard, then that used in emails I received from readers was even tougher.

Thus, Tony, a 35-year-old graphic designer in Kampala, observed:

> "People like Hinn are the last thing Uganda needs, or the world for that matter. This crazed madman with the intent of getting as much money into the bank as possible before he dies and goes to his proposed lord..... preys upon desperate and some sick individuals, asking them to pay money for a miracle that will never happen,

is absolutely appalling. Please tell me that more people then you are angry at scum like this."

While a reader in the USA argued that:

> "These so-called prosperity preachers are selling false dreams ...... they are false prophets. Where does it say in the Bible that wealth is an asset? Time after time, we are asked to relinquish wealth. These preachers are charlatans and thieves. They do not deserve the position of trust they place themselves in."

A reader called Paul thought the *Roving Eye* article had done:

> "A good job in highlighting the evils that are embedded in the religious 'sector' most especially the pentecostal churches; and also the plight churchgoers endure from these monetary leeches, also known as pastors."

At the heart of the evil that rich pastors pass off as Christianity is the sheer contrast between their lifestyle and that of Jesus Christ. Hinn stayed in Kampala in its most exclusive hotel – the *Serena*. If Jesus Christ should ever visit Uganda's capital, if Christianity means anything, then a cheap guest house might be too luxurious for him, and he might well be found sleeping out rough with the poor and the street kids in and around the taxi parks.

Such sentiments were well-captured by Paul:

> "Naïve and desperate souls flock to these 'churches' in search of an answer, most especially a divine answer, to their insurmountable problems .... these pastors are businessmen who have amassed wealth from the sheep they bleed. Some of the pastors tend to manipulate single bible verses (as short as ten words) to manipulate and extort their flock. Statements like 'our riches are signs

of blessing' are very common. Why can't these pastors live like the missionaries of the 17th and 18th centuries, that is, lives of selfless devotion to service (helping the poor), wearing brown robes instead of Creflo Dollar suits? A more recent example is that of Mother Theresa who embraced the disadvantaged groups, in contrast to the holding of the microphone with your right hand, and blaring out scriptures, while your left hand is searching your flocks' pockets for their every hard-earned shilling."

"Scum," "charlatans," "thieves," "leeches".............. I am grateful to readers of the *Sunday Monitor* for employing the sort of language that *Roving Eye* lacks the courage to use.

Pastor Kiwewesi's disgraceful wedding
(8 July 2007)

Pastor Isaac Kiwewesi, of Kansanga Miracle Centre, deserves to burn in hell, along with his wedding cake. According to press reports, his wedding last weekend, followed by the reception at the Mandela National Stadium, cost Ug Sh 360m. A newspaper reckoned it was "one of the most expensive weddings in Ugandan history." The wretched cake alone cost over Ug Sh 15m!

Judith, who is a 21-year-old prison officer, earns Ug Sh 150,000 per month. She told me:

> "It would take me over 8 years to earn the money for that cake, and that assumes I did not spend my income on anything else at all!"

The reason why the ostentatious, conspicuous consumption of Kiwewesi's wedding to Barbara Sasha Mugabi was so appalling, was well captured by J.Asiimwe in a letter to *The New Vision* (July 2, 2007):

> "The majority of the pastor's flock are poor people, some of whom live below the poverty line. As a man of God, isn't it a sin in the eyes of God to spend so much money on luxury when some of the people he leads are sleeping on empty stomachs and cannot take their children to school?"

Yes, Mr Asiimwe, it is a sin. And you are also correct when you observe:

> "If these people are truly men of God, how many textbooks would Sh 360m buy for my poor school down in the village?"

Or, one could add, how many ARV drugs for HIV/AIDS sufferers? Or boreholes in an IDP camp? And, much, much more.

But Asiimwe saves his best to last:

> "I am not saying pastors should be donors or should not have private lives. All I am saying is that they should love their neighbours more than they love themselves, just as the bible tells us."

So, what explains Kiwewesi's so obviously unchristian expenditure in one of the world's poorest countries?

David, a 38-year-old shop attendant, argued:

> "In Uganda, people are fond of showing off. They want to be seen and known. They seek attention from the evidence of their expenditure."

Mary, a 40-year-old musician, agreed with David:

> "If you have it – flaunt it. It's the Ugandan way of doing things."

And Mary pointed up an irony:

> "People from outside Uganda contribute money towards the country's poor. But you find a resident of Uganda spending money on themselves in such a conspicuous way."

Hell is a hot place and if Pastor Kiwewesi, his wedding cake and I are all down there together, there will be much to talk about, as the cake is baked for a second time.

Pastors – why no pothole miracles?
(20 January 2008)

After one month in UK for Christmas, I journey from Entebbe Airport to Kampala, and the roadside banners of rich Ugandans start to hit me between the eyes. Foremost are those of the pastors:

- One banner is about a girl-power event that requires a lime green dress code. Well, we all support women's empowerment, but the only green I associate with pastors, is the greenback dollar.
- The second banner publicises the expansion of an evangelical business empire i.e. the opening of yet another centre in a suburb of Kampala.

There are three interesting features of supposed miracles performed at these, or similar centres:

- Money changes hand at some stage in the miracle, and always into the hands of the person delivering the miracle.
- The nature of the miracle will be such that it cannot be easily proved or disproved, one way or the other. Thus,

someone is supposedly cured of HIV/AIDS. But did that person have, or not have, AIDS before the "miracle"? And did they have AIDS, or not have it, after the "miracle"?
- And given that corruption is everywhere in Uganda, can we trust the statements of the person who has supposedly benefited from the "miracle"?

What these pastors certainly never do, is to perform a miracle that can be easily proved, or disproved i.e. verified. Thus, if a pastor said he would perform the miracle of making all Kampala potholes disappear by 6am tomorrow, then tomorrow at 6am, we could all go out on Kampala roads and judge whether the potholes were still there, or not there.

And potholes are a menace – fully worthy of a miracle cure – as many accidents and deaths result from vehicles swerving to avoid them.

But pastors do not perform pothole miracles, because the potholes would still be there the next morning and it would be easy for the rest of us to see the pastors for what they really are i.e. fakes.

However, there was one occasion when a pastor made the mistake of performing something akin to a pothole prophecy – he "prophesised" that one of the candidates in a presidential election would die. Well nobody did die, and if Uganda was a better place than it is, he would have been so discredited, that there would now be none of his wretched banners to spoil my journey from Entebbe Airport to Kampala.

So pastors should stick to HIV/AIDS as this is much safer territory for bogus miracles than presidential pretenders and potholes.

Archbishop's priorities are wrong
(29 June 2008)

Archbishop Henry Orombi found time last week to attend the Global Anglican Future Conference (Gafcon) in Jerusalem.

There, according to press reports, and in line with the traditionalist objectives of the conference:

> "The Archbishops of Uganda and Nigeria attacked the Archbishop of Canterbury's failure to discipline the US Episcopal Church for consecrating an openly gay bishop {Gene Robinson} in 2003."

Internal Anglican politics have no interest for me. But what does interest me is that busy Orombi should be worrying so much about what is happening in faraway USA, spending days on something irrelevant for Uganda in Jerusalem, when he should be giving priority to his domestic agenda.

And surely topmost in that agenda is the corruption that is here, there and everywhere in our country. Whether it be the Global Fund, GAVI, junk choppers, Butabika Hospital land, ghost soldiers, ghost teachers, potholes, CHOGM cars, and much, much more – it happens in Uganda. We seem to have just about every form of corruption except ghost ghosts. But, who knows, perhaps next year there will be a Sebutinde Ghost Ghosts Commission.

And corruption finds its way into our personal relationships, so that friends that we have liked and trusted let us down big time when an opportunity comes up to benefit themselves at our expense. Or, as someone put it to me recently, "If you live long enough in this country {i.e. Uganda}, you end up not trusting anybody."

So rather than the Archbishop of Canterbury disciplining the US Episcopal Church, he should consider disciplining Archbishop Orombi for his failure to persuade people to "treat their neighbours as themselves" in Uganda. These arguments apply equally to the Catholic and evangelical churches, as well as Orombi's Anglican – they all deserve a "red card" when it comes to corruption.

While Christianity has done many good things in Uganda, on its central tenet of generating good neighbourliness, it has been a miserable failure. There would be no corruption if we treated our neighbours as ourselves. For example, we would not "eat" our neighbours' money, because we would not want them treating us in the same way. We would carry out our work duties without crookedness, because this is the way we would like other people (traffic policemen, roadbuilders, Global Fund managers etc.) to behave when their work touches our lives.

Bishop Gene Robinson is almost certainly a far more Christian man than the presumably heterosexual:

- Pastors who regularly fleece members of their flock in return for bogus healing of HIV/AIDS.
- Former ministers who, according to the Ogoola Commission, looted the Global Fund, thereby sending many Ugandans (who did not receive the medical treatment they should have received) to their deaths.

We should hold our cardinals, archbishops and pastors personally responsible for their lack of success in curbing corruption in Uganda. Instead of wasting time at Gafcon, Archbishop Orombi should have been in Uganda doing his best to ensure that the 2009 equivalent of the Global Fund scandal is not perpetrated by one of his parishioners. Sermons are supposed to serve a purpose, aren't they?

Archbishop Orombi helps set world record
(6 July 2008)

As world records go (fastest 100 metres, tallest building, longest penis etc.), it was not an important one. But last Sunday's article ("Archbishop's priorities are wrong") set a *Roving Eye* world record. It generated the largest number of emails (12) I have ever received from readers in response to a column. Now, 12 is an exceedingly modest number, but it is also the same number of disciples that Jesus had before one of them decided to do the equivalent of "eating" from the Global Fund, a fund that contains a lot more than "30 pieces of silver".

Of the 12 emails, 6 criticised the article and 6 supported it, i.e., Critics 6 - Supporters 6. But since away goals count double, I (in my completely unbiased capacity as the author of the said article) have awarded victory to Supporters.

At the heart of the article was the fact that, while Archbishop Orombi was in Jerusalem getting "hot under the collar" (under the dog collar?) about a gay American bishop, back in Uganda, a huge number of Ugandans were continuing to behave in their normal corrupt ways.

Uganda is one of the most corrupt countries in the world. Yet, it is also one of the most Christian in terms of church attendance. Therefore, by any reasonable standards of judgment, Christianity's attempt to generate "treat thy neighbour as thyself" in Uganda has been a miserable failure.

While we frequently hold politicians and civil servants responsible for corruption in Uganda, we should increasingly also hold responsible our cardinals, archbishops, bishops, priests, pastors and apostles. They appear to change nothing apart from, arguably, the size of their bank accounts.

This last point was well-captured by journalist, Agnes Asiimwe in her article "Pastors: Serving the Lord or just fleecing the flock" (*The Independent*, June 13 2008, p29). She argues that in Uganda:

> "Some church pastors are driving an agenda with Lucifer's writing all over it."

Lucifer's writing can take many forms, but a particularly evil example is "give me your money (or your car or whatever) and I will heal you of HIV/AIDS."

In days long ago, indeed it now feels so long ago that it could have been during the Old Testament, I had to carry out the annual assessments of staff that I managed. Their work performance was graded from 1 (excellent) down to 5 (very poor).

If we were carrying out the annual assessment of Archbishop Orombi, or a cardinal, a priest or a pastor, our only argument would be whether to award them Grade 4 or Grade 5. For, the fact that corruption is everywhere in Uganda, is not just due to the failure of our politicians and civil servants, but is **also** due to the failure of our men of God.

Did Christianity generate a culture of lies in Uganda?

(7 September 2008)

"Lord, Lord, how this world is given to lying." So wrote William Shakespeare in *Henry IV, Part One*.

Lies are told in every country of the world, but I have been told more lies in Uganda than in any other country in which I have lived.

One reason for such a culture of lies is obvious – corruption. Corruption is widespread in Uganda and corruption generally involves the telling of a lie.

Thus, the road engineer says, "I have inspected the road. Its construction meets the required standards." But the engineer had been bribed by the contractor and therefore told a lie. The road had not been built to the required standards and, a few months later, potholes begin to emerge.

If the telling of lies finds its way into most aspects of life in Uganda, it begs the question - why? What is the source of such widespread lying?

Of course, there may be more than one source. But on this Sunday, let me controversially argue that an important source of deception in Uganda is Christianity.

Before the coming of Christianity, Uganda was a truthfully polygamous society i.e. when a man had more than one wife, the co-wives would know of each other's existence.

But Christianity overlaid traditional polygamy with monogamy and the result was an untruthful polygamous society i.e. polygamy continued, but became based on deception. Thus, a husband might say to his 'official wife', "Darling, I will be working late at the office tonight." But it is a lie. He will not be working in his office, but will be having sex with his *kyana* in a lodge.

The relationship between a man and wife is one of the most important, if not the most important, in human society. Once lies are introduced into it, something very special is destroyed.

And once one lie is told, it becomes very easy to tell others. Thus, the same man might say he has no money to give his wife for housekeeping as his salary is only Ug Sh 200,000. Actually, it is Ug Sh 300,000, but he wants to spend the extra money on booze and other things. The wife might respond by also telling lies.

The biggest influence on children's behaviour and values are the behaviour and values of their parents. Growing up in an environment of falsehood, it is easy to see how sons and daughters are shaped into becoming liars.

Let me not overstate my case, and point out that I have met many truthful Ugandans, and I daily experience examples of truthfulness. For example, yesterday, due to my forgetfulness, when I tried to pay a butcher a second time for a half kilo of beef, he said, "No, no, Kevin, you have already paid." How easy it would have been for him to be deceitful and pocket an extra Ug Sh 1,900.

Nevertheless, while Christianity brought many good things to Uganda, it also caused the replacement of truthful polygamy with untruthful polygamy, and thereby damaged the country's social fabric so greatly that it never fully recovered.

And one result has been lies, lies and more lies.

The telling of lies in Uganda – Part Two
(14 September 2008)

Last Sunday's column considered 2 causes of the extensive telling of lies in Uganda. The first was widespread corruption since a crooked act generally requires a lie being told. The second was Christianity in the sense that the coming of monogamous Christianity to Uganda caused truthful polygamy to be replaced by untruthful polygamy.

Today, *Roving Eye*, considers a third cause of falsehood amongst Ugandans – not confronting issues.

An example is when someone comes and stays in your house. You expected them to stay one or two nights, but ten days later they are still there! A typical *muzungu* response is to bluntly confront the issue head on i.e:

> "You have overstayed your welcome. It is time for you to move on and find accommodation elsewhere."

But as Michael, a small businessman in Kampala, told me:

> "A typical Ugandan response to such an unwelcome guest is for the host to say, 'You must leave now as I've got to go on an up-country trip' (i.e. lie), rather than confront the issue."

Another example is drawn from a one-day booksigning event for my book, "Ugandan Society Observed", at Entebbe International Airport. We sold almost 20 books, but there were also at least 25 Ugandans (some passengers, some airport staff) who told me they would come back a bit later in the day and buy the book for me to sign.

Well, they did not come back, and quite honestly I don't think they had any intention of coming back i.e. they lied. I would have much preferred them to have said:

> "Kevin, I don't have the money to spare so I can't buy your book."

Or even:

> "O'Connor you've got a big nose, and an even bigger head, I would not buy your wretched book even if it was the last book remaining on earth."

But rather than confronting the issue, 20+ people lied to me – ok it was a small lie, but is it not the experience of life such that once someone is capable of telling small lies, it is much easier for them to tell big lies?

On a previous occasion, when I discussed this type of behaviour with Michael, he told me:

> "That's the nature of Ugandans. There are few of us who confront issues. It's our culture. But there is variation between tribe. Some tribes are more straightforward, direct and aggressive than others."

But for Samuel, a senior journalist, it is not a matter of tribe. He observed:

> "It really comes down to individuals. I know Ugandans who are very open about such issues and will tell you what they think and not what they think you want to hear. And I also know Ugandans who are not like this. This is just as it is in other countries. But the Ugandan education system does not encourage critical thinking, and our cultures generally do not encourage questioning of things and authority."

There are many truthful Ugandans, and it is also the case that lies are told in every country in the world. But I will leave the rather depressing concluding point of my two articles to Michael:

> "In Uganda, we know many people are liars. We expect it. There is a greater tendency of lying in our culture than in other cultures."

How religion brainwashes us

(23 November 2008)

Ethan Musolini is not a name you are likely to forget quickly. For the surname is almost the same as that of the Italian fascist dictator, Benito Mussolini. But, Ethan, it could have been much, much worse. Imagine what your life would be like if you had been called Ethan Hitler?!

Anyway, last Tuesday, Mr Musolini (that's Ethan, not Benito) had a most interesting article in the *Daily Monitor*. Entitled "Analysing your beliefs", it opened with the following ringing sentences:

> "You make your beliefs and beliefs make you. But what are beliefs? It's what you choose to accept as truth about your life and the world around you."

But what shapes our beliefs? Why do we believe what we believe?

Most important is the country/culture into which we are born. Your religious beliefs, for example, are likely to be very different if you are born not in a Christian country, but in Saudi Arabia. Then, you would go not to a church on a Sunday, but to a mosque on a Friday.

Second in importance in shaping beliefs are parents. If our parents are devout born-again Christians, then we too are likely to be – yes, you've guessed it – born-again Christians. If they are Catholic, they will probably send us to a Catholic school, where, just as at home, we will be fed that particular belief system.

Looked at in this light, we can see "faith" as what it is – nonsense. Islamic suicide bombers have faith. Born-again Christians, throwing their arms around at a Benny Sinn rally, have faith. But if it was possible to strip away the country and family influences that formed and shaped these religious beliefs during formative years, then faith would move from utter certainty through to doubt, through to, quite possibly, disbelief.

A crucial factor in the generation of religious beliefs is to get at the kids early. Of course, parents have access to them from birth. But not long after the children are able to walk and talk, they will be shipped off to Sunday school and kindergarten where the process of religious indoctrination continues.

It is interesting that when it comes to sex, we are supposed to wait until we are 18 years. When it comes to voting, we must also be 18 years. But when it comes to religion, no age is too young. And, initially at least, the choice of religion is not made by ourselves, but by others, most especially by our parents.

In an ideal world, we can see that we should not make religious decisions until we are adults. Then, having a wide variety of life experiences behind us, we could then make the choice between religious faiths (including no religious faith) in a balanced, mature way.

But such an ideal world would not be the world of priests, pastors, imams, mullahs and rabbis. The key to them having large congregations is to brainwash the kids, and to access children's brains as early in their lives as possible.

My advice to readers is to have no faith in faith.

Ug Sh 12 million wasted praising Archbishop Orombi

(22 March 2009)

His Grace, the most Reverend Henry Luke Orombi, 7th Archbishop of the Church of Uganda, is no doubt a most impressive human being with many achievements.

But the 4-page supplement, which appeared in the *Sunday Vision* of March 8 2009, showed up much that is wrong with the reality of Christian values in Uganda and with Africa's "big man" culture in general.

The supplement celebrated Orombi's 5th anniversary of becoming Archbishop. Five is hardly a big number, so, the first question is why celebrate this 5th anniversary at all, except in a modest, private way?

In a *mere* 4 pages, the supplement contained 10 photographs of Orombi. The second question is, therefore, to what extent did the supplement reflect Africa's "big man" culture, and should *Roving Eye* (the most Reverend Kevin Patrick O'Connor, 1st Archbishop of Fulham Football Club) follow suit by producing a column that includes 10 photos of His Holiness, Kevin Patrick?

But the bigger questions, and much more worrying issues for Christians, surround the huge cost of the supplement, and the better ways such money could be used.

My enquiries with the Vision's Advertising Department suggested that the initial cost of the supplement's 8 quarter-page advertisements would be Ug Sh 1,962,450 each for the 2 coloured ones, and Ug Sh 1, 142, 450 each for the 6 black and white ones. This totals Ug Sh 10.7m. The advertisers were mainly Christian organisations.

So, what was the total cost of the supplement, which also contained 2 pages of text/photos put together by the Vision's Elvis Basudde? A journalistic acquaintance told me:

> "Take the cost of the adverts {i.e. Ug Sh 10.7m}, and then double it {i.e. Ug Sh 21.4m}. The general practice here," she continued, "is to offer 40% as 'free' to the client, and require them to pay the other 60%".

If this is correct, then the supplement's total cost would be around Ug Sh12.8m (US $6,550).

Now, I am sure my financial research can be queried, but it doesn't really matter whether the cost of the supplement was Ug Sh 5m or Ug Sh 15m. For whatever the exact figure, it still represents a huge amount of money in a poor developing country like Uganda, just to "congratulate" and praise Orombi on a 5th anniversary.

If we consider some of the 8 quarter-page adverts, better uses to which the advertiser could have put these advertisement funds, spring to mind. Thus:

- Uganda Protestant Medical Bureau – more free healthcare to more people in the poor/conflict areas in which it operates.
- Bbira Vocational Training School – more scholarships to needy youngsters to acquire skills in carpentry, bricklaying, motor mechanics etc.
- Compassion International – increasing the number of children that the organisation releases "from spiritual, economic, social and physical poverty."

Basudde's article comments that Orombi is:

> "Phenomenal, vibrant and motivated....with a distinguished personality."

I would politely suggest to Orombi that if he is as phenomenal, vibrant, motivated and distinguished as Basudde suggests, he should put a stop to such useless wastage of funds on future anniversaries of his enthronement as Archbishop of Uganda.

Sodomy, pasta and miracles

(7 June 2009)

Sodomy allegations have evangelically echoed around Uganda. The end results for pastors, and their entrepreneurial prosperity preaching/healing businesses, will be most interesting. *Sunday Monitor* readers (or at least the three that read my *Roving Eye* column) may be waiting for Pasta Kevin O'Connor of Fulham Miracle Ministries to comment on this *savedee sodomy shindig*.

Pasta

So, why is Pasta O'Connor called *Pasta* O'Connor? Well, when Pasta Kevin is not preaching (to anybody prepared to listen) and writing his *Roving Eye* column, he and his wife (*Prophetless Sue*) also coach athletics. Their qualifications and experience as coaches mean they know a lot about pasta, for pasta/spaghetti/macaroni and other carbohydrate food are important to longer distance runners. Pasta's energy-giving properties, over many hours, are especially liked by marathon runners. Depending on a runner's ability, a marathon can last anything between 2 and 6+ hours. A serious marathoner will eat pasta (and any other food) about 4 hours before the race, for proper digestion.

Balakole burnout

Now, we all need energy. But any Ugandan evangelicals experiencing *balokole burnout*, as they watch some of their famous leaders accuse and argue inside and outside police stations, will need more energy than normal. And it might just be that pasta energy will heal *balokole burnout*. If so, it would be a miracle that makes Fulham Miracle Ministries happy – but they would be even happier if some money could be put into Pasta O'Connor's pocket. And even happier still if the money is put into his pocket *before* the pasta's energy has healed the unhappiness.

Adolf Mwesige

For the pastors themselves pasta is, to confuse my three readers even further, a *godsend*. Many pastors use a speaking style whose most famous disciple was Adolf. I am referring not to Adolf Mwesige, but to Adolf Hitler. The speaker starts quietly and slowly, and then gradually increases loudness until they are shouting, screaming and throwing their arms around. Like others in Africa's "big man" culture, they can speak at huge length. This marathon of a theatrical performance uses up much energy.

So pastors need pasta before they preach. And as they are not running (other than running a business), they do not need the marathoner's 4-hour digestion period. Thus, they might also eat pasta during the preaching. However, combining preaching and eating is not easy. Pastors must be especially careful, as they begin to shout, that pieces of pasta do not fly out from their mouths into their congregations.

Apostle Hodgson
Finally, Pasta O'Connor and Fulham Miracle Ministries especially wish to thank Apostle Roy Hodgson, manager of our football club. In the last match of the 2007/8 season, our team was just 10 minutes away from English Premier League relegation. Yet, in the recently concluded 2008/9 season, Apostle Hodgson took the club to 7th position (the highest top league finish in the 130 year history of our club) and therefore got us a place in next season's Europa League (formerly UEFA Cup). Now that's what you call a miracle!

Have no faith in faith

(27 September 2009)

If Uganda had been colonised by India and not Britain, most of its population would be Hindus, not Christians. Religion is nonsense. And the supposed certainty of belief, often called "faith", are distortions shaped by the accidents of history or of birth. So, you may be a devout born-again Christian who regularly throws your arms around in Kampala Watoto Church.

But had you been born in Saudi Arabia instead of Uganda, you would almost certainly not be a devout Christian, but a devout Muslim.

In a recent *Roving Eye*, I tried to sum all this up by urging readers to "have no faith in faith".

I was rather pleased with my phrase "have no faith in faith", so, it was reassuring when several *Sunday Monitor* readers emailed, complimenting me about the five words "have no faith in faith". They might not necessarily have agreed with its meaning, but they nevertheless thought it a striking expression.

Whether "have no faith in faith" is good enough to end up in a book of quotations is another matter entirely. Last week, my loving mother-in-law sent me three books of quotations (Literary; Political; Humorous).

Wondering what the strength of competition would be for "have no faith in faith" I looked at their religious chapters. The following quotation by Woody Allen would be appreciated by those who question the existence of God given events on God's earth like the Nazi holocaust and the Rwandan genocide.

> "If it turns out that there is a God, I don't think that he is evil. But the worst you can say about him is that basically he is an underachiever."

And the following anonymous quote strikes a similar note:

> "God is not dead but alive and working on a much less ambitious project."

Film star Burt Reynolds, when asked what he plans to say to God when they meet, replied:

> "I have made a lot mistakes, but, boy, you've made a lot more."

And, given, for example, that 6 million Jews were murdered by Nazis, many would go much further than Reynolds, and agree with Samuel Beckett, who wrote:

> "Let us pray to God…the bastard! He doesn't exist!"

These quotations are just examples drawn from books containing thousands of them. So, it is obvious that my "have no faith in faith" faces much competition if it is going to find its way into a book of quotations.

So, to give myself a better chance, let me offer a second *Roving Eye* quotation for consideration.

The starting point of the quotation is the question, "what have you found inside the church?" Your answer may be, "God" or "faith" or "peace" etc.

Now, when *Roving Eye* was asked the same question, he replied:

> "The only thing I have found inside a church is boredom."

Execution is always wrong

(28 February 2010)

> "News that at least 50 death row convicts" stated the *Daily Monitor* editorial of February 15, "may have their sentences reduced, following a precedent-setting Supreme Court ruling, is welcome."

But this was not welcome news to 2 Ugandans I know – both support the death penalty.

Chris is a 23-year-old electrician. He said:

> "I believe in execution of murderers because when somebody kills someone, he or she must be executed. For example, when someone poisons someone else or

when somebody is sacrificed – there have been a lot of sacrifices recently in Uganda."

Andrew, 29, thought a person should be executed "in some situations."

And what situations are these, Andrew?

"For example," he replied, "the murder of a co-wife. One kills the other because of jealousy. Another example is when a thief comes and steals, and even kills the person he has robbed. That one should be executed."

My own view is that the death penalty is wrong, at all times, and in all situations. I get rather fed up on a Sunday of people thrusting Christianity down my throat. "Have you been to church today?" Or even worse, *ogenze kusaba leero?* (Have you gone to pray today?). My answer to these questions is always "No". So it is a little strange that many churchgoers support the death penalty, while I, who does not go to church, oppose it.

For, I find it incomprehensible and unbelievable that Jesus Christ (who stands for love, compassion and forgiveness) could execute another i.e. be the executioner. For, hanging (Uganda's mode of execution) is a brutally gruesome process. As well as the mental torture to the prisoner and the increasingly well-documented psychiatric trauma it causes to Uganda Prisons staff, Ether Namugoji described, in a 2004 article, how:

"The noose tightens......death could occur when the trachea and carotid artery are blocked, cutting off the breath and blood supply. At the same time, the jugular vein, which takes out the blood is blocked and unconsciousness occurs followed by death within 20 minutes. Also the spine could snap. Other sources on death by hanging indicate that the head might actually be separated from the rest of the body and blood splash on the walls and the executioner."

In addition to its primitive, barbaric brutality, there are many other arguments against the death penalty. For example, innocent people have been found guilty of murder but because of weaknesses in the investigation methods, important evidence is overlooked. And with corruption so widespread in Uganda, how do we know that corruption has not infected the policing, legal and judiciary processes that resulted in a death sentence? And is a poor man more likely to hang than a rich man?

But on this Sunday, the most fundamental argument against the death penalty is that we cannot imagine Jesus Christ being the executioner in Luzira Prison. And if we can't imagine Jesus Christ being the hangman, surely we should not expect a member of Uganda's Prisons Department to do our brutal dirty work for us?

Missionaries brought already damaged goods to Uganda

(14 March 2010)

The 131st anniversary of the coming of the first Catholic missionaries to Uganda in 1879 was recently celebrated. However, a far more important year than 1879 in human history was 1859. For 1859, was the year that Charles Darwin's *Origin of Species* was published.

Darwin described the processes of evolution and natural selection which, by inference, drove a "cart and horses through" (i.e. showed up as nonsense) important parts of the Bible's Old Testament, such as Adam and Eve.

Kevin's conversion

This triumph of science and reason over religious superstition meant that 20 years later, when Father Lourdel and Brother Amans arrived here, the missionaries were bringing already damaged goods to Uganda.

One hundred and fifteen years after Father Lourdel, *Roving Eye*, arrived in Uganda. At that time I was an agnostic (someone who is not sure whether there is a God or not). Uganda, however, converted me from an agnostic into an atheist (someone who believes there is no God).

Where was God?

Uganda is the most church-going country I have ever lived in. Yet, it is also one of the most corrupt. In other words, going to church and the influence of Christian prayer and preaching, seem to do little to reduce corrupt "eating".

The Rwandan genocide took place a few months before my arrival. So, where was God during this genocide and during the Nazi holocaust, the 2006 Asian tsunami, the Haitian and Chilean earthquakes etc? Asleep? Gone for lunch? On holiday? Otherwise engaged?

Benny Hinn

And then there are those wretched American pastors who regularly visit here. Well, the only thing that gets healed at a Benny Hinn crusade is Benny Hinn's bank balance.

"Have no faith in faith" is the motto of this columnist. And, if as you read this, you continue to cling to your religion, ask yourself a few questions:

- If the Indians, rather than the British, had colonised Uganda, would this not then be a Hindu country, rather than a predominantly Christian one?
- From when you were a baby, what have been the effects on you of your parents (and your school) feeding your brain with a particular religion? If this brainwashing was stripped away, would you be so certain in your faith? Indeed, would you have faith at all? For, as a Jesuit once said, "Give me a child until he is seven and I will give you the man."

1859 is far more important than 1879, when the missionaries brought already damaged goods to Uganda.

The Catholic Church's funeral
(18 April 2010)

At 6am on this Sunday morning, I will no doubt have been awoken by the tolling bells of my local Catholic church.

But it is funereal bells that are tolling for the Catholic Church itself. It seems like almost every day, in another country around the world, that there are fresh child abuse allegations against Catholic priests. They are normally followed by accusations of "cover up" directed at senior clergy who are intent on stopping the abuse from becoming public knowledge. Regretfully, protecting the church comes well before protecting the children on too many a religious priority list. Accusations of cover up have even been laid at the door of Pope Benedict himself.

Whatever happened to Luke 18:16 ("But Jesus called the children to him and said, 'Let the little children come to me, and do not hinder them, for the kingdom of God belongs to such as these.'")?

One does not need a PhD in rocket science, or indeed much of an IQ at all, to work out why the Catholic Church is being troubled by so many child abuse allegations.

Sexual desire and sexual fulfilment are standard human traits. So, what happens when the rules of Catholicism require its priests to remain celibate (i.e. never have sex)? The answer is that for a certain percentage of them, their sexual desires become so repressed and distorted, that they are unleashed on children, and mainly boy children at that.

I have not heard any allegations of child abuse against Ugandan Catholic priests. But, then again, if the experience of other countries is anything to go by, we the laity would likely be the last to know.

Two other factors may explain this absence of allegations:

Firstly, there is what I have always found as a rather suffocating part of Ugandan culture i.e. *ebyomunju tebitotolwa* (whatever happens in the house should never be told to outsiders).

Secondly, what percentage of Ugandan Catholic priests are actually celibate? The pressure in wider Ugandan culture and society to "produce" children is so huge, that I wonder how many of its Catholic priests have children "in the village"?

The wretched Catholic Church's backward teachings on contraception have accelerated the spread of HIV/AIDS in Uganda and brought many unwanted children into this world. So, I for one would not mourn at its funeral but celebrate.

And as the child abuse scandal continues to echo around the world, I say to the Catholic Church, "Do not ask for whom the bell tolls, it tolls for thee."

There is no God

(26 September 2010)

"God Is Not Great" is the great title of a great book. Its author, Christopher Hitchens, provides persuasive arguments that God does not exist and that religions are manmade.

Aggrey Turyamuhaki (Bishop Barham University College, Kabale) in a letter ("Prayer for Uganda in precarious times") to the *Daily Monitor* (September 17 2010), states:

> "Our country Uganda is in need of God's intervention. We chiefly call on Him through prayer… (Blah! Blah! Blah!)… Lord hear this prayer, through Jesus Christ our Lord."

Well, all I can say to Turyamuhaki is that if you are waiting for God to intervene in Uganda (or to intercede in any aspect of your life or anybody else's life) you will be waiting for ever (or even, "for ever and ever"), as there is no God.

A prime reason religion's existence is to allow human beings to cope with the prospect of death, and of seeing parents, children etc. again. But as I say to my 87-year-old mother:

> "Mum, if you want to say anything to me, say it to me now. For we won't be meeting again in heaven or hell as there are no such places. When we die, we die. It will all go black, and that's it."

I have confidence in these statements because I was brought up as a Christian, and attended church until I was 18. So, I knew of something else before "converting" to atheism. Whereas most people of "faith", know of nothing else, having been indoctrinated from the earliest age into a particular religion by their parents and schools.

I do, though, have a preference for Christianity over Islam. The *Sunday Monitor's* cartoonist could draw a cartoon of Jesus with this article. But if he did one of Prophet Mohammed, both he and I would fear for our lives. Hitchens's Chapter 9 ("The Koran is borrowed from both Jewish and Christian myths") should be compulsory reading for all Moslems.

And on the subject of reading, the "Faith" pages in this *Sunday Monitor* magazine should include (if not every week, then at least every month) an article by an atheist to provide intellectual contrast to the traditional, rather boring, religious articles. As Facebook's *Atheist Society of Kampala* (ASK) shows, there is no shortage of atheists in Uganda who would gladly write these articles. In other words, just ask ASK!

Finally, Hitchens's international bestseller, "God Is Not Great – How Religion Poisons Everything", is available in Kampala's Aristoc bookshops for a lot less than 30 pieces of silver i.e. Ug Sh 24,000.

Sundays – to work or not to work?

(2015)

Today is Sunday. Is it a church day for you? A family day? Or is it just another work day?

I asked some Ugandan Christians, from different walks of life, about working on a Sunday.

Dorothy, 40, is a financial and management consultant and does not work on a Sunday. She said:

> "I spend that day with family. We go to church and then have a nice lunch together. As a lady and mother, I can

make a special input into our Sunday lunch. I now only work Sundays out of choice e.g. if I have some emergency consultancy work to be done. But being a consultant, I can do that at home. When I did work in an office, I did more often have to go in on a Sunday to meet deadlines especially at the month end."

Mary, 38, who owns a top of the range hair salon in central Kampala had similar views and commented that she never worked on Sundays and never would work on that day even if there were clients. A non-church going Christian, she regarded Sunday as a family day "to spend time together doing things we enjoy doing together".

In contrast, Michael, 28, who runs a small barber shop in a Kampala suburb told me:

"Why I work Sundays is simple. Poverty. We are very poor. We have to work day to day. If we don't work, we don't eat. I always work unless I am sick. I don't have a day off. I work 7 days per week. If all days were like Sunday I would go to church. But I don't go because business is so good then. It is the same for all shopkeepers around here."

Michael's comments are partly shaped by his shop being close to a large church.

Nearby, *boda-boda* motorcyclist, David, 25, said that he also worked 7 days per week, as he had many customers on a Sunday, "especially from the church and the shops." Though his *boda-boda* colleague, Patrick, 28, did not work on the Sabbath, preferring to visit his family on the other side of Kampala.

Many people, from different social strata have to work on a Sunday, though I suspect the majority are the less well off, as my not necessarily representative sample bears out.

And to make the sample even less representative, let us consider the Sunday behaviour of *Roving Eye*.

Well, to start with, I have to make no decision about whether to go to church, or which service to attend. I am an atheist so I most definitely do not go to church. That does not mean my Sundays are not affected by church. The bells of my local Catholic church frequently wake me up when they start tolling at 6am Then, there is the iron sheet roofed evangelical church that we frequently pass in our car – its screaming, screeching pastor sounds like the very incarnation of the devil (though atheism spares me from believing that there actually is a devil!)

My Sunday mornings are normally taken up by athletics coaching. So, I will be found either at Namboole Stadium, or supervising weight training in a gym. If the latter, I may persuade a trainer to play, over the gym's sound system, some of my Lucky Dube CDs, which sound much better than any hymn.

As for Sunday afternoon, I ban my normal "to do list", and am prompted by the words of the song *Lazy Sunday* by the British pop group of the late 1960s, *The Small Faces*:

> "Lazy Sunday afternoon, I got no mind to worry,
> Close my eyes and drift away."

Perhaps I "close my eyes", while drinking a beer and listening to the English Premier League on the radio. But, above all, it has to be a "Lazy Sunday afternoon."

6

Language

"Move over, I have diarrhoea!"
(13 July 2003)

You've read what feels like 25 articles on George W. Bush; another 25 on "Big Brother Africa", and it's still not 10 o'clock.

"And" to quote a line from the BBC TV comedy show *(Monty Python's Flying Circus)*, of the late 1960s and early 1970s, "now for something completely different."

A frequently heard comment on taxis *(matatu*s) in Uganda is "extend" (i.e. move over a bit).

A passenger will get on to a taxi, and needing a little more room to sit down, they will say to an already seated passenger, "extend."

Imagine if the entering passenger says, "Extend, *nnina ekiddukano*" (move over, I have diarrhoea). In other words, I do not know what might happen inside my stomach in the next 5 minutes, so my advice to you is to move away.

"Extend, *nnina ekiddukano*," when said on a taxi, crossed my mind as a possible joke. Agreed not perhaps a very funny joke, tending towards the schoolboyish, some would say crude, humour, but nevertheless a possible joke.

But it is a joke based on my cultural background. It could work in Britain (when said fully in English, of course), and is the sort of joke that might have been used on *Monty Python's Flying Circus*.

But when I put the "extend, *nnina ekiddukano*," joke idea to Michael, a journalistic friend, he replied:

> "It's no good, Kevin. The joke would not work in Uganda. People would not understand what you meant. Your humour would not cross the cultures."
>
> "And you must remember," Michael continued, "that we Ugandans tend to deny our biological functions. We are not open with our bodies. Sex, even diarrhoea, gets hushed up."

At that point, I was prepared to forget about my "extend, *nnina ekiddukano*" joke. Anyway, I lacked the courage to experiment to find out whether people would laugh or not. I thought that if I started jumping into taxis in and around Kampala, saying to anyone who was prepared to listen, "Extend, *nnina ekiddukano*," I would finish the day either at CPS (Central Police Station) or in Butabika Hospital.

Then, last Tuesday, something interesting happened. After athletics training, I jumped into a taxi with Sam (who I have coached for about a year). Sam is 23 years old, and as we sat down, I said to him, "Extend, *nnina ekiddukano*."

Well, Sam laughed long and loud. My joke had worked!

So, what was happening here? Journalist, Michael, is definitely right that in most situations the joke would be a failure in Uganda. But, why then, did it make Sam laugh?

The explanation is straightforward and lies with how human beings affect and shape each other.

Firstly, in a year of many running training sessions and telephone conversations, Sam has got used to not only my accented speech in English, but can even generally make some sense of my occasional, very limited, and highly awful speech in Luganda.

Secondly, and more importantly, Sam has had to suffer my jokes for a year. Therefore, he has got to know my sense and style of humour.

Similarly, most of my Ugandan friends do laugh at my jokes. Hopefully it is because they genuinely find them funny, and not out of respect for me.

And, of course, it is a two-way process. I have learnt, and been affected, by friendship and other contact with Ugandans, Ugandan society and culture.

Such human interaction can be called a change process, but I prefer the term "widening." For we don't need to lose anything of what we had before, and contact with people from different countries and cultures opens our eyes to other ways of looking at the world around us.

Before you rush away to read yet more about George W. Bush and "Big Brother Africa," let me too rush away as .... *nnina ekiddukano*!

And if anyone decides to chase after me then, do watch where you put your feet, as "tread softly for you tread on my jokes."

Unintended humour in a Kampala toilet

(4 February 2007)

Last week's article considered kissing ("swapping saliva") in public places and concluded that there were many advantages to couples kissing in public, rather than just in private.

This week's *Roving Eye* looks at something that is definitely not permitted in a public place, the exposure of one's private parts. The article is prompted by a big notice that I saw on the wall of a public toilet in Kampala. I looked at it once, then twice, to make sure I was not misreading, for it stated boldly, "Please Flash."

What the sign-writer had intended was, of course, "Please Flush" i.e. pull the chain or handle after use, so as to cleanse the WC with water.

I recognise, and I'm sympathetic to, the educational and literacy challenges in a Third World country like Uganda that can produce misspelled signs (e.g. "shoe shinner" instead of "shoe shiner").

Many Ugandans also have to write or speak in a language that is not their native/first one. Similarly, my awful Luganda results in all sorts of mispronunciations and misspelling when I make sorties into it.

But I could not help but smile at the unintended humour of the "Please Flash" sign.

The word "flash" has different meanings. The most common is that of sudden burst of light or flame, as in "flash of lightening". Another is a brief news item, as in "news flash".

However, a new meaning of "flash" emerged into the English language in the late 1960s. As John Ayto points out in his excellent book, *20th Century Words*, this use of flash is defined as follows:

> "Of a man - to exhibit or expose the genitals briefly and indecently, especially in a public place."

The first known use of this meaning "flash" was in 1968 in the sentence: "City parks also have their share of flashing".

A person who flashes is known as a "flasher," and Ayto suggests that the first usage of "flasher" was in a 1974 edition of the Canadian newspaper, *Kingston News*:

> "A middle aged man indecently exposed himself to a female student .... There were several reports of the so-called 'phantom flasher' in the university area."

Certainly, in the UK, the caricature of a "flasher" is a "dirty old man" who lifts his raincoat to show off his "you know what" to a young woman.

Flashing is unpleasant, upsetting and distasteful, sometimes disturbingly traumatic for a girl/woman victim, and will lead to the arrest of the flasher, if he is apprehended by the police.

Heterosexuals have no monopoly of flashing. For example, gay pop star George Michael was arrested after he exposed himself to an undercover policeman in a public toilet in the USA. But, Michael turned this setback on its head by writing and producing a highly successful pop video about the incident.

If this incident happened in Uganda, George Michael might have offered as his defence in a court law: "But, your honour, I was only obeying the sign on the toilet wall – "Please flash"!

Now you wouldn't misspell 'misspell', would you?

(15 July 2007)

Three misspellings in one newspaper advertisement. Is this a record? A national record? Perhaps even a world record?

Readers of *The Sunday Monitor* will be pleased to learn that the sports equipment advert appeared in *The New Vision*, sometimes known as "the nation's leading misspeller."

In the advert, we learnt that for Ug Sh 10,000, we could buy "*que* sticks." That is a cue for me to point out that the rod used in playing pool, snooker and billiards is called a *cue* stick. It is possible that if Ug Sh 10000 is a very competitive price, then there will be a long *queue* of people at the shop wishing to buy the sticks – but that is another matter.

The second misspelling was "*canvass* shoes." Now, there is a word "canvass." Its most common meaning is to solicit (ask for) votes for a candidate in an election. Many Ugandans walk the towns and villages wearing *silipas* (plastic flip-flop sandals), so, a pair of shoes (and not *mivumba* {second hand}, but new shoes) would be very important to them. Therefore, could these *canvass* shoes be special ones with which voters are bribed to vote for particular candidates?

The answer to that question is "no." The advert contained a misspelling. The correct spelling is *canvas* shoes.

The final mistake in the advert was offering a "pooltable" with accessories for Ug Sh 1,350,000. Leaving aside that most Ugandans have got far more important things to spend their money on than such tables, and call me a perfectionist if you like, but *pooltable* should not be spelt as one word but as two i.e. *pool table*.

Perhaps the owners of this sports shop, its advertising agency, and *The New Vision* editors should put their heads together (i.e. *pool* their resources) to ensure correct spelling in future.

But the misspelling that appeared in a Ugandan newspaper which required heads not to be put together, but to be knocked together, was "Clarrification." If that did not result in any journalist being sacked, then it must at least have resulted in more grey hairs on the editor's head.

What should have appeared next day in the same newspaper was:

> "**CLARIFICATION** – This is to clarify that yesterday's CLARRIFICATION should have been spelt CLARIFICATION."

In his book "Troublesome Words," Bill Bryson says of the word "misspell":

> "If there is one word that you don't wish to misspell, it is this one. Note -ss-."

Now, you wouldn't mispell "misspell," would you?

Is the mobile phone destroying Uganda's greeting culture?

(31 August 2008)

Consider this long Luganda greeting exchange, when translated into English:

A: You slept how?
B: Fine.
A: Um….Um

B: You slept how?
A: Fine.
B: Um
A: Um
A: How are the people at home?
B: They are fine.
A: Um
B: And you?
A: We are fine.
B: Um
A: Um
B: Thank you for the work you do.
A: All right.
B: Um
A: And you too, thank you.

B: All right.
A: Um
B: Um.

The above is from the late Dr Kasalina Matovu's "Introduction to Basic Luganda Conversation and Aspects of Culture". She is trying to show how strange these greetings can sound to a *muzungu*, to whom she points out:

> "You must always remember that many African countries were governed by the principle of a need to share in all that has happened to a person whether good or bad. If you met somebody in the morning, it was very important that you ask him/her how the night was. This made the other feel that people cared about him/her, and that they genuinely were concerned about what state of condition he was in night or day. The principle of sharing is very important."

I asked a few Ugandans whether this sharing aspect of African culture is being affected, even destroyed, by the mobile phone. After all, 'time is money', and mobile phones, often with a per second tariff, make long greetings expensive in a country where most people struggle economically.

Ronald Akiiki, 26, is an assistant in a small drug shop in Kampala. He said:

> "It depends on the person you are speaking too. Generally, if it is a new person, you begin by greeting in the normal way. When it somebody you know, you directly go to the point as you want to reduce on the income you are going to use on the phone – to use less money. Greetings would mean that you use more units."

Olama Stephen Clay, 28, has a BA in Social Studies from Makerere University and is currently unemployed. He commented:

> "Greetings are done hurriedly to save airtime and to another extent, they are omitted {altogether}. The caller goes straight away on the point that he intends to drive. Yet, in African culture, greeting is vital, a way of expressing love, unity and respect."

> "It is a great pity," continued Stephen, "that the mobile phone has damaged our culture in this way. Most time now people don't bother to greet. For example, if I rang my brother, I might say, 'Meet me at Emitex Pub now' and then I switch off immediately. But if I had met him physically, I would greet him in the normal procedure."

Domenic, a 27-year-old Muganda, said that this mobile phone greeting reduction had

> "Especially affected the Baganda. They greet so much. Other tribes don't greet as much."

As for *Roving Eye*, he too, must economise on his units, so he limits his greeting and introduction on the phone to, *"Oli otya? Bampita Muzungu Bignose."*

Will you laugh at my jokes?

(21 September 2008)

> "I now run so slowly that last week I was overtaken by an old woman carrying a pot on her head."

So, if that did not work, let my try this one:

> "One morning, I shot an elephant in my pyjamas. How he got into my pyjamas, I'll never know."

So, what have I been doing? The answer is quite simple – I have been telling (or trying to tell) jokes. The first one was my own, and the second one was by a comedian much more famous than *Roving Eye* – Groucho Marx.

The dictionary defines a joke as:

> "An amusing story; anything said or done for fun; anything that provokes a laugh."

Both jokes above made me laugh. Did they make you laugh? If not, then it may be because, of all things, it is humour that has the greatest problems in crossing cultures. So often in Uganda, because of its different cultural perspective, I end up having to explain my jokes – and if you have to explain a joke anywhere in the World, then almost certainly the humour is lost in the process.

So, humour is not a straightforward thing for a foreigner in Uganda. But it does not stop me telling jokes. Here is another one from Groucho Marx:

> "Please accept my resignation. I don't want to belong to any club that will accept me as a member."

We could twist that joke around a bit, to provide a reason for not visiting Kampala's pricey *Serena Hotel* where a beer costs Ug Sh 5000 i.e.

> "I'm not going to the *Serena*. I'm not going to any hotel that let's me through its door."

If the beers cost Ug Sh 5000, can you imagine the cost of a room!? So if *kyana* (girlfriend) suggests we spend a night at the *Serena*, my reply would be:

> "OK then. You pay for the room and I'll pay for the tap water."

Kyana is only interested in me because of my exceedingly handsome good looks. I was most disappointed, therefore, when at an audition to become a male model, Sylvie Owori told me:

> "If I had a head like yours, I'd have it circumcised."

A "double entendre" is a type of, normally sexual, joke. It is a word or phrase with two meanings, one usually more or less indecent. An example, so famous that it has already appeared in Chapter 2 of this book, was uttered by American film actress, Mae West:

> "Is that a gun in your pocket or are you just pleased to see me?"

Well, it's just possible that the man had a gun in his pocket, but more likely that the bulge in his trousers is explained by his erection on finding Mae West so beautiful and sexy!

Of course, whether Mae West's joke would work in Owino Market or Adjumani, or with you dear reader, is another matter altogether.

Bigmen, smallmen and humour
(5 October 2008)

> "We have three sizes of condom", said the chemist shop assistant. "Large, medium and *muzungu*."

From this small introduction, I would like to make two semi-important points concerning: plagiarism and humour.

Plagiarism
Did you laugh at the joke that started this article? Even if you didn't laugh, you would have read it and assumed its author was

Kevin. However, the reality is that the idea for this joke came from the Oscar-nominated Robin Williams film, *Good Morning Vietnam*.

The actual joke that Williams made about condoms was, "Large, medium and Caucasian". Since I did not wish to be accused of plagiarism (i.e. stealing from the writings or ideas of another person), it was right for me to declare that the source of the humour was not me. Otherwise, if jokes could undertake DNA testing, the results would show that it was not "O'Connor", but "Williams" who was the father of the joke. I will not confuse readers by adding "because O'Connor was wearing a condom, he could not father the joke."

Interestingly, the Latin word *plagiarius* means "kidnapper". And, I suppose I had indeed kidnapped the Robin Williams joke.

Plagiarism rears its ugly head in many areas of life. In academia, sometimes a masters or doctoral thesis has been stolen from elsewhere. In music, Chameleone was accused of copying the song *Bomboclat* from the Tanzanian artist, Professor Jay. Another area for plagiarism is journalism. There is nothing wrong in using the internet to research an article, provided the writer declares the sources of quotations. But "kidnapping" someone else's article in its entirety, and passing it off as one's own is a different matter. A percentage of articles that we read in our newspapers are plagiarised from the net.

Humour

The Robin Williams joke that opened this article, as well as the Kevin O'Connor joke (*"Bampita muzungu* Bignose Smallpenis") used in a recent *Roving Eye*, represent a type of humour I use a great deal. The writer/speaker satirises themselves i.e. pokes fun at themselves. Am I right in thinking that such humour is rather un-African? We live amidst the culture of the African bigman. Women kneel before such big men. And above all, what such big men do not do, is to make fun of themselves.

But I am not African. And not only that, I am a non-African who lacks self-confidence and who has, at the best of times, a pretty low opinion of himself. So, it is easy for me to say:

> "Yesterday, my biggest achievement was to use the toilet 10 times before midday. I had diarrhoea."

But would an African bigman even admit to having diarrhoea, indeed even going to the toilet at all, and using such non-bigman things as latrines and toilet paper?

We are told to respect our elders. But should not respect be earned, rather than automatically given?

I love Africa. But I don't love its bigman culture. Fortunately, African women are increasingly starting to recognise when the bigman is a smallman.

The story about "storage"

(14 December 2008)

A few years ago, not long after I had started the journey to the tiny amount of Luganda, spoken in a horrible London accent, that I now know, I walked past some *boda-boda* cyclists in a Kampala suburb. One of them shouted "storage!" at me.

> "Why is this man shouting 'storage'," I thought to myself. "Does he need somewhere to store the spare parts to his motorcycle? Perhaps he wants to set up a warehousing business with me? Or, tired of being a *boda-boda* cyclist, maybe he wants me to find him employment as a storekeeper?" 'Storage' – the possibilities of what the man might mean seemed endless. And, to make matter

worse, it was only 7.30 in the morning, so my brain was still half asleep.

Fast forward five fully fantastic fun-filled years, and my Luganda, while still awful, just about realises that what the *boda-boda* man was shouting was not "storage," but "*sitole ki?*" And for an explanation as to what he meant, let us turn to "Wes" a Ugandan friend of mine in his early twenties. I should add that Wes is not his real name but his new nickname, after his favourite footballer, Wes Brown of Manchester United.

> "*Sitole ki?* is how you would say it and spell it with a real Luganda accent," explained Wes. "I would translate it as 'what's up?' But the literal translation would be 'what's your story?' The normal answer is *sirina*, which literally means 'I don't have' {i.e. I don't have any story}, but the better translation of the reply is 'nothing's up'."

Just as with *oli otya?* (how are you?), where the reply appears to be *gyendi* (I'm fine), even if you are asked while lying in a bed in a Ugandan hospital's intensive care ward, then also with *sitole ki?* The reply is inevitably *sirina*, even when you do have a huge story such as, "Diarrhoea is rapidly travelling down the inside of my trouser leg." Or, "Yesterday I won much money on *Deal, or No Deal*." At this obvious contrast between the reply to a Luganda greeting, and the actual state of body/mind of the person replying, Wes looked at me with his intelligent gaze, and said:

> "Don't worry, Kevin. It's just our behaviour, our culture."

I have noticed that when I say *sitole ki?* to Ugandans, they generally <u>smile</u> at me before replying. So, I asked Wes why they should think it funny, when *sitole ki?* is an expression that is so widely used.

"Well, Kevin, that term *sitole ki?* is most especially used by the youth."

"Now, you say that," I interrupted, "I remember someone else told me it was the language of the streets."

"That's right," Wes continued, "It is the Luganda of the streets. So, they are not expecting *a gentleman*, let alone a *muzungu* gentleman like you, to use *sitole ki?*"

There we are then. I always knew I was not a gentleman. So, just as the *boda-boda* cyclist once shouted it at me, let *Roving Eye*, on Sunday December 14 2008, shout to all readers, "Storage?" Sorry, wrong again, just blame my London accent, for I really mean, *Sitole ki?*

"Apology" and "forgiveness" – more than just words

(4 January 2009)

Journalistically, something must be going wrong within a newspaper when it has to print two apologies within its first four pages. But such was the case in a recent edition of one of Uganda's daily newspapers.

On the front page there was an apology to two very senior judges for a story alleging they had taken bribes. Not to be outdone, page 4 included a school photo with a caption apologising that the Saturday December 20 edition had named someone as the owner of the school, who was in fact not the owner of the school!

Sometimes such newspaper apologies result from court cases, or from the newspaper fearing that it would lose a court case. The newspaper may have to pay damages to a person as well as publish an apology. For example, a few years back, the same newspaper had to pay Ug Sh 5m in damages because of certain stories written by one of its leading sports journalists.

Apology is therefore an important word in journalism, and more generally in life. The word in English originates from Greek, and is defined as an expression of regret for a fault i.e. regret for something said or done that is wrong/incorrect.

We human beings often do not find it easy to apologise, to say those three magic words, "I am sorry". Looking back on my life, I can remember examples when I have apologised, and other occasions when I should have apologised to someone, but did not. But when an apology is genuinely given, it can defuse unhappiness and tension, and produce something in the person receiving it that is as important a quality as the *apology* itself...................*forgiveness*.

Forgiveness, and praying to God for forgiveness, play important roles in Christianity. Mathew makes the important point that God's forgiveness of humans is closely related to human forgiveness of others (Matt 5:23-24; 6:12).The Bible tells us that forgiveness is a duty, and no limit should be set to the extent of forgiveness (Luke 17:4). And again, that an unforgiving spirit is one of the most serious of sins (Matt 18:34-35; Luke 15:28-30).

There is no point in forgiving, then continuing to carry around a lingering resentment. For that would mean that the act of forgiveness had not been a truly genuine one.

One result of not forgiving someone for an action committed against oneself, is that the action recurs in the mind, sometimes obsessively so, years, even decades, later. For example, 45 years ago, a boy called Ernest tripped me from behind when we were playing football in the school playground. I fell over, bruised and bloodied my knee, tore my trousers and cried a great deal. As the years at secondary school passed by, Ernest and I disliked each other more and more. For whatever reason, I could never bring myself to forgive Ernest, and the result is that 45 years later, I still think about that playground incident. In 2009 in Uganda, my brain could surely be put to better use than thinking about something that happened almost half a century ago in a boys' secondary school in West London!

Forgiveness and apology are more than just two nouns. They are two of the most important words in the English language and capture two of the most important qualities open to a human being.

Keep English simple

(19 April 2009)

My fellow columnist, Kadumukasa Kironde II, has a long name, wears a long chef's hat and likes using long/tough words.

In contrast, Kevin O'Connor the first, agrees with George Orwell, who wrote in his *Politics and the English Language*, "Never use a long word where a short one will do."

Here is an example of unnecessarily complicated Mr Kironde in full flow:

> "…….given the *al fresco* setting, *ceteris paribus* we see no reason…….."

It is noteworthy that Kadumukasa Kironde II, like Queen Elizabeth II, uses the royal "we". And then there is his use of non-English words. "Ceteris paribus" is Latin and means "everything else remaining the same". While "al fresco" is Italian and means "outside" or "in the fresh/open air".

Now, there are Ugandans who understand such tough language. But most Ugandans have faced educational challenges, and Mr Kironde's columns would be understood by more readers if he used simple language. For, as Nicholas Bagnall observes in *Newspaper Language*:

> "Good writers........go through their work and ask themselves whether they have written anything which can be put in a simpler way."

Thus, in the same March 29 article, Kironde writes, "with no iota of consideration whatsoever towards patrons." This can be rewritten as, "without the smallest amount of consideration towards regular customers", without any loss of meaning

"Iota" is a Greek word, while "patron" comes from Latin. And to quote George Orwell again:

> "Bad writers are nearly always haunted by the notion that Latin and Greek words are grander than Saxon ones."

But "big words" are not just for "big men". Dear old Lillian - why use a short easy word when you can use a long complicated one - Barenzi returned to Uganda from her British government scholarship at Leeds University, and just to prove that she now held a Masters degree in journalism, started using words that sent the rest of us looking for our dictionaries.

I doubt if Nicholas Bagnall could have been one of Barenzi's tutors in Leeds, as he has commented of Lillian-type writers:

> "You are supposed to be telling your readers of something they didn't know before, not persuading them how clever you are."

Or as Galen, a doctor and philosopher who lived almost two thousand years ago, put it:

"The chief merit of language is clearness, and we know that nothing detracts so much from this as do unfamiliar terms."

So, the conclusion of today's article is:
- Eschew polysyllabic labyrinthine verba in order to augment the intellection of the bibliophile.

Sorry, that should have been:
- Avoid long difficult words in order to increase the understanding of the reader.

Ugandan greetings made easy
(28 June 2009)

Renowned linguistics (language) expert, Professor Kevin O'Connor, will today show how word association has helped him to learn some greetings in different Ugandan languages.

But what is word association? It is the linking of a word (or words) with something else in order to memorise that word or remember a fact.

Here is an example. I could never remember whether Jose Mourinho was the manager of A.C. Milan or Inter-Milan. Now, Inter begins with "I" and Jose begins with "J". "I-Jay" was, before they had, as Ugandans would say, "a misunderstanding", the pop group which comprised Iryn Namubiru and Juliana Kanyomozi. So, when I need to remember of which Milan football club Mourinho is the manager, I just have to think of Iryn's beautiful face and, in *Red Pepper* prose, her "bootylicious" body. The "I" in Iryn prompts me to remember that Mourinho's team is Inter-Milan.

Turning to greetings, as I can speak kindergarten Luganda, I have no problems remembering greetings such as *oli otya?*, *wasuze otyanno?*, *osiibye otyanno?* etc.

For reasons I do not know, I have also always been able to say, without deep thought, the Lugbara *ngoni?* and its reply *muke*.

And, although my pronunciation is absolutely awful, the Acholi *kopango?* and *kope* do not trouble the memory cells in my brain.

But the Banyankore greeting of *agandi?* was more troublesome. Then, I hit upon the word association method of linking that greeting with, in this case, Mahatma Gandhi, the famous Indian statesman and nationalist leader. However, the Banyankore reply of *nimarungi* is far harder. Indeed, I may have to be sent on a training course, funded by DfID (the UK's Department for International Development), or one of those other First World donors who enjoy throwing their money around in Uganda, in order to remember, and then how to pronounce, *nimarungi*.

Finally, I recently met up with a Tororo athletics coach, who I have known for many years. Rather than ask him to explain the current squabbling over districts in Tororo, or why Uganda increasingly seems to have more districts than Sudhir Ruperelia has dollars, I asked him to tell me a Jopadhola greeting. Well, first of all, he told me some terribly tough word, but seeing the dazed look of incomprehension on my face, he said, "I think you will find this one easier – *yoganoi?*" My friend was right. For, in order to remember *yoganoi?*, and the reply *yoga*, I only have to think of those funny poses and exercises that comprise yoga.

Word association has many more uses than remembering Ugandan greetings. For instance, in its "10 Tips for effective studying" the *Daily Monitor* (17 June 2009, p19) listed at number 10, "Use of memory prompts: use word association to help you remember facts".

Thus, if you need to remember who is the best team in the English Premier League, just think of a big fat man who is *full* of *ham*.

How to find the meaning of fascinating phrases
(6 September 2009)

Poor old Oryem Okello! At the infamous news conference in Kampala with the Chief Prosecutor of the International Criminal Court (ICC), Luis Moreno-Ocampo, Uganda's Minister for International Relations could:
- Either say that President Bashir of Sudan *would* be arrested if he set foot in Uganda (and thereby offend Sudan and the African Union).
- Or, say that he would *not* be arrested (and thereby offend Ocampo and the ICC).

Several newspapers said that Okello had been caught "between a rock and a hard place", which describes a situation when someone is in difficulty because they are faced with a choice between two unsatisfactory options.

More interesting than Mr Oryem Overweight Okello is the phrase, "between a rock and a hard place". Why does it mean what it means?

The internet has made all sorts of educational information easily available, including the answer to the above question.

The Phrase Finder website www.phrases.org.uk provides the meanings and origins of over 1,200 sayings, phrases and idioms found in the English language.

Furthermore, on this website, anybody can subscribe, free of charge, to "a phrase a week", whereby the explanation for a different phrase is emailed, once a week, to your inbox.

So what does *The Phrase Finder* tell us about the origins of "between a rock and a hard place"?

Well, it seems that in Bisbee, Arizona (USA), in the early years of the twentieth century, a dispute between copper mining companies and mineworkers developed. In 1917, the workers, some of whom had organised into labour unions, approached the company management with a list of demands for better pay and conditions. These were refused and subsequently many workers at the Bisbee mines were forcibly deported to New Mexico.

Thus the mineworkers were faced with a choice between harsh and underpaid work at the rock-face (i.e. "a rock") on the one hand, and poverty in New Mexico (i.e. "a hard place") on the other.

The website provides the origin of phrases like "between the devil and the deep blue sea" which has a similar meaning to "between a rock and a hard place", and to hundreds of other very different phrases, e.g. "as sober as a judge", "back to square one", "movers and shakers" and "rule of thumb".

Returning to Mr Oryem Overweight Okello, it is obvious that he has attended too many posh lunches and dinners with visiting dignitaries, and now needs to shed more than a few kilos. Here are two options:

- Okello spends a few hours every week working at the rock face in the Kilembe Mines.
- Or, he begins pounding (potholes permitting) along the hard roads of Kampala, in preparation for November's MTN Marathon.

Faced with such a tough choice, it could be said, for a second time, that Mr Oryem Okello had been caught "between a rock and a hard place".

Why do Ugandans say "Er?!"?

(13 September 2009)

Lawrence (Nationality – Ugandan; Age – 24; Occupation - Shop Assistant; Tribe - Muganda) and Kevin (Nationality – British; Age – 56; Occupation – Male Model; Tribe – Fulham FC) are sitting on a wooden bench in a Kampala suburb, on a hot, humid Wednesday morning.

It is the male model who breaks the silence:

> "Now, Lawrence, I have noticed that you, like many Ugandans, puncture discussions with the sound 'Er'. In what situations do you say 'Er'?"

Lawrence explained:

> "The actual sound we make is somewhere between 'Er?' and 'Eh?', and you do it when you are doubting something someone has told you. Or, when someone has told you a new thing – something that you did not know before."

> "The equivalents of 'Er', if I was speaking in English," continued Lawrence, "are 'Is it?' and 'Really?' Here is an example. My friend says to me, '99% of ladies have a bigger left breast than right breast, because most gents

are right-handed.' In English my reply might be, 'Really?!', but in Luganda it would definitely be, 'Er?!'"

At this point, Lawrence and Kevin are joined by Alvin (Nationality – Ugandan; Age – 27; Occupation - Driver; Tribe – Muganda), who exclaimed:

"I agree with Lawrence about 'Er?!' I do it a lot myself, especially when something surprises me. It is something that is done by all tribes in Uganda, but they often do it differently. For example, a Manyakore would say, *Er yamawe*."

Lawrence then interrupted Alvin with the observation:

"The Banyakore 'Er' is a bit different. It is a bit longer i.e. more like *Err yamawe*! And then there are the Alur, Acholi, and Langi - they do 'Er', but the conc ones who are deep in the village, and don't speak to other tribes, make a completely different sound which is similar to the smacking or kissing of lips."

At this point, I must admit, that when I am in conversation with Lawrence and he says, "Er", I then respond with an "Er", in imitation.

So is my "Er" a racist "Er", or even tribalistic "Er", as when I learnt that Chelsea had beaten Fulham 2-0 at Craven Cottage, my response to this defeat by the old enemy was definitely, "Er!?".

No, my "Er" when I imitate Lawrence, is neither racist nor tribalistic, but just plain sarcastic, and I hope readers of the first paragraph of this article ("Kevin, Occupation – Male Model) will recognise that making jokes at my own expense is part of my humour. For, while Kevin O'Connor has many strengths, being handsome/beautiful is not one of them, and of all the occupations open to me, 'male model' is about the least likely in which I would be successful.

Uganda has an over-abundance of long-winded, pompous 'big men'. So, if I say that "Uganda would be a better country if more of its 'big men' were prepared to tell jokes at their own expense", would your reply be, 'Er?!'?

Ugandans' overuse of "over"
(21 March 2010)

> "I'm very busy," said Jim, a 31-year-old electrician. "I got started late. I was overdisturbed this morning."

Well, "overdisturbed" is not a word in my vocabulary, so, I asked Jim why he had combined the word "over" with the word "disturbed".

> "We use that word 'over' a lot," Jim replied. "It means *going beyond*."

I thought deeply, scratched my head, and then, after rubbing the resulting dandruff off my shoulders, said to Jim:

> "Yes, but it is often used with words when the 'over' is unnecessary. For example, 'overspeeding'. You can't overspeed. A driver is either speeding or not speeding. They can't overspeed."

So, what is happening here, grammatically? When Jim uses 'over' in this way, he is normally combining it with a verb. This is generally fine. Thus, Jim can work, but on some occasions, he may be overworked.

The problem arises when the verb already carries with it the meaning of doing too much of something. Thus, if we said that a driver is speeding, it already means that they are travelling too fast. Hence, to say that the driver is overspeeding adds nothing to the meaning – the "over" is unnecessary/redundant.

Similarly, if I am boozed, I have consumed too much alcohol and am drunk. I can't be "overboozed".

"Overdisturbed" is a little trickier. If I say I have been disturbed, it means that I have been subject to too many interruptions. The implication of "too many" in the meaning indicates that it is unnecessary to add the "over" to "disturbed". In fact, I would go as far as to say that the use of "overdisturb" disturbs me!

The British often said of American troops stationed in the UK during World War 2 that they were "oversexed, overpaid and over here" i.e. the Americans used their money to impress, date and take to bed a lot of British girls.

Well I am over here (in Uganda). But I am definitely not overpaid, and whether I am oversexed or not, I will leave to the ladies to decide.

Anyway, my words have got over (sic; or possibly sick as in sick joke) and before I overdisturb the *Sunday Life* editor by making this article overlong, let me conclude by saying that "it's not over till it's over".

Enkya never comes

(4 July 2010)

> "The problem for us Ugandans," exclaimed Simon, a book publisher, "is that we don't confront issues."

So started my article "What happened to the aggressive Ugandan" (20 March 2006) and which is reproduced in my book "Ugandan Society Observed", a selection of the best, or should that be, the least worst, *Roving Eye* columns.

The frequent use of the word *enkya* (tomorrow) in Luganda provides a key to not confronting issues. So rather than saying "no" to a request (like "lend me 30,000 shillings"), the reply is often *"enkya."*

I asked two Ugandans for their explanation of this aspect of Ugandan culture.

Joseph, a 26-year-old assistant in a small hardware shop, said:

> "Sometimes we Africans we don't trust each other. That's why sometimes I keep telling you *enkya* in order to keep you in touch as my friend even if I will not give you that money. But the point is that we Ugandans we don't know how to be frank or straightforward. Sometimes we fear enmity. We are cowards."

While Norman, a 21-year-old student, pointed out:

> "It's not just Ugandans. It is most Africans."

> "The truth is," Norman continued, "is that they don't have money. It is difficult for them to admit that every penny they hold is most times accounted for. They think that if they say 'no I will not give you' to a friend, they might get annoyed. So, it is better to keep on responding with *enkya* until the person finds the money somewhere else."

Due to the renowned generosity of the *Sunday Monitor's Lifestyle* magazine editor, it gives me great pleasure to announce a *Roving Eye* column competition. The first reader to email me at the address below will receive a First Class British Airways business class return ticket to London plus an all expenses paid, two week tour of the UK.

The lucky reader will receive their prize ……… *enkya.*

Proverbs and culture

(15 August 2010)

Every morning, on BBC World Service, "Network Africa" begins with a proverb drawn from a different part of the continent.

There are many definitions of "proverb". Mine would be that a proverb distils the experience of previous generations into a relevant reminder to the living.

However, while a proverb may "distil the experience of previous generations," it may also capture their sexism, their gender bias etc.

Thus, in Luganda we have, *omwana omugezigezi asanyusa kitawe, naye omwana omusilusilu anakuwaza nyina.* (A clever child makes his father glad, but a foolish child makes his mum sad.)

But from the perspective of the year 2010, we might ask "Why should a mother not take credit for a clever child?" and "Why should a father not take responsibility for a foolish child?"

Therefore, proverbs can be good, bad and even indifferent.
One that I hate totally and utterly is:

"A woman's place is in the home."

In my local bar in Kampala, I never see any women. So, being a controversial soul, I ask: "Where are your women?" The boozed-up men reply: "They are not here, they are at home cooking. It's our culture." In other words, they truly believe that "A woman's place is in the home". I feel like saying "To hell with the culture." The culture may be right, or may be wrong, but it is definitely there to be challenged and changed for the better.

Some proverbs are extremely funny. For example: "A young doctor fattens the churchyard"

In other words, even doctors have to begin to learn their profession, and as they learn from their mistakes, their first patients will sometimes meet an earlier death than otherwise might be expected!

And, in Uganda, we have few doctors, but we have many chemists and drug stores. Behind the false status that a counter provides, the young assistant may have no more knowledge of the effects of the drugs than a fat traffic policeman or a *Speke Hotel* prostitute. How many of the eager buyers of the drugs have fattened "the churchyard,", or since most Ugandans are not buried in churchyards, have "provided income for the coffin-maker."

Life, death, sorrow, success .... there is a proverb to capture them all. Human beings must find meaning in their lives, and the only proverb that is missing, is the one that says, that there is no meaning at all.

Are you able to mimic?

(2 November 2010)

So what has been your worst exam result? I remember I got a very low grade indeed in oral French O-level. Yet I got the top grade in written French. So, why did I do so badly in spoken French?

Well, the only way I can speak is the way I speak. Tell me to speak English with an American or Russian accent (let alone with a specific American or Russian regional dialect) and I still end up sounding exactly like me.

Let's move from inability to ability to sound like someone else. Some time ago, Ruth, a MUBS graduate, told me:

> "There was a guy who came to Uganda from Zambia and he could put on voices that sounded like different African leaders such as Presidents Museveni and Mugabe and former President Mandela."

Ruth was referring to Ben Phiri who is a mimic (sometimes called an impersonator). A mimic tries to sound in voice, or behave in manner, like somebody else, and is often a comedian.

Interestingly, the word *mimic* comes from the old Greek (*mimos*) and Latin (*mimus*) languages. Such are the origins of familiar English words like: imitate, mime and pantomime.

And even the mockingbird (an American bird which imitates the songs of others) is a member of the *Mimus* bird family.

Mimicry is common on Uganda's FM radio stations. Ruth told me that she often finds such mimics funny. She continued:

> "The favourite target of FM radio presenters who can mimic is the President. But they can imitate anyone like northerners, the Baganda as well as westerners and Indians. They sometimes do it in the vernacular languages and sometimes in English. For example, they mimic how some Baganda exchange 'l's' and 'r's' in English."

Mimicry is not limited to imitating other people. A discussion with several children showed the uses of imitating the sounds made by domestic animals. For example, Margaret, 14, told me:

> "I make the sound of chickens {clucking}. You call them like that to get them to come to you, so you can give them food."

It is often said that the ability to mimic is the key skill required for speaking foreign languages. So, dear reader, are you a good mimic? Can you mimic another person? Or mimic speech from a different region of Uganda than your own? Or perhaps you can imitate the sounds of a domestic animal, such as a chicken?

If you can, then you are likely to have the ability to master speaking foreign languages and avoid my type of disastrous oral French exam result.

There may be other *oral* areas of life that I am good at, but if I try to explain them, I am sure I will be censored by the *Sunday Monitor*.

"OK please" is OK
(13 February 2011)

"We are all Ugandans now" is a phrase I use to capture something of the reality of my life in "the Pearl of Africa". Of course, I will never actually be a Ugandan. But, as I live here longer and longer (it will soon be 17 years since I first stepped off a plane at Entebbe Airport), I find myself taking on more typical Ugandan mannerisms, while something of Ugandaspeak (words and speech pattern, intonation and accent) also rubs off on me.

Ugandan friends tell me that when I call them by telephone from the UK, I sound "more English", which presumably means that I sound a little more Ugandan when I am here.

In a previous *Roving Eye* column ("O'Condom and hand movements" March 28 2010), Kevin O'Condom drew attention to the way many Ugandans throw their arms/hands from an upward position to down by their sides in order to emphasise a point. Just as in "Why do Ugandans say "Er?!" (September 13 2009), the same O'Condom looked at why Ugandans often puncture discussions with the sound 'Er'.

In 2011, I, too, often throw my hands down my side and say "Er?!" This is in some part due to me having lived here for so long (i.e. what's good for the goose is good for the goose), but in large part is due to me being a sarcastic sod, or as we would say back in *Bazunguland*, I love "taking the mickey" or, ruder, I love "taking the piss". So, when a Ugandan acquaintance says "Er?!" my frequent reaction is to reply "Er?! Er?!" And in my local trading centre, I so often throw my arms down by my side in imitation of friends, much to the amusement of everyone, that it has become a novel way of keeping fit.

If you ask the typical *muzungu* what Ugandanism they will fondly remember after returning to their home country, I suspect it would be "OK please".

Alvin, a 27-year-old driver told me:

"I use 'OK please' when I want to agree with something. For example, you might ask me, 'Will you come to my place?' And I can reply by saying, 'OK please'".

If you ever hear me saying "OK please" then you really will know that "We are all Ugandans now".

A book you can't put down

(22 May 2011)

I am not sure whether the word *unputdownable* does or does not exist in the English language.

However, every now and again, one reads a book that one can't put down, i.e. it is unputdownable.

Twenty four hours ago I picked up a book entitled *A Place of Execution* by Val McDermid. At over 600 pages, I thought to myself, "This is going to be a long read", perhaps taking me 10 days or a fortnight to complete. But I am already on page 450, and am just taking a break from reading in order to write this article.

Yes, *A Place of Execution* has got me by the "short and curlies" – a crime thriller which has its hands round my throat, just like its killer had his hands around the throat of a 13-year-old girl.

Do Ugandans get addicted to books in the same way? It is often said that Uganda lacks a reading culture. The recent physical extension of the *Aristoc* bookshop in Kampala's Garden City could be used as evidence against this assertion. However, it is rarely the case that one sees books in the hands of Ugandan youngsters, other than school books. The one exception is a book that is an excellent cure for insomnia and is a fable full of untruth i.e. the Bible.

We live in the television age, and except in schools and colleges, how many libraries does one see in Uganda? Yet, in every trading centre there are numerous video/DVD libraries. And, of course, there are many internet cafes. So are books a relic of the past, increasingly superseded by the TV and the computer?

As regular readers of this column will know, I am a great fan of the BBC World Service Radio's *World Book Club*. It is broadcast on the first Saturday of the month. It features a different novel every month and authors are drawn from all continents. A studio audience asks the author questions about the book, but questions can also be phoned in or emailed.

I don't enjoy every book it features. But every now and again, there is an *unputdownable* one, such as *A Place of Execution*. Suddenly, I am no longer in hot humid Kampala, but have been transported both geographically and historically to a cold

December in Derbyshire in 1963 England where a terrible rape and murder of a 13-year-old girl have been committed. Give me a good book rather than a good DVD any day of the week.

Some unusual names
(31 October 2015)

Gardening, and articles about gardening, I avoid like the plague. But there was something in Constance Obonyo's "What it takes to have a neat garden" (*Daily Monitor*, August 5 2015) that caught my eye. Before reading her article, I had always associated transplants with hospitals (heart transplants, liver transplants etc.). But from her paragraphs about transplanting a young seedling from the nursery to its own individual bag, I learnt that "the in-charge of the nursery and plant propagation," quite a verbal mouthful in itself, "at *Plants for Africa* on Kasenyi Road in Buziga," is called Brighton Onyango.

He, should it be the case that this particular nursery focussed on young plants, would be the in-charge of the "Nursery And Plant Propagation Youthful," which would have the acronym NAPPY. One does associate nappies with a nursery, but that is nursery in the sense of babies, not flowers and plants.

Charles Onyango Obbo
This was the first time in Uganda, or anywhere else for that matter, I had come across someone with the first name of Brighton. There is a famous seaside resort on the south coast of England called Brighton. The UK has many other seaside towns, and with different fortune our friend from the nursery might have been called Southend Onyango, or Eastbourne Onyango, or moving to the west coast of Scotland, Oban Onyango. If we switch that last name around we get Onyango

Oban which has similarities to that of the renowned *Daily Monitor* columnist, Onyango Obbo.

English Gardner

Brighton Onyango's name made me think of the whole subject of unusual names. Staying with gardens and nurseries there is a 100m female runner called English Gardner. Her personal best of 10.79 seconds, set in 2015, ranks her in the top twenty all-time for the 100m. An interesting thing about Ms Gardner, 23, is that she is not English. She is American!

The Beckhams

It is not impossible that Mr Onyango was conceived in Brighton, and his parents gave him that name, or that they supported Brighton Football Club. Many people think that David Beckham's eldest son was conceived in Brooklyn, New York, and therefore called Brooklyn. However, this is not correct, for as Victoria Beckham explains in her autobiography:

> "I had always liked the name Brooke and then we suddenly thought about Brooklyn. I'd always liked it as a place - it's very multi-cultural, very grounded. And it was only afterwards that I realised how appropriate it was because it was in New York that I found out I was pregnant."

Davin, Dalvine and Josel

Joseph, 32, owns a small beauty parlour in Kampala, which (surprise, surprise) is called "Joseph's Beauty Parlour". He told me:

> "Davin is unusual. So is Dalvine. Both are men's names. I saw these names in the newspapers and had never heard of them before."

Peter, 40, is a Ugandan friend. He said:

> "Peter was one of Jesus's disciples, and it is a very common name in Uganda. In contrast, Josel is not common. I don't remember where and when I heard it. But a kid was called Josel. Also a baby was named Clinton, after the American President visited Uganda."

Bill Clinton

Indeed, on this last point, the baby was actually called Bill Clinton, and President Clinton held him in his arms during his 1998 visit. According to ABC News, when the former President visited Uganda again in 2012 to inspect health and education projects supported by the Clinton Foundation, he asked to meet his now 14-year-old namesake (full name Bill Clinton Kaligani) and encouraged him to stay focused on his dream of getting a medical degree.

Inzikuru

A Ugandan athlete who speaks Lugbara told me that the word "inzikuru" translates into English as "no respect" or "having no respect for you". Well, at the recent Ugandan National Athletics Championships, a greatly overweight Dorcus Inzikuru ran in the 3000m Steeplechase, and was almost lapped. Once a much respected renowned athlete, it was certainly the case that many coaches had little respect for her decision to participate, when she was so unfit.

And, finally with my own name, Kevin, it is only given to males in my country of birth (UK). So, I was surprised when coming to Uganda, to find females also called Kevin.

7

Sport

Lessons from the MTN marathon
(3 December 2006)

The MTN Kampala Marathon and 10km races showed up both pluses and minuses in Ugandan society.

Let's start with the positive. MTN and the Uganda Athletics Federation (UAF) have created something very wonderful. Our newspapers have been full of plaudits for the event. For example, Isaiah Rwanyekiro writing in *Red Pepper* ("MTN Marathon Lights up Kampala", 22 November 2006, p12), observes:

> "What started a few years ago as a sports event, is fast establishing itself as a social event on Kampala's social calendar. With several socialites taking part, the MTN marathon can no longer be perceived as a sports event *per se*. The event has become a social gathering for the city socialites."

Community

Well, socialites, also known as bigwigs or the "A class", are often pompously too full of themselves, and I can take them or leave them. It was not the participation of Kampala's elite that stood out for me. It was the feeling of community that the event unleashed amongst participants and spectators. There was a spirit of buoyant camaraderie, of togetherness. And participants were not just encouraged by spectators, but also encouraged each other. For a few short hours on that Sunday morning, young and old, rich and poor, black and white, able-bodied and disabled, all came together in a spirit of unity while doing something worthy (raising money for charity) and in the sporting test of completing the course.

Before my prose runs away from me faster than a marathon winner, and becomes even more gushing, let me turn to two negative features.

Wrong practices

Regrettably, wrong practices seep into just about ever aspect of Ugandan society. The "big men" eat money in one way and therefore the small men find their own ways of doing it. Dan Tukwasibwe, Ali Matovu and Festo Tushabe finished 3rd, 4th and 6th. They wanted the big prize money (Ug Sh 1.8m, 1.2m and 0.6m, respectively), but fortunately, the organisers had spotted that they had run only part of the course, and they were rightly disqualified.

This sort of behaviour by some competitors came as no surprise. Earlier this year, in Iganga, I was following (by car) athletes participating in the 20km National Road Running Championships. I spotted a runner in the group ahead of me jump on the back of a bicycle *boda-boda*, and speedily cover part of the course. He then jumped off the bike, and started running again! Unfortunately for him, I had noted down his vest number, and rather than getting prize money, he just got disqualification.

Selfish commuters

So what was a second unsavoury incident at the MTN marathon? Let me point out that I was not running myself. As an athletics coach, I prefer to be out on the course supporting and advising the athletes that I coach. At Constitution Square, there was a temporary marshalling hiccup, and some *matatu* taxis were trying to drive across the closed side of Kampala Road, straight in front of the runners. After 9km of the 10km race, hundreds and hundreds of runners were streaming past. And the very last thing a tired runner is going to expect, let alone notice, is a *matatu* cutting across from their left.

I have been associated with running for more than 40 years, and I know what it is like to be a tired runner – and how one pays little attention to traffic, and only cares about reaching the finishing line. Added to that:
- The road was closed to vehicles.
- The closures were well-publicised in the media.
- The event takes place only on one morning, once a year, and it is reasonable to expect commuters to be both patient, and caring of their fellow human beings.

I really lost my temper, big time. Especially with one bespectacled, fat-faced passenger, who told me he was "late for an appointment" and continued urging the *matatu* driver to cut across the runners. The passenger and I almost came to blows. I apologise for hurling abuse at him, but I am pleased to say that a little bit of the O'Connor humour still shone through, when I told him:

> "Given how fat you are, you should be taking part in that 10km race, running some of that flesh off."

Fortunately, the police and marshalls then got their act together, and sanity was restored – the passengers disembarked (including "His Fatness"), and the *matatu*s were sent back up Constitution Square.

Conclusion
But, all in all, the event was a wonderful success both for athletics and for humankind. Well done MTN, and well done the UAF!

Why more Ugandans should support smaller Premiership teams
(7 January 2007)

I am in Luzira – not the prison, at least not yet anyway. I am in a bar in Luzira watching, live on Supersport, the English Premier League team I support, Fulham.

Fulham are at home, at our picturesque ground (Craven Cottage) next to the River Thames. Since they are playing Arsenal, I am surrounded by Arsenal fans, some dressed in the club's red replica football shirts.

At one point during the match, Mr Red Replica turns to me and asks:

"Why do you support Fulham?"

I understand why the question is being asked, as virtually all Ugandan fans support one of the big successful teams i.e. Man U, Arsenal, Liverpool or Chelsea. A Fulham supporter in Uganda is as common as a thin traffic policeman.

"Look at the TV screen," I reply. "You see the goal on the left. Well, my late father's ashes are scattered behind that goal."

So what is the explanation? My father was born in the West London suburb of Fulham in 1924. This was an era when geography of birth, not wealth and success of a football team, dictated a young person's supporting loyalty.

Today the world is different, and it is boringly predictable that Arsenal supporters are as numerous in Kampala, Nairobi and Dar-es-salaam, as they are in North London.

So Dad, despite the ups and many, many downs of his team, always stayed loyal to Fulham.

And when Dad passed away and was cremated in early 2004, his ashes were scattered in two places which meant much to him:

- The running track where he had trained with Sir Roger Bannister in the months before Bannister ran the first sub-4 minute mile in May 1954.
- And Craven Cottage, home ground of Dad's beloved football team.

The club was most helpful when approached about the scattered ashes. I had not realised what a common request this is to the club chaplain, Rev. Gary Piper, who scattered my father's ashes behind the goal, at the popular "Hammersmith End" of Craven Cottage.

It was a moving ceremony for our family gathered in the empty stadium.

My mind went back to 1959, when my father had taken me, aged six, to my first match at Craven Cottage. In those fargone days, most spectators stood, and Dad had to hold me up in the air so I could see over the heads of the fans standing in front of us.

'Like father, like son', so I am, of course, also a lifelong Fulham supporter.

Back in Luzira, Mr Red Replica was interested by my reply, and understood why I could never support Chelsea, Man U, Liverpool etc. And the result of the game we were watching on TV? It was Fulham's first victory over Arsenal for 40 years – a match I had attended as a teenage boy in 1966.

Perhaps more Ugandans should support smaller Premier League teams. The big victories will come less often, but when they do come, they provide truly unforgettable moments.

Let's kill off American sports scholarships
(11 February 2007)

Renowned athlete and 1500m national record holder, Julius Acon, has announced his intention to promote American sports scholarships in Uganda. I do not regard this initiative as being good for Ugandan sport. While such scholarships can have many benefits for the individual, for the improvement of Ugandan athletics, they have been a terrible failure.

In recent years, many more than 30 Ugandan athletes have won sports scholarships to the USA. But with the exception of Acon himself, virtually none have made an impact on the international athletics scene, indeed very few have actually returned to Uganda.

A classic example of what goes wrong from the sporting angle was a talented female 400m runner, who represented Uganda on many occasions. At the risk of sounding sexist, she had the face and body of a catwalk model. The start of a 400m women's race would see photographers huddled around her, snapping away. After her scholarship, she returned briefly to

Uganda for an introduction ceremony. She, though, did not light up any Ugandan tracks, as she had grown hugely fat.

So, what goes wrong with American sports scholarships, from the sporting angle? At the very beginning, the theory appears simple, straightforward and all beneficial. An athlete gains a scholarship to an American college and within the context of much better resourced, indeed hugely resourced, education and athletics systems, both their studies and sporting performance will surely prosper. Initially, all goes well.

A Ugandan Athletics Federation (UAF) official told me:

> "They normally continue to compete for some time and then slowly disappear. I am not aware of any improvement of them when in the USA. Our experience is that they are lost from Uganda athletic activity."

So why does this happen? Most Ugandan athletes come from poor backgrounds, and the USA, not athletics, provides an opportunity for a permanent escape from poverty.

Hit or miss affair

In contrast, success (and therefore income) at the uppermost end of international athletics is a "hit or miss" affair, with far more misses than hits. So, it is not surprising that eventually one or more of the following become more important than athletics to Ugandans on American sports scholarships:

- Work.
- Further studies.
- A green card.
- Marriage.

The American occupations of our former athletes include truck drivers, pastors, policemen, fitness trainers and, of course, *kyeyo*.

And even for the very few who remain dedicated to athletics, the cost of international travel between the USA and Uganda, makes it difficult for themselves, or the UAF, to fund their travel to national trials and other competitions in their home country.

USA hugely rich

The USA is a hugely rich country, and while sports scholarships may appear an act of American generosity, they are really akin to the current brain-drain from Third World to First World.

Rather than scholarships, a far better use of American resources would be to directly assist the development of athletics in Ugandan clubs and universities.

They need gyms, and especially synthetic running tracks. An American athletics coach would find it difficult to believe that Uganda still has only one synthetic track (at Kampala's Mandela National Stadium). Funds for coaching workshops and training camps would also be helpful. But all these activities should take place in Uganda.

And is there something else, deep in the psyche of Ugandans and Americans that explains why there is not this American investment inside Uganda, but instead a continuing preference for scholarships to the USA? Another UAF official told me:

> "This exodus on sports scholarships reflects the poor attitude and inferiority complex of Ugandan youth, and superiority and "bossiness" of Americans, that there is nothing good in Uganda for Ugandans except paradise in USA!"

Let America invest directly in the fast improving UAF/MTN Ugandan athletics scene, rather than in scholarships to individuals who will rarely grace Ugandan tracks again.

Making the right choices

(1 April 2007)

Last weekend's World Cross-Country Championships in Mombasa were more than just running. On two counts, the choices made by Ugandan runners showed up some of the fundamental choices that we human beings regularly face.

Selfish and unselfish

The first choice is that between self and team; or put more strongly, between selfishness and selflessness.

In the Men's Senior Race, both the renowned Ethiopian, Kenenisa Bekele, and Uganda's Boniface Kiprop, "dropped out" when in sight of the finishing line. Despite the horribly humid conditions (which must bring into question the suitability of Mombasa as a venue for such championships), both runners were surely capable of finishing the race if they had thought more about their team (and less about their personal disappointment of not running as well as they had hoped). For it meant that:

- Uganda did not win a team silver medal, but "only" a bronze.
- Ethiopia did not win a team medal at all in the senior race, as 3 of their other runners also dropped out. They had just 5 finishers, and therefore did not close a team owing to the "6 to score" rule.

OK, it's only sport, not war. But it is fair to argue that had Bekele and Kiprop thought a little more beyond themselves, they would have brought increased happiness to other team members, and to their fellow countrymen and women. For just as in the economy and in the body politic, as in running - the pursuit of self-interest has to be balanced by the pursuit of the public good.

Inzikuru

In the Women's Senior Race, Dorcus Inzikuru also dropped out – though not at the end, but in the middle of the race.

The choices facing Inzikuru were a bit more complicated. She is both a nice lady and a hugely talented athlete, and whatever the reasons for her "dropping out" decision, I do feel that there is one challenge that she needs to face up to – how to deal with failure.

She won Gold Medals at the World Junior Championships, and then as a senior in the World Championships and the Commonwealth Games. These last two were at the new event of the Women's 3000m Steeplechase. Every year, more and more women, all over the world, are learning the techniques of steeplechasing. Competition is therefore becoming more intense, and so it will be more and more difficult for "Inzii" to win Gold at steeplechase, for instance, at next year's Olympic Games. In other words, it is likely that Inzii will get beaten more often, and so she will have to learn how to cope with defeat and perceived failure.

Coping with defeat

Actually, it is not that tough. Anyone, who has been a runner knows that you have good races and you have bad races. Sometimes, when you expect to run well, you run badly. And sometimes when you expect to run badly (say after a bout of tummy trouble the night before), you surprise yourself and run extremely well.

These uncertainties are part of the wonder of racing, and of sport in general.

I give the following advice to the athletes I coach. When you get beaten in a race, all you need to do is simply go over to the victor, shake hands, and say "Well done. You ran well today." But at the same time, you can be thinking to yourself, "But I am going to get you next time." For, perhaps, a change in race tactics or a change in training, can bring you future victory.

Victories and defeats lie ahead for all runners, but two simple words "Well done" combined with a simple handshake can take away most of the fear of failure.

Journeymen runners like myself, unlike Dorcus, never had to face the world's media after a race. But again, all a star needs to do is to keep it simple e.g. "she ran better than me today, but I hope to do better in future."

Dropping out

And one final piece of advice to runners is, unless you are badly injured (and continuing would therefore worsen the injury) – never drop out. For, "dropping out" can be a bit like a disease, that once a runner becomes infected with, quickly spreads i.e. dropping out becomes a habit, it becomes easier and easier to do so in future races. It is normally better to finish the race, even if it means slowing down, and jogging through to the finish. Just as in life, it is generally better not to give up.

Athletics has shown me Uganda
(24 June 2007)

Last weekend I was in Adjumani. Nice place though it is, I had no reason to visit Adjumani, except for one – a national athletics selection trial was being held there.

So, not only did I learn a bit more athletics, I also learnt, for example about the awful condition of the murram road between Gulu and Atiak. Since this is also the main highway to Sudan, it highlighted in my mind one of the many developmental challenges facing northern Uganda and southern Sudan.

It was another athletics meeting – 2 years ago in Lira – that enabled me to make my first visit to an IDP (Internally Displaced People) camp. It was memories of this visit that caused me to write in last week's *Roving Eye*, when considering "us and them":

> "If you have bathed in a urinal today, or are waiting in a long line with your jerry can to reach a standpipe in an IDP camp, there can be little doubt that you would regard 8-showers-in-his-family-house Mukula as one of "them", brave boy though he was for showering in unheated water in Luzira Prison!"

In short, whether it be Kabale, Gulu, Ntungamo, Sironko, Tororo and innumerable other places in Uganda, athletics has taken me there over the last 13 years. One of the most wonderful things that has ever been said to me is when a Uganda Athletics Federation (UAF) official observed:

> "An athletics meeting would not be an athletics meeting unless the O'Connors are there!"

Well that is a big exaggeration, but what I would say is that athletics has provided a wonderful doorway into Ugandan life. For as one travels to meetings around the country, the insights one gains are not just into athletics and geography, but into Ugandan society and culture.

A further dimension is added by coaching athletics. My wife and I specialise in coaching middle distance running (800m and

1500m). Since we do this in our spare time, on a voluntary basis, we limit ourselves (currently) to three athletes, but aim to deliver them a high quality service. We meet for training 3 or 4 times per week, and speak additionally on the telephone.

Our many conversation are, of course, not just about racing and training. We get many insights into the lives of young Ugandans.

For example, a 20-year-old 1500m runner, in paid employment, has no children herself, but is still responsible for the school fees of several children – her brothers and sisters. This oh-so-common reality in Uganda, would be more or less unknown in my own country of origin (UK).

There are many reasons why I, and my father before me, need to say a big "thank you" to running. And an important one for me is that athletics has enabled me to learn much about Uganda, though, as always in life, there is a vast amount still to learn.

Ludo a sport? How ludicrous!

(1 July 2007)

The headline in the *New Vision* sports pages hit me between the eyes – "LUDO: Bwaise are YMCA champs".

Ludo a sport? You must be kidding! If ludo is a sport then so is passing gas (farting) and chewing gum.

But given that it was President Lyndon Johnson who said of another American President, Gerald Ford, that he is "so dumb that he can't fart and chew gum at the same time," I decided to do a *Google* internet search for "ludo" in case anybody accused me of being "dumb." And from *Wikipedia* I learnt that:

> "**Ludo** (from Latin *ludus*, "game") is a simple children's board game for two to four players, in which the players race their four tokens from start to finish according to dice rolls."

The suggestion, therefore, that "a simple children's board game" is a sport, is ludicrous. It is surely no coincidence that "ludo" and "ludicrous" come from the same Latin root.

Call me anti-ludo Luddite if you like. Accuse me of having a prejudice against ludo – and it won't be the first sport I have had a prejudice against, even though ludo is not a sport.

Let me freely admit that I am the owner of much sporting prejudice.

Where does such prejudice come from? A frequent conclusion of sociology is that people's behaviour, interests and views are shaped, at an early age, by their parents. Religion is a prime example.

But, returning to sport, I was a middle-distance runner because, you guessed it, my father was a middle-distance runner. Amongst all the accompanying mental baggage, I inherited his irritation for our fellow athletes – the sprinters, who delay and disrupt meetings by their many false starts.

Even if the new IAAF rules on false starts bring improvements, I can always fall back on a completely uncalled-for personal piece of prejudice – you are not a real runner until you can do 25 X 200 metres, with a short recovery in-between each one.

Such exercise would kill off the average Ugandan rally driver, whose chubby, helmeted features frequently peer at readers from the sports pages. My definition of motor-rallying in Uganda is:

"Rich, fat men playing with cars."

And what about golf? Is that a sport?

In my totally prejudiced view, proper sports - like football, cycling, boxing and running - require vigorous working of the heart and lungs.

Don't listen to all that nonsense about golf and "exercise." Should a round of golf shed a micro-fraction of a kilo from the many fat stomachs found on golf courses, then some golfers put that weight immediately back again by boozing on the "nineteenth hole" i.e. in the clubhouse.

It was American actor, W.C. Fields, who said:

> "I am free of all prejudice. I hate everyone equally."

So, let me make an important statement to *Sunday Monitor* readers:

> "I am free of all prejudice. I hate everyone equally………..
> except not-so-fat, middle distance running, non-ludo playing, Fulham supporters."

In other words, I know what I like, and I like what I know. And it is such self-centredness which provides the basis for most prejudice, in different spheres of life, throughout the world.

Pity those who don't understand sport
(6 January 2008)

I love sport. Correction –I love the sports I love such as running and football. In contrast, I hate motor sport, which in Uganda seems to be no more than fat rich men playing with cars. And talking of fatness, isn't rugby played by fat thugs? I am exaggerating, but it's certainly true that some of Uganda's national rugby team would be better players if they lost their fat stomachs.

Even though I would prefer to have a bout of diarrhoea than watch a game of rugby, I do have some understanding of this wretched sport. For example, I know what a scrum is, and a lineout and a try, and much else.

For people who are disinterested in, or lack knowledge of sport, a sporting event is disaster area. They don't know what the hell is going on. And when conversation or the media turn to sport, these people's understanding of the activity is less than a virgin's in a brothel.

A close second to their sporting ignorance, is their boredom. This is not surprising given that halfway through the Premier League season, newspapers, even in Uganda, are full of the same predictable headlines, barely distinguishable from those of previous years. If it's not Man U, it is Chelsea. If it's not Chelsea, it's Liverpool. And if it's not Liverpool, it's Arsenal. And who cares a monkey's arse about Arsenal, other than that they share the same four letters? Even people that enjoy football (and there's no better sporting spectacle than a good football match) get fed up with the repetition. Can't somebody else win something in the UK other than the "Big 4"?

In Uganda, tears were shed last year when the Cranes, albeit unluckily, failed to reach the finals of the Africa Cup of Nations for the umpteenth time. And with each football failure, journalistic venom is unleashed on yet another piece of FUFA maladministration.

And so it goes on. Week in, week out. Month in, month out. Year after year.

But can you imagine what all this means to someone who is actually bored by sport? To someone who thinks 4-2-4 is the name of a 24-hour supermarket? Or believes that a "sweeper" is the job done by a Ugandan doing *kyeyo* in the USA?

However, if football is tough for them to understand, then cricket is like trying to understand Chinese, even Martian, languages. What sense can they make of cricket's impenetrable jargon?

Bowlers bowl "off-breaks", "googlies", "chinamen" and "yorkers". Sometimes, they even "bowl a maiden over" which is what some men try to do at discotheques, often with the help of booze, and sometimes with the help of condoms. And for all you cricketing virgins, let me tell you that what the expression actually means is bowling an over (6 balls) without a run being scored.

Batsmen hit "off drives", "on drives", "hooks", "sweeps", "cuts" and even "late cuts".

Fielders field at "cover point", "square leg", "mid off", in the "slips", in the "gully" and even at "silly mid off".

And these are fairly standard terms in cricket. It is possible to get far more technical and obscure in sport.

For instance, when an athlete I coach has a big race, we will often have a detailed conversation about the pluses and minuses of running the first lap in 68 or 70.

Now only an athletics fanatic would wish to listen to that, so it is little wonder when I start ranting on to friends in Uganda about athletics, I will often see glazed expression in their eyes, and their body language starts to indicate that they need to move on to an urgent –if imaginary –appointment elsewhere.

So, those of us, who are deeply interested in sport, should spare a thought for the many that are not.

Beijing Olympics – there will be no medals for Inzikuru

(10 February 2008)

Dorcus Inzikuru will be bringing back no medals from the Beijing Olympics in August. Ugandans may ask, "Who is to blame?" And the simple answer is, "You Ugandans are to blame". Or put more accurately, the level of socio-economic development in Uganda is to blame.

In Uganda, an average woman has 7 kids. In rich countries, the average woman will have 2 or less children. Both a cause and a result of a country's development is reducing family size.

Back to poor Third World/Seven Kid Uganda. The socio-cultural pressure on a childless (I prefer the term "childfree") Ugandan woman in her mid-twenties to "produce" is huge.

So, Inzikuru conformed, and no doubt there were wild celebrations in Arua when she "produced" in late December.

But many people in the athletics world did not celebrate when they learnt of Inzikuru's pregnancy. For the timing of the birth made athletics nonsense. It meant that:

- She did not defend her World Championships steeplechase title in Japan in 2007.
- Her preparation time for the 2008 Beijing Olympics has been so slashed, that she will do remarkably well just to reach the Final, let alone win a medal.

For God's sake, Inzikuru is only 25 years old. Uganda already has more pregnant women (and resulting poverty) than it knows what to do with. We really did not need a pregnant Inzikuru.

The contrast with the UK's outstanding marathon runner, Paula Radcliffe, is striking. She waited until she was 33 years before she had her first child. Yet, the same methods of family planning were available to Inzikuru.

Running is a cruel sport in the sense that when you stop for any significant period, the fitness quickly disappears. Thus, for Inzikuru, when she begins serious training again, it will be like starting from zero. And now there is just not enough time to reach the very high standards needed for her to win a medal in Beijing.

It is arguable whether even a fully fit Inzikuru would have won Gold – the women's steeplechase is a relatively new event. All over the world women are taking it up, so standards are rising much more quickly in female steeplechasing, than in other events.

Inzikuru is a wonderfully talented athlete whose World and Commonwealth Gold Medals mean that she will always have a special place in Ugandan sporting history. But the ultimate prize was to have joined John Akii-Bua and become the only Ugandans to have won Olympic Gold in any sport. She had a chance of Gold. But the timing of the pregnancy, through her conforming to the norms of Ugandan society, and doing what so many of her fellow Ugandans expected of her, means that she now has no chance.

Author's Note
Marathon runner Stephen Kiprotich became the second Ugandan to win an Olympic Gold Medal in London in 2012.

God bless the underdog
(1 May 2008)

The very lifeblood of sport is its unpredictability and uncertainty. This is no better illustrated than when an "underdog" beats a hot favourite.

The word "underdog" stems from "the dog that gets the worst of it in a fight" and is, therefore, *under* the stronger dog. An underdog is not expected to win, but when one does in sport, it is normally a memorable occasion. On the few occasions that Fulham have beaten one of England's "Big 4" (Man U, Chelsea, Arsenal, Liverpool), it is definitely the case of the triumph of the underdog, of a David beating a Goliath.

The unexpected success of an underdog is found in all areas of life, not just in sport.

Militarily, a small nation sometimes defeats their bigger neighbour. For example, in the early years of the twentieth century, Japan inflicted a humiliating defeat on Russia in the

Russo-Japanese War. In some ways, it was reminiscent of boxing. An ageing champion, long past their best (as Russia was in the final decades of the Imperial Tsars), was demolished by the young up-and-coming challenger – Japan – a country which would later go on to a bigger stage, in war and in economics.

In politics, elections can throw up huge upsets, as when the famous wartime British Prime Minister, Winston Churchill, was swept from power in 1945 Britain by the Labour Party of Clement Attlee.

Even in the office, a long-serving executive may expect, and is expected by all, to gain promotion into a vacant post. And then the innovative managing director gives the job to a young, talented, but rank outsider.

In the Uganda of 2008, the homosexual is an underdog. Long having gained their freedom in other countries, including South Africa, here homosexuals are persecuted from all sides. Bigotry begets bigots, such as Pastor Martin Ssempa, who mobilise to deny homosexuals basic freedoms. And when Prime Minister Apollo Nsibambi last weekend spoke out against homosexuality, playing the boring and false card that it is un-African, he did so with a selective memory, conveniently failing to inform his audience that a long-dead Kabaka is commonly known to have been a homosexual.

Returning to sport, another underdog example was provided by Hungary in 1953. England's national football team had never lost on home soil to continental opposition. But they were totally outclassed by Puskas's stylish Hungarians. That 6-3 defeat for the English was the end of football as they knew it. Coinciding in period with the end of Empire, the match seemed to capture the passing of an era. The "winds of change" were blowing through Africa. In 1957, Ghana gained its independence, followed in 1962 by Uganda. And in 1990, the "winds of change" began blowing in football, when an African team, Cameroon, came very close to beating England in the World Cup.

Sportslovers, however, should not become too besotted with the thrill of an underdog victory, at the expense of the broad predictable rhythms of sport.

For although Uganda, Kenya, Tanzania and Zanzibar have all had football matches they unexpectedly won as the underdog, there is no mistaking the brutal truth put forward a few years ago by Hezekiah Wepukhulu:

> "None of the four ....has ever managed to qualify for the World Cup Finals or the Olympic Games ...... East African football...remains an underdeveloped and losing proposition." (*The East African*, 18 June 2001, p35).

But let us put harsh realities to one side. There are few more thrilling experiences than supporting the unexpected winner. Occasionally, God does bless the underdog.

FDC calls for unlimited term limits
(11 May 2008)

Today is a big day for the FDC. I refer not to the Ugandan political party – the Forum for Democratic Change, but of course to **F**ulham for **D**emocratic **C**hange, of which I am the Life President.

The reason for today's importance is that it is the last day of the English Premier League season. And while some readers will be focussed on unimportant matches involving Man U and Chelsea, FDC supporters will only care about today's big match – Portsmouth V Fulham. If we lose today, and other results go against them, Fulham will be relegated from the Premier League.

Whereas Arsenal have never been relegated from the top tier of English football, Fulham have been up and down more times than the penis of a teenage boy who has just discovered masturbation.

This grim reality for "the Cottagers" has led the FDC to call for a radical change in policy – the abolition of term limits i.e. Fulham's time in the Premier League should be unlimited. When they lose, they will win, just like Robert Mugabe.

If it was the case that Benny Hinn actually did perform miracles at a Namboole Stadium crusade, he would be claiming responsibility for our achievements in the last few weeks. It is indeed a miracle that they have reached the final match of the season and still have a chance of remaining in the Premier League. After not winning an away match all season, they have now won two in succession. And one of those (at Manchester City, when losing 2-0 with only 20 minutes remaining, we somehow managed to score 3 goals, the last one being in the final seconds of added time) was a rising from the dead that has only been matched by Lazarus.

Indeed, until this recent turnaround, so bad were Fulham's results, that the FDC was seriously considering changing its name to ZANU-PF i.e. **Z**ero **A**waygoals **N**ot **U**nusual – **P**athetic **F**ulham.

So who cares about Chelsea vs Bolton, let alone Wigan vs Man U? These big teams are the First World of the Premier League, the World Bank and the IMF of football. In contrast, Fulham are the Third World of soccer. So, the FDC is calling its supporters out on the streets of Kampala this afternoon to demonstrate in support of the Uganda of the Premier League – Fulham.

Ugandan patriotism destroyed by English Premier League

(24 August 2008)

The day is Sunday August 17 2008. The scene is a bar in a Kampala suburb. I have gone there with my wife to watch the Beijing Olympics athletics, most particularly to watch Uganda's Boniface Kiprop run in the 10,000 metres final. We cannot watch at home because we don't have satellite TV and it is often unclear which of the various Olympic sports UBC will show. DSTV, though, has a channel which broadcasts only athletics from the Games.

Awaiting us in the bar, huddled around the television, are a group of around 10 men, mainly middle-aged, mainly overweight, all Ugandan. Where their women are, and what they are doing, would alone require a *Roving Eye* column, but not today's.

Chelsea vs Portsmouth is about to begin on the TV. So, I ask them, "would you not prefer to watch 'your boy', runner Boniface Kiprop, on another channel, since he has a very real chance of winning an Olympic medal?"

Their faces register utter astonishment, that is, to the extent that rounded, bloated faces – so typical of Kampala's more expensive up-market bars – can register anything. It is a bizarre situation. My wife and I are *English*, but want to watch a Ugandan. Yet the Ugandans want to watch the *English* Premier League. Consider also the following:

- No Ugandans play for Chelsea or Portsmouth.
- Indeed, no Ugandans play in the English Premier League.
- The League is annual, is now only won by a small number of dominant clubs ("the Big 4") and it seems only yesterday that the last season ended.
- In contrast, the Olympic Games are held only every 4 years, and long predate the Premier League. Every country in the world participates.
- Uganda has only ever won 2 athletics Olympic medals (John Akii-Bua and Davis Kamoga). Most of its sportsmen had already been eliminated from the Beijing Games, and its medal chances by last Sunday rested with just a small number of athletes, of whom Boniface Kiprop was the most notable.

I am a human being with very many faults, weaknesses and shortcomings. And one of those weaknesses is that I support Fulham. But I can genuinely say, that if I had the choice of watching Fulham playing in the Premier League on one TV channel, or a genuine Ugandan Olympic medal prospect (which could foreseeably only be in boxing or athletics) on another channel, I would always watch the Ugandan. After all, I have lived in this country for 14 years, and it has given me so very much.

At the bar, we accepted defeat (and eventually watched Kiprop fail to win a medal at a friend's house on the other side of Kampala).

But what the bar incident showed, is just how powerful neo-colonialism is. So powerful that, as regards sport at least, it has destroyed Ugandan patriotism.

Sitting and standing in football stadia

(19 October 2008)

Last Sunday, the Ugandan Cranes won the battle but lost the war. They beat Benin 2-1 at Namboole Stadium, but previous poor performances, especially away from home, meant that they were still eliminated from Africa Cup of Nations/World Cup qualification.

Home advantage

The Cranes' excellent home record means that their home ground has sometimes been referred to as "Fortress Namboole" and begs the interesting question of why football teams generally win many more points at home than away. After all, football pitches are much of a muchness wherever they are located i.e. pitch size and width (within stipulated dimensions), grass, goalposts etc.

The reason for home advantage is surely that the huge noise generated by the home supporters (who almost always massively outnumber the away supporters) both intimidates/worries the away team and drives the home team to higher performance levels.

All-seater stadia

In Britain, there has been a debate about whether the conversion of major football grounds from standing to all-sitting arena, has had a marked effect in reducing home advantage.

In the 1960s and 1970s I regularly went to football matches in London to watch Fulham. I can virtually never remember sitting in a seat. The seats in the (confusingly called) stands were for the rich, the snobs and the infirm.

But standing areas are more prone to crowd trouble and violence. It was the tragedies at England's Hillsborough Stadium and Belgium's Heysel Stadium that ushered the rapid introduction of all-seater stadia in the top leagues.

Sitting and standing

So, why should spectators sitting, rather than standing, reduce home advantage? The starting point is that when we human beings experience moments of passion and excitement, we will normally be on our feet, standing.

An exception is sex, though, there will be some energetic readers who disagree, and whose standing sexual positions require more energy and changes of position than that achieved by the talented Man U forward line on the football pitch.

Moving away from sex, a heated argument is best conducted while standing. How many orators have cast their spells over an audience from a sitting position? Adolf Hitler did not wave his arms about at the Nuremburg Rallies from an armchair. Born-again preachers, whose speaking styles this column has compared to those employed by Adolf Hitler (*Born Again or Hypocrites?* 12 January 2003) will rarely reach their sermon's climax while seated.

In contrast to standing, sitting is generally associated with resting, relaxing or with calmly, methodically working. One would therefore expect there to be less noise and passion in all-seater stadia.

Manchester United

Thus, while Manchester United may have enjoyed incredible, almost unbroken success under Sir Alex Ferguson, Old

Trafford has been described as a "great stadium with a poor atmosphere."

Ferguson once said that United fans:

> "Sit and admire the ground and wait to be entertained as if they were at a theatre......that may be all right for some people, but it is of no use to me or my players."

"Theatre of Dreams", maybe, but theatre good for home teams, possibly not.

The impact of all-seater stadia has been well captured by Simon Barnes of *The Times of London*:

> "If you sit down to watch football, you are a *spectator*. You say, 'Here I am. Entertain me'. But a person who stands up is a *participant*, and not a negligible one."

Crowd safety

So, that our Mandela National Stadium at Namboole is not all-seater may be a factor in the Cranes' excellent home record. But we should never forget the implication that this has for crowd safety.

A few years ago, my wife and I thought about inviting a large number of school parties (with free entrance) to a national athletics meeting at Namboole Stadium. In contrast to up-country, the attendance of spectators for athletics at the Mandela National Stadium is pathetic. The atmosphere is so lacking that my standard joke is that "I have experienced more excitement at a funeral". But, when I started to think about tens of thousands of school kids inside Namboole, with its absence of crush barriers, I became fearful of the possible consequences, and I did not put my plan into action. So, apart from the athletes, the number of spectators for a national athletics meeting in Namboole, rarely reaches double figures, and the noise and excitement generated is close to zero.

When neocolonialism won at the Cecafa Cup
(18 January 2009)

Last weekend's *Sunday Monitor* back page headline was, "Cecafa Cup semis kick off at noon" and the article began, "The Cecafa Senior Challenge Cup semifinals have been brought forward by four hours........."

This meant that the second semi-final (between Uganda and Burundi) would now start at 3pm rather than the originally scheduled 7pm.

Let's look at some possible explanations for these changed timings.

Possibility 1 – Electricity
The original evening kick-off would have required floodlights. Perhaps loadshedding was expected and, given rising fuel prices, using the standby generator, would be too expensive for the Cecafa organisers?

Possibility 2 – *Kyana*
Despite his receding hairline and thick Scottish accent, Cranes' coach, Bobby Williamson has been a big hit with the local ladies. His current *kyana* had noticed how exhausted a big international match leaves Bobby. And that however many goals the Cranes score, Bobby is unable to score in her "Match of the Day" afterwards. She therefore demanded that if Bobby wanted to meet her as per their normal arrangement in Room 131 of Kampala's *Sheraton Hotel*, the starting time of Uganda vs Burundi had to be brought forward to 3pm.

Possibility 3 – Burundian soap opera

The original 7pm kick-off clashed with the famous Burundian TV soap opera, *That's Life Fattu*. Indeed, last Sunday's episode was the climax of this long-running series, in which the overweight star, enraged by a failed attempt at dieting, murders all his co-stars. As this TV programme is so popular in Burundi, a senior Bujumbura policymaker intervened to ensure that kick-off of the Uganda vs Burundi match was brought forward to 3pm.

Possibility 4 – Neocolonialism

The three possibilities above all provide wrong explanations for the changed kick-off times. For the correct explanation, let us now insert the missing words in this article's opening sentences:

> "The Cecafa Senior Challenge Cup semifinals have been brought forward by four hours …..to allow fans to watch the English Premiership game between Manchester United and Chelsea."

You may ask yourself whether the colonialists ever went home, because neocolonialism (i.e. the *new* colonialism) is alive and well, at least in Ugandan sport.

Let's step back a moment and consider. The timing of a club match in the, note, English Premier League, is determining the timing of two important international matches, taking place many thousands of miles away, in a former colony. In comparison with the Premier League, Ugandans rank their own football in about Division 87, and that's being kind. How many Ugandans do you see wearing SC Villa, KCC or Express shirts? How many do you see wearing Man U, Arsenal, Chelsea or Liverpool shirts?

Neocolonialism is defined as the quasi-colonialism practised by strong countries in dominating weaker, though politically independent, countries by means of economic and other pressure.

The bringing forward by 4 hours of last weekend's Cecafa semifinals is a small, but nevertheless, good example of neocolonialism in practice. Why was it the Cecafa matches, and not the Man U V Chelsea match, that were brought forward by 4 hours? You may laugh that this question is even posed, but in a non-neocolonialistic world, it would be a valid question to ask.

Idi Amin's Golden Age?
(30 August 2009)

Was your life better in the past than it is today? "Yes" is the most likely answer to this question as the human race generally looks back through "rose-coloured spectacles."

Thus, writers in Britain in the early nineteenth century remembered nostalgically times before the Industrial Revolution, which they termed "the Golden Age."

Of course, the Golden Age had never existed, and was the product of sentimental imaginations, since life for most in pre-industrial, agricultural Britain was "nasty, brutish and short."

Simon Barnes (the *Times of London*) has argued that "sport is more open to nostalgia than any other area of life."

Idi Amin

Ugandans often look back to the 1970s, to the Idi Amin regime, as the country's Golden Age of sport. Akii-Bua won Uganda's only Olympic Gold Medal, the Cranes reached the Final of the African Cup of Nations, and there were various boxing triumphs.

An Idi Amin Golden Age is indeed a bizarre concept, for his regime killed many innocent people, and wreaked economic havoc by expelling the Asians. But there is a case for arguing that Amin's considerable personal interest in sport, resulting from his background in boxing, raised Uganda to a level of sporting success not achieved before or after.

I doubt, though, whether Akii-Bua's Gold Medal can be laid at Amin's door. A far more important factor was that Malcolm Arnold was Uganda's National Coach in the late 1960s and early 1970s i.e. mainly before the Amin regime. Arnold not only went on to become Britain's Chief Athletics Coach, but remains one of the World's top hurdling coaching specialists. Arnold's coaching was crucial to Akii-Bua's success at 400m hurdles.

Football

Whereas the jury might be regarded as still out on Uganda's Golden Age of sport, more generally the Golden Age concept is false.

Thus Barnes says of football's supposed Golden Age in Britain – in the first half of the twentieth century – "like every Golden Age, it was filled with scandal, immorality, horror, greed and turmoil."

There were riots at Cup Finals, examples of match fixing and fouls aplenty. Racism was present as it has been since the time of the very first black footballer in Britain – Arthur Wharton, who played in the late nineteenth century.

Further, the technical quality of football was much lower in the supposed Golden Age. Players were relatively unfit and slow-moving, formations and tactics were stereotyped.

Better today
It is true that a sportsman should never be judged out of the period they were competing in, but surely the most persuasive argument against a sporting Golden Age is that in every sport which can be measured (like swimming and athletics) standards are hugely higher today.

And, as in sport, as in life. You may think that you were happier in the past, that there were no potholes in the road and that public officials did not take bribes. But take off those rose-coloured spectacles and you may well find, to use the famous words of former British Prime Minister, Harold MacMillan, that "you've never had it so good!"

An athletics training experience for Cranes' footballers
(4 January 2010)

It is always good to be involved in something worthwhile that has never been done before. Such was the case recently when my wife and I led an athletics training session for 4 members of the national football team (the Cranes). We were helped by Assistant Cranes coach, David Otti. 800m National Champion, Achola Janet (who we had coached for 5 years). Athlete Charles Felix Mukasa (Nkumba University) also participated.

"Unique"
Veteran Otti commented:

"I am not aware of anything like this ever taking place before in Uganda i.e. where an athletics coach has done a training session with members of the national football team. Today was unique, and we footballers greatly value this collaboration."

The scene was Kampala's Mandela National Stadium where the home-based players of the the Cranes were in residential training, preparing for the Africa Nations Championship (CHAN) return leg against Burundi.

We put 4 midfielders (Kaweesa Malco, Mudde Musa, Semakula Noah, Serunkuma Simon) through an athletics session. We suggested midfielders to the Cranes' coaches, as they must do a massive amount of running (between defence and attack) during any match. It was a middle distance (800/1500m) session which we thought good for footballers, as middle distance combines speed and endurance.

The session
The session consisted: 25 minutes jogging; 20 minutes flexibility exercises; a fitness test (situps in one minute); strides and the main part of the training – 6 x 400m with 90 seconds recovery between each 400m.

Cross-training
This Namboole session was an example of cross-training i.e. where participants of one sport (in this case football) do the training of another sport (in this case athletics). Cross-training is becoming increasingly popular – for example, many athletes do some swimming training, especially when they are recovering from injury. Sports have so much to learn and gain from each other.

I have met many national football coaches while training athletes on Namboole's track over the last decade. I have on several occasions talked with them about the possibility of a joint session, and it is to the credit of Bobby Williamson, Jackson Mayanja and David Otti that they turned this idea into a reality.

Pop music

Pop music (by the late, great South African reggae star, Lucky Dube) was played during the session for motivational purposes. It seemed appropriate in the circumstances, that it included one of his most famous tracks – "Different colours, one people".

Two World Cup memories
(30 May 2010)

Well, the football World Cup is almost here. And, for those readers who do not enjoy soccer, booking a rocket trip to the moon may be the only way to escape the huge media coverage!

But for those of us interested in football, a wonderful festival lies ahead, which will etch memories in our brains. When I asked Paul, a 23-year-old Kampala shopkeeper for his favourite memory from past World Cups, he replied:

"That's when Senegal reached the quarter-finals in 2002".

This was the first time Senegal had got to the World Cup. They memorably beat holders France in the opening match and were only the second African team (the first being Cameroon in 1990) to reach the last eight of the tournament.

"I especially remember El Diouf and Sylva," continued Paul. "El Diouf could dodge all the defences, and then even laugh at them. And if Senegal had reached the semi-

> final or final, then Sylva would have been the goalkeeper of the tournament."

The impression on Paul was all the greater because this was his first experience of world cup matches, and he even remembers the TV he watched them on!

> "In 2002, I was too young to go to a bar. But fortunately, I was able to watch at my neighbours'. It was fantastic because we only had black and white pictures, but he had a colour TV."

As regards my World Cup memories, I will cheat by choosing a favourite one away from the pitch. My family watched the 1966 Final on TV in our flat over the bank in the heart of London, where my Dad worked as a caretaker. England beat West Germany in the Final at Wembley. Afterwards, we stood on the steps outside the bank watching the traffic stream down from Wembley. The Portuguese team coach, stopped a few yards from me, at the traffic lights. In one of the window seats, was the great African footballer, Eusebio. For a brief moment our eyes met, and we smiled at each other. Then the traffic lights changed, and the Portuguese bus disappeared into the heart of London.

As a young schoolboy, I was too young to appreciate the colonialist reasons why Eusebio played not for Mozambique, but for Portugal. I did know, though, that he was an exceptional player. And he scored 9 goals in the 1966 tournament which made him its leading marksman, helping Portugal to take third place.

Eusebio will, of course, not remember me. But I have a wonderful 42-year-old memory of us smiling at each other across a busy London road.

Namboole Stadium – learning from the past
(27 February 2011)

My wife and I recently made a brief visit to Namboole Stadium to look at its renovation under the Chinese aid project. And very impressive it is too.

That the 6 lane warm-up track has been transformed from tarmac to tartan meets a requirement that will enable the stadium to host major international track and field games.

And the orange and green of the newly-laid tartan in the main stadium is so bright that I almost had to put sunglasses on to view it. This re-laying was made necessary by damage to the old track, such as holes and tears in the tartan. And this damage was regretfully not caused by running as, despite Namboole having the only synthetic track in Uganda, it was hugely under-utilised both as a competition and as a training venue.

The damage was caused by music concerts and, above all, by religious crusades, where people were allowed to stand on the uncovered track and football pitch. The wretched pastors should have been asked to perform the miracle of removing all the holes from the track, since they and their flock had caused them. But, of course, they would have not accepted this challenge, since the holes would have still been there the next day, and we would have seen their healing as the *bicupuli/* fake nonsense it really is.

Some damage to the track was due to stages and speaker systems being erected on it. But the worst damage was caused by ladies wearing high-heeled shoes. It may be that Jesus laid his hands on people's heads, but if I am allowed to lay my hands on the legs of such babes, I personally volunteer to remove their high-heeled shoes.

There should be no crusades at Namboole Stadium - full stop. After all it is *the* national sports stadium and not a born-again church. But if these, or other large non-sporting functions, are to go ahead, the stadium management must first be allowed to purchase the protective covering carpet for the track and football pitch that has been recommended by the Chinese. I understand that this covering cannot be funded by the aid project and will have to be paid for by the Ministry of Education and Sports.

So, let us remember the 3Cs i.e. no **C**overing **C**arpet = no **C**rusades. While Uganda has been making good progress in sports such as rugby and cricket, for the foreseeable future, it is only at middle and long distance running that it can achieve medals on the world stage. And for that, Uganda needs its only synthetic running track to remain in good condition.

Namboole Stadium – a national disgrace

(19 June 2012) (published under a pseudonym)

The National Track and Field Championships were scheduled for June 22 and 23 June at Mandela National Stadium (more commonly known as Namboole Stadium).

This seemed all very sensible as:
- Namboole has Uganda's only synthetic (tartan) track.
- The meeting is just 5 weeks before the opening of the Olympic Games in London.
- Athletics (given boxing's current shambles) is the only Olympic sport in which Uganda has any chance of winning medals.

However, although the Uganda Athletics Federation (UAF) presented its calendar, and paid its invoice for different meetings at Namboole, at the start of the season, it has just been informed by the stadium management that it cannot use the facilities on 22 and 23 June.

The reason is that some hugely wealthy and strange Japanese cult called "Happy Science" will now be using the stadium on those dates.

I say "strange", because according to Wikipedia, the leader of the cult, "World Teacher" Ryuho Okawa, "claims to channel the spirits of Muhammad, Christ, Buddha and Confucius."

So, the first question to Namboole Stadium is, that while we all support freedom of speech, should they really be introducing Ugandans to such a bizarre belief system?

The second question is what damage will Okawa and his followers do to the surfaces (football pitch and tartan track) at the stadium?

Namboole, built under the Chinese aid programme, was opened in 1997. But by the new millenium, holes were already beginning to appear in its tartan track. These were not caused by running, but by non-sporting events such as evangelical crusades, pop concerts and political rallies.

Just over a year ago, at great expense, the Chinese government refurbished the track. But Namboole management soon began repeating its same mistakes.

Last Good Friday, some wretched pastor, whose name I forget, held a huge crusade at Namboole. The damage to the stadium's surfaces was horrible, and delayed the Saturday Uganda Athletics Federation National Trial. Photos show scaffolding being dropped from a great height on to the tartan and the football pitch.

It would be possible to hold crusades etc. at Namboole if it had the necessary "carpet" to roll out over the pitch and tartan to protect the surfaces. But the stadium does not have one.

Until the "carpet" has been purchased, and is in place, it is obvious that no more crusades and the like should be held at Namboole. But, Ryuho Okawa will be there on 22 and 23 June, destroying our country's only tartan track.

And, instead of Uganda's National Track and Field Championships being held at Namboole, it will now be held on a bumpy grass track in Kampala. What wonderful preparation for our athletes for the London Olympics!

60th Anniversary of the 4-minute mile
(6 May 2014)

Today is the 60th anniversary of the first sub-4-minute mile (3 min 59.4 sec) run by Roger Bannister on 6 May 1954 at Oxford University's Iffley Road track.

To commemorate this world famous historical athletics event, the Ugandan Athletics Federation (UAF), in conjunction with Kevin and Sue O'Connor, will hold Men's and Women's mile races (replacing the 1500m) at the 4th UAF National Trial on Saturday 10 May 2014 at Mandela National Stadium in Kampala. One mile is 1609.34 metres i.e. just over 4 laps of a 400 metres track.

Prizes

Readers of the UK magazine *Athletics Weekly* have provided some special prizes for this special event:
- 60 copies of the hardback book "Showdown in Moscow" signed by author Hugh Shields. The book captures the epic confrontation over 800m and 1500m between Steve Ovett

and Sebastian Coe at the 1980 Moscow Olympics. They both held the world mile record at different times. Each participant (up to a maximum of 60) in the mile races will receive a copy of the book, and if there are any remaining, they will go to runners in the 800m races (as Bannister also often ran the 2 lap race).

- The men's winner of the mile race will receive an additional book – "The Four-Minute Mile" by Sir Roger Bannister.
- Inscribed gold, silver and bronze medals for the first 3 men and the first 3 women in the "A" races.
- Cash prizes of Ug Sh 150,000, Ug Sh 100,000 and Ug Sh 50,000 for 1st, 2nd and 3rd places respectively, in both Men's "A" and Women's "A" Miles.
- Bonuses of Ug Sh 100,000 for each man under 4 minutes and each woman under 4min 36.23 sec (equivalent to a sub-4-minute Men's mile, according to the IAAF 2014 Scoring Tables).

UAF Organising Secretary

Faustino Kiwa, the UAF Organising Secretary, has commented:

> "We are delighted with this initiative. The last mile race run on a Ugandan track must have been over 40 years ago when the world of athletics fully converted from imperial distances (440 yards, 880 yards, one mile etc.) to metric distances (400m, 800m, 1500m etc.) It would be great if we could get some Ugandan men under 4 minutes on 10 May, but even 60 years on, it is a tough call."

Family connection

Kevin's late father (Pat O'Connor, whose one mile personal best time was 4 min 12 sec) trained with Roger Bannister at

Paddington Recreation Ground in West London during the winter of 1953-54. Their standard training session was 10 x 440 yards with 2 minutes recovery, the metric equivalent of which (10 x 400m) Kevin and Sue still sometimes use in their coaching in Uganda.

Author's Note
The above was a press release, not an article. However, as the event meant so much to myself and my family, I have included it in this book.

The Margaret O'Hogartaigh Women's 5000m Memorial Race

(23 March 2015)

Summary

A Women's 5000m, in memory of the late Dr Margaret O'Hogartaigh, and sponsored by her husband Professor Ciaran O'Hogartaigh, will take place on 30 May 2015, as part of the 5th UAF National Trial in Kampala. There will be a generous and innovative money prize structure, plus trophy for the winner and medals for the first three. The UAF will add a Ug Sh 100,000 bonus if the national record is broken. If deemed a success, the race will become a permanent feature of the Ugandan Track and Field Calendar.

Dr Margaret O'Hogartaigh

Margaret was an outstanding Irish academic and a Fellow of the Royal Academy of Medicine in Ireland. In 2000, she was awarded a Fulbright scholarship and spent the following year in Boston at Boston College. This was the beginning of Margaret's long connection with academia in the United States and she was to return frequently to teach at Boston College and at Harvard.

Margaret was a resilient cross-country runner and, more recently, competed in field events for Ireland at Masters (veteran) level. She won a silver medal for Ireland in athletics at the European Masters' Games, Sweden, as well as Northern Ireland and New Zealand athletics titles, plus five All-Ireland medals.

She was also an avid athletics fan. As part of her historical work, she published several papers on athletics, many of which are collected and published in her collection of essays *Quiet revolutionaries: Irish women in education, medicine and sport, 1861-1964*, one of the six books which she authored/edited. Margaret was a generous supporter of Ugandan athletics, and provided, over many years, a huge number of athletics magazines and books for distribution to Ugandan athletes. Regretfully, Margaret passed away just before Christmas 2014 at the age of 47, due to cancer.

Memorial race

Margaret's husband, Ciaran, suggested that one fitting tribute to his wife would be a memorial race in Uganda. As she frequently wrote about gender issues, it was thought that this should be a women's race, and that it should be a distance race, as she particularly liked competing in and watching such races. In conjunction with the Ugandan Athletics Federation (UAF), it was decided that the "Margaret O'Hogartaigh Women's 5000m Memorial Race", should take place on May 30 2015 at

Kampala's Mandela National Stadium, as part of the 5th UAF National Trial, in which a W5000m was already scheduled.

Margaret was and is in her essence a generous soul and it is hoped that this memorial race will be a testament to her generosity and her interest in athletics.

Prizes
In her memory, Ciarán is sponsoring a generous and innovative set of prizes:
1st Ug Sh 400k plus engraved trophy and medal;
2nd Ug Sh 200k plus engraved medal;
3rd Ug Sh 100k plus engraved medal;
4th – 6th Ug Sh 20k each;
7th – 10th Ug Sh 10k each.
The UAF will provide a Ug Sh 100,000 bonus to the winner should she break the National 5000m Record.
Ciaran will be present on 30 May to award the prizes.

Review
In the week following the race, Beatrice Ayikoru, Ciaran, Kevin and Sue O'Connor will conduct a review. If the race is deemed a success, the "Margaret O'Hogartaigh Women's 5000m Memorial Race" will become a permanent feature of the Ugandan Track and Field Calendar.

Author's Note
The above press release was included in the book as a tribute to a remarkable lady. It has now been agreed with the UAF that the memorial race will take place every year.

Did Cheptegei "choose money over honour"?
(4 July 2015)

The *New Vision* (June 29 2015, p61) has reported that athlete Joshua Cheptegei (20) has withdrawn from the Ugandan team for the 2015 Summer World University Games which are being held in Gwangju, South Korea. The reason is that he prefers, on July 9, to run in a race in the USA for which the prize is a reported $30,000. The timing of this race clashes with the athletics (8-12 July) at the Games.

"Hell hath no fury like a woman scorned", and if the Association of Ugandan University Sports (AUUS) was a woman who had just lost her man to a rival, we could say she was well and truly heartbroken. For Cheptegei, the reigning 10,000m IAAF World Junior Champion, provided Uganda's best chance of winning a medal at the Games.

According to journalist Charles Mutebi, a highly disappointed President of the AUUS, Peninnah Kabenge, commented that Cheptegei had, "chosen money over honour." While Mutebi himself added that the athlete, "was just the latest case of a sportsman putting self before country, always a controversial if rational choice."

But is Mutebi's point surprising? After all, most Ugandans do not support local football teams. They prefer following clubs (Manchester United, Arsenal, Chelsea etc.) from the land of the former colonial masters. So, if Ugandan patriotism does not score in football, it is hardly likely to register in Cheptegei's brain when faced with a choice between dollars and representing his country.

Returning to Peninnah Kabenge's acute disappointment, it must surely have been matched by that of the Ugandan Games contingent, as they set out on their arduous 24 hour journey from Entebbe to Gwangju, on learning that their best medal prospect was not now travelling with them. Perhaps Cheptegei lacked the team spirit to recognise this.

Interestingly, Mutebi indicates that Cheptegei's international manager was deeply involved in the decision to race in the USA. Generally, such managers operate on the basis of a percentage commission. Thus, the manager could earn income from the USA race, but not from the World University Games, where the prizes are medals, not money. In other words, when it comes to managers, it is all the M's. Managers are Motivated by Money, not by Medals.

Let me step back from the controversy and make some other key points.

Firstly, what we are dealing with here may be selfishness, but it is not corruption. There will be politicians, civil servants, road engineers etc. who, by corrupt means, will make more money than Cheptegei in July 2015, and expend an awful lot less energy.

Secondly, unless Cheptegei's $30,000 is appearance money, he may get less (or perhaps nothing at all) if he does not win the race.

Thirdly, the Summer World University Games are held only every two years. So, will Cheptegei still be able to compete in 2017? Will he have another chance to add a World University Games Gold Medal to that he won at the World Junior Championships?

Lastly, Cheptegei was one of the two leading Ugandan athletes who were being fully funded by the international university sports federation (FISU) – the other is Shida Leni, who my wife and I coach, and who I can guarantee has definitely travelled to South Korea. Given the lateness of his withdrawal, was there time to switch Cheptegei's FISU funding to another Uganda sportsperson? Did Cheptegei or his manager consider this when making their USA decision? – I doubt it.

So, Peninnah Kabenge, you may be "a woman scorned", but I fully agree with you – Cheptegei has indeed "chosen money over honour."

8

Music

Music to soothe the soul
(29 April 2007)

Oh my God! It's Monday tomorrow. Will the week start with another day full of too many challenges and too much stress?

If so, there is a remedy - why not get out of bed on a Monday and put on some inspirational music?

Best music varies
But, just as "beauty is in the eye of the beholder", then inspirational music is "in the ear of the listener." That is, music that inspires will vary greatly from person to person. Thus, for some it may be traditional music; for others it will be gospel or pop music.

For me it is definitely pop music. Waking up on a dark, dull, depressing Monday morning, here are some of the tunes that would make me want to jump out of bed, and face the challenges of the day ahead:
- Ragga Dee's *Digida*.
- Jose Chameleone's *Bomboclat*.
- Afrigo Band's *Toni*.

- Rachel Magoola's *Obangaina*.
- Lucky Dube's *False Prophets*.
- John Lennon's *Imagine*.

Stress

And what about music and stress? Stress is a real monster that does not respect the borders of time provided by the end of the day in the workplace. After dinner, you try to unwind, but your mind keeps flitting back to the office, to the in-tray, to tasks undone, to phone calls unmade, to personnel problems amongst colleagues, to that all-important contract not yet signed. You drag yourself to bed, hoping that sleep will bring sweet relief from the mental burden of responsibility, but you toss and turn through the night until the alarm loudly heralds the start of another pressured day.

But music can have a role in reducing the stress the day has generated in your brain. For as the English dramatist, William Congreve, observed in the late seventeenth century, "music has charms to soothe a savage breast."

Afrigo Band

For as the words of the Afrigo Band's popular song, *Music,* say, "*okera kumacha muma tulutulu, nozibya obude nga ononya nsimbi. Bwodayo eka eyo osokera ku music akawumuze olwo okole ebirala.*" (You wake in the morning and work all day looking for money. When you return home the first thing you turn to is music. It relaxes you and then you can do other things).

It is little wonder that the clubs and bars around Uganda that offer live music at the weekends are rarely short of business. You only have to look at the happiness on the faces of those dancing the night away to their favourite tunes to know that, as the Afrigo Band song says, *"esanyu mu balamu lye gandalo lyo. Mukaseera ako buli kimu kibera bulungi. Music lyesanyu, music ewumuza ebirowozo. Music alinga eddagala, akusokera buli kanyomero komubiri. Omubiri olwo ne gwetta."* (Happiness in your life is your leisure, at which time everything feels fine. Music provides happiness and rests the mind. It is like medicine, reaching every part of the body and relaxing it).

Panadol
So whether it be the start of the day, or the end of the day, put that music on and – if it is to your taste – turn it up loud. For the *panadol* of life is not a tablet, it is music.

The *sagala* song hits Uganda
(14 October 2007)

> "Sagala Man U,
> Sagala Chelsea,
> Sagala Arse,
> Njagala Ful-ham.
> Ful-ham, Ful-ham,
> Ful-ham, Ful-ham."

I sing the above song loud and often to friends at my local trading centre in a suburb of Kampala. When I reach the line, "Sagala Arse," I bend over and slap my buttocks.

And for readers whose Luganda is even worse than mine, let me tell you that *Sagala* means *I don't like*, and *Njagala* means *I like*.

It is true that Arsenal is, so to speak, the butt of this joke. It is also true that the tune of the song is the same as for the "Pompey Chimes". "Pompey" is the nickname of Portsmouth Football Club. And the simple words of the Pompey Chimes are:

"Play up Pompey,
Pompey play up."

And whether it be coincidence, fate or plain juju, last Sunday Portsmouth beat Fulham 2-0. So it can be said that Pompey certainly did "play up".

Although I have stolen the tune, the song is otherwise my own i.e. composed, written and sung by, The Rt. Hon. Eng. Sir Kevin Muzungu Bignose O'Connor MP OBE CBE.

When he had a spare moment from considering Sir Kevin's beatification and imminent sainthood, Cardinal Emmanuel Wamala said recently that if you want to be immortal you must either have children, plant trees or write a book. Perhaps he should have added a fourth source of immortality – composing a song.

Given Uganda's HIV/AIDS pandemic, a low life expectancy of somewhere in the 40's and the appalling number of accidents on our roads, death is an all too frequent uninvited guest in "the pearl of Africa." So it may therefore be wise to leave something behind for after one's own burial – be it a child, a tree, a book or a song.

As my coffin rots, and the worms and ants begin to eat my body, it would be a fitting memorial to my life if the following could be sung all around Uganda:

> "Sagala Man U,
> Sagala Chelsea,
> Sagala Arse,
> Njagala Ful-ham.
> Ful-ham, Ful-ham,
> Ful-ham, Ful-ham."

But there are 2 problems here. Firstly, I don't want to be buried, I wish to be cremated. Secondly, and more importantly, there are very few Fulham fans in Uganda, so who will do the singing? Well, Queen Elizabeth of England did not make me "Sir Kevin" and award me the OBE and CBE, without good reason. Yes, I have a brain in my head, and it would be very easy to change the song according to which team the singer supported. Thus a fan of Manchester United could sing:

> "Sagala Ful-ham,
> Sagala Chelsea,
> Sagala Arse,
> Njagala Man U.
> Man U, Man U,
> Man U, Man U."

And the entrepreneurial businessman in me feels that the saying "there's money to be made in them there hills" should become "there's money to be made in them there songs." So stand aside Jose Chameleone, Ragga Dee, Bobi Wine and Juliana. Make way for Sir Kevin Muzungu Bignose O'Connor and the forthcoming biggest hit in the history of Uganda pop music – "Sagala Man U".

And when the British High Commissioner to Uganda (can't remember his/her name as they change so often) reports back to Queen Elizabeth her humble subject's musical success, I am confident that it will soon not be Sir Kevin but Lord O'Connor!

Lucky Dube's songs will never die
(28 October 2007)

It is now 10 days ago that Lucky Dube was murdered. Yet, it is still hard for me to believe that he is dead. For his:
- Concerts were the most memorable I have ever attended.
- Lyrics often find their way into my own articles.

- Music inspires me. And by way of aside, its effect on my mood is such that I feel more at ease, and safer, when driving while listening to one of his cassettes.

There is only one other pop star whose music has affected me as much as Lucky Dube's. That is John Lennon whose songs (initially written with Paul McCartney as members of *The Beatles*) shaped me during my growing-up years. Like Dube, Lennon was killed by bullets from a murderer's gun. Then it was 1980, when the radio awoke me with news of a great man's death. And again on October 19 2007, with radio just turned on in bed, another early morning bulletin sent similar shockwaves shuddering through my brain.

Though Lucky Dube is dead, we still have his music by which to remember his brilliance. There are so many Dube songs that I love, it is difficult to choose two favourites – but here goes!

False prophets

The first is *False Prophets* from the album *Prisoner*. When Lucky sings:

> *We see them every day*
> *Movin' up and down*
> *Holding their bibles in their hands yeah*
> *Going to church every Sunday*
> *Telling people they' re Christians yeah*
> *... False prophets lies and elution*

I always (rightly or wrongly) think of those hideously rich, hideous-everything, American pastors, and their Ugandan counterparts, whose corrupt crusades offer cures to HIV/AIDS sufferers in return for the giving of money. I use the word "corrupt" because there is (as of yet) no cure for HIV/

AIDS, though the taking of antiretroviral drugs greatly reduces its incidence in the body.

Kiss no frog

By way of introduction to my other favourite Lucky Dube track, let me repeat the story of Mary, a 21-year-old Ugandan woman, who has many plans and ambitions over the next 5 years, and whose salary pays for her siblings' school fees. She therefore does not wish to get pregnant until her mid to late twenties and used condoms when having sex with her boyfriend, David.

A few months ago, just after a sex session, David told Mary, "I removed the condom because I want you to 'produce'".

After crying, and shouting at David, Mary was relieved to find out, some time later, that she was not pregnant and was still HIV-negative. But she realised that trust had disappeared from the relationship. She gave David "a red card" and currently has no boyfriend.

At this stage in her life Mary should remember the words from Lucky Dube's *Kiss no frog*:

> *Better to be alone and happy*
> *Than being with someone*
> *And be unhappy*
> *All your life*

Sensitivity

I asked Dube about these very words at a press conference I attended during his last tour to Uganda. How did he manage to write such inspirational lyrics? He said he tried to put himself in the mind of the person he was writing about, so in this case, he added, "I imagined myself as a woman." A Ugandan female friend later told me:

"I find it very difficult, indeed impossible to think of a Ugandan man ever coming out with that phrase, 'I imagined myself as a woman.' We Ugandans are too stuck in our cultural and sexual stereotypes, and that is perhaps why *Kiss No Frog* could be written by Lucky Dube but not by a Ugandan male musician."

At that press conference, I was sitting just 10 feet away from Dube, and what struck me was not so much that he had a strong character, with firm views, but the gentleness and sensitivity of his eyes.

Perhaps it is that combination of strength and sensitivity of character that produced the wonderfully insightful lyrics of his music. And although his life is over, his songs and their melodies will never die.

UB40 – No money to go
(2 March 2008)

Given a choice between attending a UB40 concert OR a Lucky Dube one, I would always choose Lucky Dube. But since it will be Obote 3 before I go again to a concert of the late, great, Lucky Dube, I must say that I really enjoyed last weekend's UB40's show at the Lugogo Cricket Oval in Kampala.

Down amongst the silver ticket holders, my wife and I danced and sang. I particularly enjoyed singing along to "Can't Help Falling in Love" i.e.

"Wise men say,
Only fools rush in,
But I can't help,
Falling in love with you".

And each time the chorus reached "I can't help falling in love with **YOU**", I pointed not to my wife, but to a different beautiful "brown babe" dancing near to us. Fortunately, *mukyala*, Sue, like her husband, has a sense of humour, and I didn't get a red card, or even a yellow one.

And those ticket prices! The snobs, the "toffs" (as we would say in the UK), and the "big stomachs" who bought platinum tickets (Ug Sh 300,000) would have needed a pair of binoculars to see the stage from their position on the distant balcony of the new *Oasis* restaurant, adjacent to the Lugogo Club House. Of course, they could look at the big screens, but so could we in *lumpen* silver.

And as for the gold tickets (Ug Sh 120,000), it hardly seemed worth paying an additional Ug Sh 95,000 for merely a slightly raised position right next to the silver proletariat.

Of course, using the terms *lumpen* and proletariat (which both refer to poor social groups in the community) would be entirely wrong in describing we silver ticket-holders. For, as a visit to my local trading centre demonstrated, even a ticket priced at Ug Sh 25,000 would exclude most of the Ugandan population.

Albert, a newsvendor, or Albert Newsvendor as I call him, came straight to the point:

> "I had no money. Money, money, money, that's the problem."

While Peter, who runs an electrical repair shop, said:

> "My rent for where I stay is Ug Sh 30,000 per month. If I pay 25,000 for a UB40 ticket, then that's almost a whole month's rent! If I went to UB40 this means that

> the expenditure would have been too big compared to my earnings".

Rose sells vegetables from a small stall, and her explanation as to why she didn't go to the concert was as follows:

> "Not enough time. I was busy. I was selling my things {vegetables}. Even the money I couldn't afford".

While this was the view of the large majority of people I spoke to in the trading centre, it was not that of everyone. Thus Geoffrey, a butcher, said:

> "I went. They advertised it a long time ago and I kept saving, saving, saving. I had to go – it will surely be the only time they come to Uganda, and I heard that the main singer {Ali Campbell} would be leaving the group after the concert".

Those, above, who said they could not afford to see UB40 are all reasonably successful small businessmen and women – they are not among the huge number of really impoverished Ugandans. For words that say something about *their* plight, we should turn to another UB40 song ('One in Ten' – a proportion that, of course, is much higher in Africa):

> "Malnutrition dulls my hair
> My eyes are black and lifeless
> With an underprivileged stare".

To the extent that such poor people buy any tickets, they are not platinum, gold or silver, but stone ones. Such human beings are indeed:

> "A statistical reminder
> Of a world that doesn`t care".

Is Juliana getting fat?

(16 November 2008)

Henry Ssali's *Kiwani* is showing in Garden City's Cineplex and I am greatly enjoying the film. Juliana Kanyomozi appears on the screen, and the 3 young women seated behind me immediately start laughing. One whispers, "She's getting fat."

The first photo with today's column shows Juliana performing in 2000. Eight years later, at the recent PAM Awards, the second photo captures not only an older, but also, yes, a fatter, Juliana.

If her former lover, boxer Kassim Ouma, had been eating the same food, he would have to move up from being a Lightweight to being a Heavyweight! But does it matter if Juliana is getting fat? She is, after all, not a boxer, nor a catwalk model. She is a singer, famous for her voice, not for her body. At the PAM Awards, she won "Artiste of the Year", not the *Miss Uganda* title.

If there was a *Miss Obesity* award, it would surely be won by Straka, and Juliana has no worries yet about reaching that level of fatness. Nevertheless, the plumper, chubbier face of 2008 Juliana may show a woman on a journey to losing her extremely pretty features. With a weak chin, a big nose and a pointed head (no wonder my nickname at school was "Diamond Head"), I've never had to worry about being called "handsome", but if I was as beautiful as Juliana, I would certainly want to keep my good looks.

Her outfit at the PAM Awards cost her over US$500 in Los Angeles and *Red Pepper* observed:

> "Juliana could not have chosen a better dress to receive her award.........It was a very flattering long leopard

print dress, and was a PERFECT tribute to what she has accomplished throughout her career."

Perfect? Well, you can't always believe what you read in the *Red Pepper*, and I thought that the dress made Juliana's hips look as wide as the *Titanic*. And when I watched the PAM Awards on WBS, I could see the dress also highlighted her not-so-pretty tummy, sticking out from somewhere in the middle of her body.

But "beauty is in the eye of the beholder" and it is a culture, many thousands of miles from Africa that has shaped my outlook. Yes, I like my women tall, and although I use the word advisedly in Uganda, I like my women *slim*. But in Africa, fatness has traditionally had a positive association with wealth. And many African men find "big bums" on women to be extremely attractive.

Such was the view of 30-year-old Eric. When I showed him the two photographs, he could not see any difference in Juliana's size. Indeed, the 2008 photo caused his *Arsenal beat Man U 2-1* smile to be replaced by a look of worry for Juliana's matrimonial future. He said:

> "I understand that Juliana is not married and yet African men like fat women. Her small size will affect her chances of getting married."

So, there we are then. I think Juliana is fat. Eric thinks she is thin. As they say, "one man's meat is another man's poison." All emails, rightly accusing me of sexism, should be sent to: kevin@imul.com

The late, great Lucky Dube lives on
(11 January 2009)

Mr Lucky Dube plays a huge role in my life. There is no hymn, and no pop song, not even from my growing-up years by the great pop group, *The Beatles*, whose words have had a greater effect on me.

So, it was after much searching, and at great expense (Ug Sh 40,000), that I was at last able to find and buy in Kampala his CD "Respect". This was the last one he recorded before he was murdered. And the CD is fantastic.

I hope I am not a Lucky Dube groupie, for whom he can do, or sing, no wrong. There are some tracks on "Respect" that do nothing for me. But most of them I like. My favourite tracks are "Shembe" and the title track itself, "Respect".

Given my religious beliefs, or rather lack of them, it is most unlikely that Shembe "is the way". But on the track "Shembe is the way", the drums hit you just when you are not expecting them. What sort of drums they are, and where they come from, I have no idea. But when I hear them, I want to dance. And, as with its equivalent the rock air guitar, I, in my stupid *muzungu* way, start beating imaginary drums. God (even though you don't exist) bless you, Lucky Dube.

Then there is the track, "Choose your friends". It has the amazing line, "You can choose your friends, but you cannot choose who you're related to." So very true, Mr Dube. I have one or two relatives who I certainly wish I was not related to. But because they are relatives, it is hugely difficult to give them a "red card" to expel them from my life. And, also, there are definitely a few people, who are not relatives, but with whom

I became friends with over 30 years ago, and who are still dear friends today.

In "Celebrate life", Dube sings, "Say yeah!! Yeah!! Celebrate life. Say yeah!! Yeah!! Life is good." To be fair, the same song also describes some of the darker sides of life. When applied to myself, I can associate with "Celebrate life, life is good," for part of the time. But what about all those many times, when I feel anxious and depressed? And then I also think about the women, near my home, who I see chipping stones into pieces, for very little money, and without any protection over their eyes and mouths. Are these ladies ever able to sing, "Celebrate life, life is good"?

The second track on the CD is called, "Shut Up", and has the line, "If you can't say something good about somebody, just shut up." Now, that line really makes you think. Because just about every human being, who has ever existed, has at least one or two good points. Even those wretched relatives mentioned above, do have something good about them. And, many years ago, on management courses, I was taught that when criticising the performance of a junior member of staff in their job discussion/annual assessment, I should precede the negative point with a positive point. In other words, "If you can't say something good about somebody, just shut up."

And before I "shut up" today, let me just add that a bullet may have robbed us of Lucky Dube, but his music lives on to always allow us to remember a great songster and a great man.

What music at your funeral?

(5 July 2009)

As my late cat (may his soul rest in eternal milk) demonstrated, sooner or later, we are all going to die. So, let me ask you this question. What music would you like played at your funeral?

Kitty had no music at his burial since I could not find "Onward Christian Cats" in the hymn book. But the Ugandans I interviewed had musical funereal tastes which were quite similar to each other.

Michael, a 24-year-old student, said:

> "I would want slow gospel music. Also hymns. I don't like any particular hymn. As long as it is a hymn, that would be enough."

Fiona Mukasa

Peter, 33, supports Arsenal, a crime that, after his funeral, could earn him a place in hell, if such a place exists. He shared Michael's taste in gospel music, but added that "it should be by local artists such as Fiona Mukasa."

I then spoke to S6 leaver, Edgar, 19, who commented:

> "I'm not too sure about what music I would want. I have not been to many funeral services. But I would want something that ensures a safe journey to the next life. And, as for our dog, he wouldn't want music. He would just want to be buried with a bone or a piece of meat."

I then interviewed Kevin. So that readers do not conclude that I was talking to myself, let me add that Kevin is female and also a 19-year-old S6 leaver. She said:

> "I would like Christian music. But not music that makes people so sad that they mourn too much."

No heaven and hell

As for me, *Roving Eye*, there will be no gospel music or hymns at my funeral. I am not religious. There is no heaven and no hell. These are just myths created by human beings so that they can feel they will meet up again with their loved ones after death.

Lucky Dube

When my coffin is carried into the crematorium, I would like played the Lucky Dube anthem, "Different colours, one people". And then, as the coffin heads towards the gas incinerators, Gracie Fields will start singing, "Wish me luck as you wave me goodbye."

Let's face it, should I be wrong about the existence of hell, I will need luck in large quantities!

Disco music and much else spoils my football viewing

(28 November 2010)

I am not a multitasker! And, if you share this characteristic and are already distracted doing something else, you may urgently require me to repeat this phrase – I am not a multitasker!

Being a "one thing at a time" type of person has reduced my pleasure in some bars and restaurants in Kampala.

Two matches

Recently, I was watching the English Premier League. On adjoining screens there were two different matches. I had gone to watch the Man U match, but on the other TV screen only 2 feet away from Man U, was the Liverpool game, with the volume turned down.

As much as I tried strictly to discipline myself and focus my eyes solely on Man U, an invisible force (possibly called Gerrard), kept dragging my eyes towards the Liverpool screen.

In doing so, I missed some key shots and passes at Old Trafford, so my enjoyment of the Man U match was definitely reduced, and was not offset by whatever shots/passes and other scraps of info that I picked up on Liverpool.

In other words, the Liverpool screen needed a red card so if it was not sent off, then at least was turned off, enabling *Roving* "one thing at a time" *Eye* to maximise his enjoyment.

Disco music

Another bar I frequent has a similar problem. At some stage during the football match, normally halfway through the second half when the game's orgasmic climax is almost upon us, the DJ arrives and loud throbbing disco music starts up, drowning out the commentary coming all the way from Anfield, Stamford Bridge or wherever!

Don't get me wrong, whether it be Chameleon, Ragga Dee, or the late great Lucky Dube, I enjoy a wide variety of music, and even occasionally try something faintly resembling dancing. But for goodness sake, we don't need loud music when most of the patrons are watching (and *listening* to) the EPL!

The two (football and music) just do not go together. Can you imagine that instead the scene was a crowded discotheque? The dancers try impress each other with their rhythmic moves. Or perhaps, the music is slow and sultry, and the couples shuffle around the dance floor in loving embrace, perhaps the hors-d'oeuvre (starter) to the main course later that night in a lodge. But, suddenly, the music is abruptly replaced by a football commentary, and the startled couples feel they are in the wrong place at the wrong time.

So, just as a football commentary has no place in a disco, then disco music should be banned from bars showing live Premier League football. A bar-owner once told me that he was giving his customers "something extra", free of charge, for their satisfaction. But for Sir Kevin, it was most definitely, "something less".

Formula 1

A final example from my "one thing at a time" life occurred at a Chinese restaurant. Looking stupid as I pretended to know how to use chopsticks, I was about to sample my oh-so predictable order of sweet and sour pork and egg fried rice, when one metre from my nose, perched on a nearby counter, the TV was switched on, showing recorded highlights of Formula 1.

I am not so much of a "one thing at a time" man to recognise that a little Chinese music in the background can enhance the pleasure of a Chinese meal. But Lewis Hamilton, Jenson Button, Sebastian Vettel etc. have no place in a posh, or even not so posh, Chinese restaurant, unless they happen to be eating there!

Unhappy and happy New Year's Eves
(16 January 2011)

New Year's Eves they come and go. But all we can really be certain about is that we are one day closer to death.

They seem a big thing at the time. But how many past ones can you actually remember?

Two stick in my mind. One unhappy, the other happy.

I had a particularly desolate New Year's Eve in 1982. Without a girlfriend, indeed without many friends at all, December 31 saw me in my lonely bed by 9pm I was awoken at midnight by the raucous noise of other people's celebrations, from parties in neighbouring houses, reaching me under my sheets. So depressed was I that I did not have the energy or desire to lower my right hand to my manhood and welcome 1983 with a masturbatory orgasm. "New Year's Eves," I thought to myself, "can't come much worse than this." I was quite wrong, of course, since I had never spent December 31 in a Nazi concentration camp, or with a bloated empty stomach in famine-ravaged eighties Ethiopia.

My most memorable New Year's Eve was timely since it ushered in the millennium. Exotic it was for *muzungu* me, as it was spent under the stars in the Kampala *Sheraton Hotel* gardens, watching and listening to the Afrigo Band. As midnight approached, Rachel Magoola broke into "Obangaina", one of the biggest hits in the history of Ugandan pop music.

Magoola's amazing stage presence reached out to touch the crowd, lifting them to even higher levels of happiness and expectation as the historical landmark approached. As midnight struck, Magoola cleverly changed the words of the chorus of the song from "Obangaina" to "Happy New Year". Even I, whose dancing style has often been likened to a man trying to knock pooh-pooh off the sole of his shoe, was on his feet attempting to mimic the African rhythms of the dancing Ugandans who surrounded me.

So, 17 years after an unhappy New Year's Eve, I experienced a memorably happy one.

New Year's Eves they come and go. But all we can really be certain about is that we are one day closer to death.

What music motivates you?

(25 October 2015)

As footballers get off their bus for an English Premier League match they will often be wearing headphones, as will athletes as they prepare for Diamond League races. They will generally be listening to music, and to tracks that motivate them, and hopefully inspire them on to a better performance.

My wife and I coach two Ugandan women at running and there are two motivational tracks that we play in the car on the way to races, or over the gym's loudspeaker system during long, hard weight-training sessions.

The first is Tina Turner's, "The Best". The song is about things other than sport, but its chorus would surely inspire any sportsman or woman i.e.

> "You're simply the best
> Better than all the rest
> Better than anyone
> Anyone I've ever met
> …..You're the best."

The second song is from Paul Simon's classic *Graceland* album. It is "Diamonds on the Soles of her Shoes". And when a female runner speeds to victory, we can truly shout from the rooftops, "She's got diamonds on the soles of her shoes."

But these two songs have a bonus for our two young athletes. They are in the repertoire of *Code 9*, a band that plays at *Jazzville*, in Kampala's Bugolobi. When the four of us attend, bandleader, Chris Ireland, will dedicate the two songs "to Joyce and Shida", and athletes and their coaches will dance along.

In my local trading centre in Kampala, I asked several Ugandans, "What music motivates you? What music makes you feel good?"

Fiona, 38, is a vegetable seller. She said:

> "I like gospel music, especially Judith Babirye. It washes away my sorrow and makes me feel relieved from the pain I had before."

Brian, 19, a butcher, also voted for gospel music:

> "I have faith in its words because I am Christian," which was all very appropriate given that my questions were being asked on a Sunday.

Peter is a 32-year-old barber, and his response was very different. He remarked:

> "Jazz and country music. Only that, nothing else."

"And why Peter?" I queried.

> "That question is funny. It is like asking 'why do you eat food?' Or 'why do you work?' Or 'why, Kevin, are you wearing that yellow T-shirt?' I like Don Williams and listening to *Bob FM*, which only plays country music."

Joseline, 19, is a marketeer with *Blue Wave Beverages*. She provided a more youthful insight:

> "I enjoy slow music and R & B. I like Celine Dion, Westlife, Backstreet Boys and many others. They make my mind become calm."

Chandi, 30, is currently unemployed. When he can get it, he does some casual work "every now and again", such as labouring on a building site. His reply was more wide-ranging than the others':

> "Any music that I think is good, I will listen to. It doesn't matter what type as long as it is good. There is even some music that I don't understand, because I don't know the language, but I can still like it."

So what music motivates Kevin? Well, I generally prefer pop music to classical music. And readers will be tired of being told that I am a fan of Lucky Dube, and that I would like his, "Different Colours, One People" played at my funeral (which just might motivate me to get out of the coffin!). However, there is one piece of classical music that never fails to cause my pulse to race and my heart beat faster. It is Tchaikovsky's 1812 Overture. As Burnett James writes, its wonderful and noisy climax includes "in addition to full symphony orchestra, bells, canon, military band, and of course, plenty of percussion."

Therefore, for me, Tchaikovsky's 1812 Overture is "simply the best".

9

Education

MUK graduates, I have no money for your parties!

(5 March 2000)

"The next graduation ceremony of Makerere University is due on March 17," writes Julius Mucunguzi (*The Monitor*, February 29), "and prospective graduands are already roaming from office to office, dishing out their hefty budgets to potential donors."

My advice is, if approached by one of these privileged graduates (known as graduands in Uganda) - and anyone who has had tertiary education in a developing country, is firmly in the upper reaches of the privileged elite - asking for money for their party, that you should respond with a firm "no."

And you should be confident and proud of your negative response. Graduation parties seem to be an African phenomenon. I never came across them in England. Indeed in the radical 1960s and 1970s, not only were there no parties but many graduates deliberately did not attend their own graduation ceremonies (receiving, instead, their degrees through the post).

The gowns, the mortarboards and the tradition of the ceremony stank of establishment privilege, so that some young people (at least in their radical youth) wanted nothing to do with them.

Africans have meekly accepted the graduation traditions of their former colonial rulers and, as is often the case, given them an added twist, in this case, in the form of exorbitantly expensive graduation parties.

These huge parties will bring some families near to bankruptcy. They are a disgraceful spectacle in Uganda, one of the poorest countries in the world.

I agree with a recent comment of Minister of Internal Affairs, Prof. Edward Rugumayo, when he said "graduands should not hold parties if they can't afford them."

But I would go further and argue that they should not hold parties even if they can afford them.

Let me start my arguments with a simple observation. Late in the evening after Makerere's graduation ceremony, one of the biggest traffic jams in Kampala will be at Bugolobi because of the sheer number of parties taking place. Why so many parties there?

The reason is that the average number of graduands per thousand of population will be much higher in Bugolobi than in the less prosperous suburbs. Educational research shows that most important factor predicting a young person's success in the educational system is the social background of their parents.

Bugolobi is a "posh" area. If you were born in Bugolobi (or Kololo or Nakasero), went to an elite school like Kings College Budo and predictably on to Makerere, then the resulting university degree is not mainly because of your intelligence, not mainly due to your ability at the rote memorising from books required by an examination-based system, but mainly because you "chose your parents well."

Graduands at the ceremonies in England, preening themselves in bizarre clothes, look like clowns. But in Uganda, they look even greater clowns because the clothes and the ceremony are a colonial import, drawing nothing from Africa's rich traditions and cultural heritage. Indeed, a Ugandan friend joked that the only African aspect of a graduation ceremony or party is the over-long nature of the speeches.

The clothes serve a similar function to the equally archaic pantomime outfits worn by the judiciary. They result in social distance between the wearer and the rest of us. In a court of law, this helps to intimidate and ensure that we are humble and do not answer back too often.

But for the graduates, their fancy dress gives them a standing, by making them for a few hours look so different from the rest of us, which serves to confirm their social elevation, their right to increased economic fruits based on supposed higher level of skills and knowledge.

Of course, their belief is nonsense. A university degree, is often not a good predictor of performance in workplace, especially of the combination of problem-solving and interpersonal skills that are crucial to working in company teams and dealing with clients and contacts. This is hardly surprising, since a degree is a better measure of ability to memorise from books and regurgitate in rote fashion in 45 minute chunks in the exam room.

But don't expect a graduand to agree. At the ceremony, the gown and mortarboard have a noticeable effect on the graduand's bearing. They - especially the young men - adopt a completely different walk from normal, a sort of arrogant swagger.

Afterwards, our graduand strutters keep their uniform on for the party, and at every opportunity for several days (do they sleep in them as well?).

For, their purpose, and that of their families, is to shout loudly: "look at me everybody, I'm a graduand" and therefore I fully deserve the fruits – economic and status – of obtaining a degree which bypass other larger and "less capable" sections of my fellow citizens.

So, if you are asked for money for a graduation party, politely tell the graduand to "get lost" and to get on with the rest of their lives, hopefully deploying some of their privileged education to help drag Uganda out of the brutal, grinding poverty which is the daily reality for the vast majority of the graduand's fellow citizens.

PLE results boredom

(27 January 2008)

And so it goes on in our newspapers. Page after page, day after day – the same old photos of wretched smiling parents and their wretched smiling children who have done "well" in PLE (Primary Leaving Examination). Once you have seen one photo, you have seen them all. It's enough to make you fall asleep while reading the newspaper.

I was wondering if my reaction was that of a stupid *muzungu* who does not understand Ugandan culture. So it was reassuring when a letter was published in the *Daily Monitor* (January 23, p11) from Ojoatre Kaaka of Gulu:

> "I'm dismayed by the undue attention which the print media has devoted to writing about the 'successful' PLE candidates. I have been buying both *New Vision* and *Daily*

Monitor for the past two days only to discover that I have not much informative news."

Not only is it not informative news, is it news at all? After all, these exams are held in predictable fashion every year, and equally predictable is that a certain percentage of candidates will get good grades. I don't remember seeing similar coverage in the UK, and what limited coverage there is, for example, of the O and A levels results, is devoted not to smiling individuals, but to an overall analysis of the grades to try judge whether the country's educational standards are rising or falling.

So, why do Ugandan newspapers vomit out these awful pages at PLE result time?

Sarah, 29, a senior Ugandan journalist told me:

> "The explanation in the past for the huge media coverage of the PLE results was that it sold more newspapers i.e. it was a marketing tool. Parents were keen to see if their kid was mentioned, and how their kid and kid's school compared to others. But while this tool may have worked in the past, I doubt if it does today, and newspapers should actively seek out new ways of covering exam results."

I would add another reason for the excessive newspaper coverage. It is lazy journalism. Often the scribe won't even have to go to the premises of the likes of Greenhill Academy to get the story. The school and the kid are sufficiently aware of the advantages of institutional and self-advertising that they will turn up in person at the newspaper offices.

And what is newsworthy about a kid from bloody Greenhill Academy scoring Aggregate 4? A parent who sends a child to Greenhill will not have much change from one million Ugandan shillings *per term*! So, if you have a hugely resourced school, educating privileged kids from wealthy families, getting some outstanding exam results is as predictable as night following day.

Investigative journalism, as opposed to lazy journalism, would identify an up-country school whose results were not nearly as good as Greenhill's but whose achievements (their "value-added") were far greater given the lesser resources of both the school and the pupils' families.

If I was an editor to whom a journalist brought me the typical Greenhill PLE story/photo, I would tell them to stick the Aggregate 4 up Greenhill's a*** and then bring me some real news.

Journalistic corruption and PLE results
(3 February 2008)

Sometimes I am a really stupid *muzungu* – and many people would say not just sometimes, but all the time. For, in last Sunday's *Roving Eye* ("PLE results boredom") I overlooked one additional and extremely important cause of the horribly excessive coverage of PLE results in our newspapers – **CORRUPTION**. It was John, a journalist who prefers that I don't use his real name, who pointed this out to me by email:

> "Journalists themselves who cover education get some 'motivation' {money} from school head teachers and proprietors (private schools) who are eager to have their excelling kids splashed in newspapers so they can show the Board how good they are doing. It means a lot to these head teachers for their schools and kids to appear in newspapers and they reward scribes generously."

And parents similarly bribe journalists to get their kids into the newspapers.

I remember a former managing editor of a Ugandan newspaper telling me about the "brown envelopes" that many journalists receive, in return for covering particular stories. But before my fellow scribes vote to "shoot me at dawn", let me point out that in the 13 years I have lived in Uganda, the media has improved enormously – whether it be television, radio or newspapers. But, as always in life, much remains to be done.

Take another area for improvement, this time from last Tuesday's *Daily Monitor* (p2). There was a photo by Stephen Wandera with the following caption:

> "*Daily Monitor's* Sumin Namaganda celebrates after she was awarded a masters degree at Makerere University yesterday. A total of 547 students were awarded degrees in various disciplines."

A couple of questions – firstly, is the Makerere graduation "news" at all (let alone "news" placed on the key p2 with its hugely important stories, like the continuing turmoil and bloodshed in Kenya)? After all, Makerere's graduations take place with predictable monotony, as do those of Uganda's many other tertiary educational institutions.

And secondly, in the unlikely event that the Makerere graduation was actually "news", of the 547 students, why should it be Ms Sumin Namaganda's photo that appears? Well, dear reader, I'm sure you know the answer to that question.

The Makerere (or any other) graduation should only appear in a newspaper if something unusual happens to make it genuine news. For example, imagine these headlines:

- Severe diarrhoea outbreak ruins many gowns at Makerere graduation.
- Homosexual kisses Makerere University Vice Chancellor when receiving degree.

Finally, let's return to those wretched PLE results (and similarly those for O and A levels). My advice to newspaper editors is to prohibit any coverage except:

- An overall analysis of the results with its implications for the country's educational standards.
- An up-country school which has achieved exceptional results despite limited resources.

If smiling kids, parents and teachers want to publicise themselves with those boring photos of, yes, themselves, let them do so by buying newspaper advertising space. For what we are dealing with here is indeed not news but advertising.

And as for journalists accepting "brown envelopes", perhaps editors should try reduce this practice by paying journalists a bit more – starting with none other than me, Sir Kevin Bignose O'Connor MBE OBE.

Don't send children to single sex schools
(26 July 2009)

The recent comments of two Ugandans about the disadvantages of single sex schools made me remember my own unhappiness during a secondary school education where all my fellow pupils were, regretfully, male.

In an excellent letter to the *Daily Monitor* (13 July), Mark Kigozi sketches the wider mixed society in which our school education takes place:

"Every human being needs to interact, in a healthy way, with members of the opposite sex. But if this need is denied, this individual develops a state of imbalance psychologically."

Kigozi's statement also has relevance to the Catholic Church, which in USA, Ireland and other countries around the world, has incurred huge legal damages, after some of its supposedly celibate priests defiled young people:

"Our families are gender inclusive and so are our communities," Kigozi continues. "Why then would an institution break the norm…..I appeal to the Ministry of Education to explore the possibility of making every school mixed. After all, students from mixed schools adjust quickly and better socially."

Conformity

I went to a mixed London primary school. But my parents decided I should attend a single sex secondary school. This school provided me with a wonderful academic education, but there were disadvantages which I have always associated with its single sex nature.

Firstly, conformity ruled! The school's sub-culture required one to go with the group i.e. to be part of the herd. It was therefore not easy for kids whose behaviour was different from the norm, or in some way eccentric. Such pupils would be targeted for bullying, though I appreciate bullying has many and varied causes.

Immaturity

Secondly, we often seemed to behave in a way that was younger than our years i.e. widespread immature behaviour.

Linked to this, and lastly, was something described in Erique Mununuzi's article (*Sunday Vision* 12 July), "In single boys' schools, girls are a very rare delicacy. By default you were suspected of being gay (we called them backstabbers) and had to spend your entire life proving everyone wrong."

"Homo" obsession

Mununuzi is right. My recollection is that just about every day, especially in the S1 to S4 years, there would be accusations flying around our classroom that "you are a homo" (or "a queer" in our London slang), or that such and such teacher was "queer". All these accusations and denials! Such wasted energy. Yet, statistically, the very large percentage of both teachers and pupils would have been heterosexual.

My wife (who attended a mixed secondary school) tells me that although issues of sexual orientation did get raised and discussed, there was not the immature obsession with the subject that I experienced in my single sex school.

I do not feel single sex schools should be abolished (parents should be allowed a choice). But otherwise, I fully agree with Mr Kigozi. My advice is to send children to mixed, rather than single sex, schools.

Oral communication skills are key to your career

(30 August 2009)

She sat opposite me. I cannot remember whether she was beautiful or ugly, young or middle-aged, or whether she was dressed smartly or not so smartly.

The encounter took place 14 years ago. Such a long time gap has reduced my ability to remember the exact details. So what do I remember?

Well, firstly, I was chairing a selection board in Kampala. She was applying for a job in the international organisation that then employed me.

Secondly, the lady was Ugandan and had obtained a Masters degree at a Canadian university.

Thirdly, the subject of this Masters degree was relevant to the job. Indeed, it was a prime reason why she had been shortlisted.

Next, and this became apparent when she telephoned after learning that her application had been unsuccessful, she felt that she must be the best candidate precisely because her masters degree was from a *First World* university.

Lastly, while much knowledge undoubtedly resided in the lady's brain, she lacked the communication skills to pass that knowledge on, both to the selection board and to any future team she was part of.

I was reminded of this lady by Ethan Musolini's article, "Public speaking; the way to survive" (*Daily Monitor*, August 11).

The article began with the ringing sentence:

> "If you were to grill me under oath concerning the two most important life skills a person can survive on, I would mention selling skills and public speaking."

Leaving aside that a grilled Ethan might appeal to, indeed might sell to, a cannibal, I would agree with his emphasis on public speaking. However, public speaking is a subset (part) of oral communication skills, and this whole wider area is crucial in the workplace. For while a manager will, from time to time, give a speech/talk to a large audience (i.e. public speaking), he/she will have to speak to smaller groups and to individuals on a constant basis.

I spent 9 years recommending British courses for public officials from many different developing countries. Their training was funded by the UK's aid programme and the courses were in areas like economics, management and finance, often at postgraduate level.

Just like the lady at the Kampala selection board, many of these officials, at the end of these courses, still lacked the ability to communicate their enhanced knowledge and skills to other people.

One of the happier memories of my previous professional life was working with the Universities of Bradford (Development and Project Planning Centre), Birmingham (Institute of Local Government Studies) and Manchester (Institute of Development Policy and Management) to overcome this weakness by incorporating oral communication skills modules into their courses.

And to Ugandans studying in Uganda today, my advice is to always be on the lookout for ways to improve your oral skills. And if your institution does not have such training, do try to persuade them to include it in your education. Whether it be in front of a selection board, or contributing to a boardroom discussion in the distant future, your employability will benefit.

"Back to school" and bullying

(31 January 2010)

A UK supermarket has, printed on its large *kaveera* in big multi-coloured letters – "Say K**NO**W MORE to bullying" i.e. say 'no' to it, and 'know' more about it.

Bullying can occur in any sphere of life (e.g. in the workplace) but is particularly associated with schools.

As we enter the "back to school" period in Uganda, this British *kaveera* emphasises the international nature of the bullying problem. It haunts parents and kids everywhere.

I first asked two former Ugandan students about bullying.

David, 24, finished at S6, and now works in a travel agency. He said:

> "I went to a day school and in my mind I link bullying more with boarding schools. But even at my school, it was widespread. For instance, an older student finishes some tea and orders an S1 (or any student he regards as weak) to take the cup back to the canteen. If they refuse, he will threaten to beat them up and sometimes does it."

"Bullying", continued David, "is more widespread in single sex schools than mixed schools". Interestingly, my wife (mixed school) and I (single sex) studied in the UK around 40 years earlier, and we agree with David.

Joan, a 28-year-old domestic worker, said:

> "An S1 student can wake up in the morning and S3 and S4 will have removed the S1's clothes. That means that the S1 will spend time looking for them and worry about arriving late for class. At night they might even pour water on the new student's bed."

I then asked two current Ugandan students about bullying.

Mary (15 years, S2) emphasised that it was:

> "When pupils are new to a school that they get bullied by older students that had been at the school for a long time." She provided the example of being forced to do huge amounts of washing.

Judith, (18 years, S4) added:

> "Sometimes it is about the dressing of the new students. When I started S1 at a boarding school in Mukono, it was 2 months before I got a school uniform, so I had to wear my casual wear. The older students made fun of my clothes."

These Ugandan experiences made me think of my own secondary (day) school. S1's were called "weeds", and a pupil in my class, who knew absolutely nothing about sex, was mercilessly mocked because he thought that when he was born he had emerged out of his mother's bum. Other students had ink flicked at them which stained their uniforms.

Also written on that supermarket kaveera is "Helping the children who need it most" and this serves to emphasise that it is not just first year students that are bullied - emotionally sensitive and physically weak schoolchildren are vulnerable at any age.

It is timely, therefore, that Kampala's All Saints Cathedral Nakasero is beginning a campaign against bullying in schools and that this has been highlighted in the press. It follows a report that over 60% of Ugandan schoolchildren are bullied.

This is a wonderful initiative by All Saints and let's hope their efforts succeed in reducing the horrible 60% statistic.

Examination worries

(6 June 2010)

The recent "back to school" period made me think that it would soon be "back to exams" and above all "back to exam worries".

Exam worries can take all shapes and forms. But when I spoke to Rachel, a 20-year-old university student in Kampala, her worries were fairly general in nature, probably shared by most Ugandan students. Thus she said:

> "Basically, if you haven't read enough, that's when you really fear. Often you want to please your parents and relatives. And at university you get scared because you look at the huge cost of the course – and fear getting few marks when someone's paid a lot for you to do the course."

Someone for whom exams caused great worries is Dorothy, a 50-year-old *muzungu* who has lived in Uganda for many years. Interestingly, her memories of those worries focussed on one particular examination room incident. It was a 3-hour A-level examination (appropriately) in Biology which took place during her menstrual period. She said:

> "Before the exam began, to my horror I noticed a pool of blood on the chair. This was my greatest nightmare come true. For the whole 3 hours I couldn't concentrate on the paper, all I could think about was how I could leave the exam room having messed myself in that way. As a result, I failed the paper."

As for myself, a keen athlete at the time, a few months before my final exams at university I stopped competitive running to concentrate on studying. This was a big mistake, and only heightened my worries and fears concerning those exams.

It is a mistake that is repeated today by many Ugandan students who compete in sport. "I can't race tomorrow", they say, "I've got to do more reading for my exams."

It is well known that the endorphins released by physical exercise generate a "feelgood" feeling in the brain. A big reduction in physical exercise, therefore, can have an equally big effect on mind and body and can create increased worry and anxiety.

It is also beneficial to have educational targets balanced by sporting targets. By removing the volleyball games, or the football matches, or the running race, a person's life can be thrown into major imbalance by suddenly having only one target i.e. the examination.

Examinations will always be there, and every student has to cope with the stress in their own way. But to those students involved in sports, my advice is to continue playing your sport up to, and during, exam time.

Study less for higher grades
(20 June 2010)

Helen, 14, is an S2 student. She told me that during school holidays she is able to do some additional study by setting her alarm clock for 1.30am (in the middle of the night) and reading her school books for up to two hours before going back to sleep.

She would be better advised to get an undisturbed night's sleep, and fully refreshed, undertake her studying during more normal daytime hours.

Helen is one of many Ugandan students (and of many students worldwide) who study excessively long hours and sacrifice quality for quantity.

Joseph, 19, is another. He is a day student at a Kampala school and will be sitting his A-levels (History, Economics and Geography) in November. He told me his term time routine and to say I was surprised would be an understatement – I was absolutely staggered by his self-imposed hard labour prison sentence! Joseph sets his alarm for 3.30am, reads his books until 5am, then bathes, reaches school at 6am and works until the formal beginning of the school day at 8am. For most students, the school day finishes at 5pm, but Joseph said that he and other exam candidates keep working until 8pm. He then returns home, before studying some more and going to bed at 11pm.

This is madness! Joseph is trying to study for this huge number of hours on the basis of only 4 hours sleep. I asked him how he felt during the day at school. Not surprisingly, his reply was, "I often feel tired, even dizzy."

I have advised Joseph to cut out his 3.30am. study session, sleep continuously from 10pm to 5.30am, and go to school a bit later. I hope to persuade him to reduce his study hours even further, but as with most efforts to change human behaviour, "one step at a time" should be the order of the day (or night!).

Students must remember that we are human beings, not machines. If we study for too many hours, our brains become tired and dulled. We take in and retain less information, and understand less. Our exam results suffer. And on the day before the exam itself, an hour or two's study is enough, allowing the student to enter the exam room feeling fresh and mentally energetic.

Yes, it really is possible get better grades by studying less!

Good and bad memories

(5 September 2010)

There is a famous song, from a bygone era, called "Thanks for the memory."

Our lives are full of memories. Some are good, some are bad, some are neither and they can be drawn from any time in our lives.

Michael is a 23-year-old Ugandan who has just completed a diploma, and is currently looking for a job. I asked Michael to give me some examples of big memories from his life.

The first example involved the death of a relative. His Aunt died in 2007. She had paid his school fees and helped him in many different ways. Perhaps, with slight exaggeration, he added, "she would give me anything I asked for." But there was no doubting the sadness of his concluding comment, "Since her death, I became so miserable because I am constantly missing her."

Michael's second memory takes us back to his primary school days:

> "The teachers," he recalled, "would cane me whenever I reached school very late since I used to come from far. And at times, they would beat me whenever I got things wrong in class. But I could not blame them because they were shaping me to become a good adult in future."

The third memory is of an S3 school tour. Michael had no money for it but his class teacher kindly paid for him. The trip was to Jinja to see the Source of the Nile, and learn about John Hanning Speke and much else. Michael emphasised, "It was such an interesting school journey that I will never forget it in my life."

The final memory concerned his obtaining government sponsorship for his Diploma:

> "Very many students had applied for sponsorship, but among the few who were successful," he joyously remembered, "my name was there!"

So, of Michael's four memories, two were good and two were bad. In considering this 2-2 draw, is it the pessimist in me that would conclude that this is not typical, as we human beings generally remember the bad memories more than the good ones?

Finally, virtually all Michael's "big" memories related to his education. Uganda has a young population, with large numbers in primary, secondary and tertiary education, recently completed, or unable to be completed due to lack of fees. Michael's bias in his selection of memories towards education may therefore be quite typical.

Memories of teachers

(24 October 2010)

I was once shown around a primary school in a Kampala suburb by the headmistress. All the classrooms were neat and tidy, with visual aids, produced by the children themselves, covering the walls. The energy, enthusiasm and abilities of one particular teacher stood out. The children in her class were attentive, obviously hanging on her every word. They looked happy, and without describing other factors which contributed to what I saw, I thought that this was education working at its best.

We often think back to our own school days, so let me give you a circuitous introduction to an important aspect of this by telling you about a cinema visit I made many years ago in London's famous Leicester Square. The screen was wide and the seats comfortable. To be frank, I don't remember anything about the film, but what I do vividly remember is the advert that preceded it!

This advert featured a series of famous people drawn from various walks of life (sport, films, politics etc.). They appeared on the screen for just a few seconds, each recalling a person's name. About 15 celebrities, including the British Prime Minister, spoke the name of someone about whom the audience knew nothing: "Mary Roberts, Bill Bloggs, David Williamson, Jitendra Patel, Jean Tully etc."

The advertisement seemed to make no sense whatsoever until the final caption in huge bold letters appeared – "**NO-ONE FORGETS A GOOD TEACHER**".

It was a government advert aimed at boosting teacher recruitment.

It is true, isn't it? No-one forgets a good teacher. If you think back to your own childhood, hopefully there is at least one teacher who was inspirational, and whose influence on the development of your abilities and character was profound. Who would it be for you? Almost 50 years on, I still sometimes think about the superb teacher in my last 2 years at primary school.

I am willing to bet Ug Sh 100 (OK, let me be particularly daring and bet Ug Sh 200) that in the year 2030 there will be adults, who were once pupils at that Kampala primary school described above, who will still fondly remember the inspirational teacher I observed that day.

Ugandans' educational concerns

(2015)

The *New Vision* newspaper organised a national sample survey in Uganda between June 12 and June 20 2015. It covered a sample size of 6,626 households, and was conducted in rural and urban areas across the country, with the target audience being those over 18 years.

The first results publicised were political e.g. the support for different candidates in next year's Presidential election.

Those polled, however, were also asked about issues they wanted candidates to address. Ranked sixth was education (23%), below health (44%), roads (36%), water and sanitation (35%), poverty (31%) and national security (24%).

Issues that ranked lower than education were: employment (22%); agriculture (15%); corruption (14%); energy use (13%); high cost of living (9%); cultural issues such as witchcraft (7%); land, e.g., land grabbing (6%); domestic issues like child marriage (3%); children issues such as child sacrifice (3%); floods/poor drainage (2%); hooliganism (2%); planning and development (2%); environment, e.g. poor waste disposal (1%) and media such as digital migration (1%).

Let's take a closer look at the education sector. The concerns there surprised me. I would have assumed that school fees and the inability to pay them would have been top of the educational ranking. My wife and I are being constantly asked if we can help out with school fees.

But school fees were "only" second on the educational list. Top of the ranking (in which I have rounded percentages to the nearest digit) was inadequate teachers both in number and in quality, and this accounted for 27% of all respondents. But the concern with teachers was not spread evenly throughout the country. The greatest complaints on inadequate teachers came from north-eastern Uganda (39%), and then the east with 31%.

So, what was third on the educational ranking? It was poor curriculum/cheating in exams (14%). It is not clear why the survey lumps together poor curriculum and cheating in exams. They are very different issues. Cheating in exams is just another form of corruption that one finds in so many areas of life in Uganda, whether it be undertaken by the "big fish" in the Ministry of Health and National Social Security Fund or the smaller fish who take performance enhancing drugs in sport.

Ranked high at four was "none" at 10%. I am not sure what this means. It does not mean "don't know" since this was ranked twelfth with 2%. Nor does it mean "refused to answer", with a paltry 0.1%. Presumably "none" means that the respondent has no concerns in the education sector. Everything is wonderful. But surely one in ten cannot think that?!

Below "none", we have more, so to speak, and there are some very important issues amongst them: low teacher salaries (9%); poor school facilities (library, labs) (9%); few primary schools (6%); long distance to school (5%); many school requirements (5%); school drop outs/early marriage/high levels of illiteracy (4%) – I don't understand why the third issue is lumped together with the first two; poor accommodation and feeding (2%); poor student attitudes towards studying (2%); corruption/low funding (2%); few secondary schools

(1%); girl-child pregnancy (1%); lack of career guidance (0.4%) and insecurity in school area (0.1%).

One has to be careful in interpreting national sample surveys. Even those in the much better resourced First World countries are prone to spectacular errors. For example, in the May 2015 UK General Election, almost every poll predicted a "hung parliament" i.e. no political party would have an overall majority, so there would need to be a coalition government. The actual result was very different. The Conservative Party won with an overall majority of 12, and David Cameron formed the first Conservative majority government since 1992.

And samples surveys are surely more difficult in a more heterogeneous Third World country such as Uganda, with sharper demographic differences between urban and rural areas, and within these areas.

Nevertheless, I found this particular survey helpful in highlighting the issues that were of concern to Ugandans within the country's educational sector.

10

Media

Truth, lies and advertising
(19 November 2006)

Advertising invades our lives, each and every day. Turn over the pages of this very *Sunday Monitor*, and you find the ads staring out at you – some are small, some are quarter or half page, and occasionally they are full page. Go on – count the number of adverts in today's edition, and you will be surprised by just how many there are.

Advertising everywhere
You cannot escape adverts, and as surely as night follows day, they will impinge on your consciousness in some way or the other. Put down the newspaper, and you will hear them on the radio and see them on TV. Walk or drive along a road, and unbearable billboards bombard. Even surfing the internet, they appear, uninvited, on your monitor screen.

It has been said that "advertising is a necessary evil"- the fuel of commercialism that drives the engine of economic growth.

Even more interestingly, Jerry Della Femina observed that "advertising is the most fun you can have with your clothes on."

But, just like having sex with the wrong person, advertising can also be dull and boring.

Mobile phone ad

An example is provided by the current radio advertising campaign of a mobile phone company. In order to associate its product with positive human attributes, it sings the good points, or should that be supposed good points, of East Africa and East Africans. We are asked "what makes East Africans so unique and yet so much the same?" The answers, provided by the advert, are:

- Friendliness.
- Economy.
- Cuisine (cookery).
- Games (sports).
- Drive.
- Networking.

Some of these claims can be questioned. For example, Uganda is a staggeringly fertile country, capable of producing a huge range of agricultural products. Yet, typically a bar or restaurant can offer you nothing more exciting than chicken and chips, or posho and beans. In a league table of cuisine, Uganda would be down near the bottom, with relegation beckoning. Up at the top would surely be India, with its striking range of dishes and spices.

And as for sporting achievement, you must be joking! Without an Olympic Gold Medal since 1972, and not having qualified for the African Cup of Nations at football since 1978, sporting achievement is not one of Uganda's strengths.

Alternative claims

So, the claims of adverts are often wrong, and sometimes are downright lies. But, they also open up possibilities for humour. And as it is better to laugh than cry, let us return to the mobile phone company and its advertising campaign. The question "What makes East Africans so unique, yet so much the same" has many alternative answers to those provided in the advert. So let us get started.

East Africa is famous for its POTHOLES. Driving in Kampala between the Jinja Road and *Celtel* roundabouts has distinct similarities to negotiating the craters of the moon. Indeed, we have the "Mountains of the Moon" in western Uganda, and the "Craters of the Moon" in Kampala!

East Africa is famous for its CORRUPTION. At some stage, Uganda was ranked as the third most corrupt country in the world. Had things got any worse, I would have changed my name to Kevin O'Corruption, or possibly Kevin NO'Corruption, if somebody had offered me a bribe to do so.

East Africa is famous for its DIARRHOEA. Really, I do seem to suffer from the old *ekidukaano* more often than I should. I wash my hands scrupulously many times each day, but despite such precautions, I will often still feel that uncomfortable motion in my stomach, which means I must run to the toilet faster than I can say *ekidukaano*.

The advert ends with a question – *have you embraced the spirit of East Africa?* So what should the reply be? Here is one possibility:

> "Yes, I have embraced the spirit of East Africa. I end every day with a glass of *waragi*."

And if this is not true, then what does it matter? Who said adverts are true?

The advantages of journalists' misspelling
(25 March 2007)

So there's spelling and there's misspelling.

Some people have the ability to spell, others don't. But given all the many jobs and professions in this world, one hopes that at least those who have chosen the profession of journalism can spell, and spell well.

So, it is with some unhappiness, that, I regret to inform you that there are journalists who can spell no better than a P1 student drop-out or a seller of *yous'd* (sorry, *used*) cars.

Do I have any evidence to back up this statement?

Well, here it is ---- last Monday, I opened a Ugandan national newspaper, and here are some of the headlines that greeted me:

Courtesy of the Ezra Tract Team Board Ltd (ETTB)
Now, it is true that Mike Ezra has much money, and nobody knows where it comes from. But, unless Mike has become a born-again fanatic, selling religious tracts, I think we can agree that his "Tract Team Board", should, in fact, be his "Track Team Board".

The next strange headline was:

Ivory Coast rebels intergrated into army
In my short life (well, that's what I tell my *byana* (girlfriends), that it has been short), I have met a few inters. To start with, there has been *Inter Milan*, a successful Italian football team. Then there has been *inter alia*, which is Latin, and means "among other things". But, never in my short life, have I met

inte*r*grated. Perhaps, the journalist concerned had been out on the booze, had fallen on his *r'se*, and therefore decided to add another *r* to the existing *r* in *integrated*. Who knows? Even he/she probably doesn't remember, as booze is responsible for far worse sins than adding an unnecessary 'r' to *integrated*.

And finally, there was:

GUID race: MAK NRM wing splits

So what is a "guid"? In UK slang, people sometimes say "30 quid", rather than "30 pounds" of money. But "quid" is not "guid". And therefore I decided to do a *Google* search for *guid* and the result was:

> "A **Globally Unique Identifier** or **GUID** (IPA pronunciation: [gwɪd] or ['gu.ɪd]) is a pseudo-random number used in software applications. While each generated GUID is not guaranteed to be unique, the total number of unique keys (2^{128} or $3.40282366 \times 10^{38}$) is so large that the probability of the same number being generated twice is very small. For an application using 10 billion random GUIDs, the probability of a coincidence is on the order of 1 in a quintillion."

Well, dear readers, I am sure you are more intelligent than me, 'coz I don't understand anything in that definition of "guid".

So what to say about "guid"? The journalist, meant to write "*Guild* race: Mak NRM wing splits." But it is that journalist's misspelling that has given us so much information about "guid". And because of that mistake, the result is that "guid" has gone worldwide in today's *Sunday Monitor* internet edition. Indeed, that error is the journalist's Globally Unique Identifier, and will be so, forever. A better *guid* (sorry, *guide*) than me would be able to identify many more advantages of misspelling.

USPA should right its shameful omission
(26 August 2007)

The Uganda Sports Press Association (USPA) is rightly commemorating the tragic deaths of four of its members (Kenneth Matovu, Leo Kabunga, Simon Peter Ekarot and Francis Batte Junior) who perished in a horrific car crash on the Jinja–Kampala road on August 28 2001.

Yesterday (August 25) there was a function at the scene of the accident in Lugazi where UTL and City Tyres are funding various USPA road safety activities. And on Tuesday, there will be a memorial service at Christ the King Church in Kampala.

The fifth man

You would be forgiven if you did not realise that a fifth man died in the accident. Since in 2001, and again now, the scribes' total concentration has been on their fallen colleagues.

The fifth man killed in the accident was the driver (Festo of Nsagazi near Lugazi) of the oncoming pick-up. According to police reports at the time, the journalists' car, at great speed, had recklessly tried to overtake a trailer on a bend, and had hit the pick-up truck, which was in its correct lane.

Innocent victim ignored

Festo was the innocent victim in this accident. He left behind a wife and children. Yet the USPA memorial monument in Lugazi made no mention of Festo, nor was there mention of him at the journalists' funeral service nor in the press coverage. It was as if Festo had never existed or was a nobody, unworthy of mention. It was left to the Presidential Press Adviser, Mr John Nagenda, to speak the truth in a letter to the *New Vision* – he pointed out that an innocent man had been killed by Kenneth Matovu's reckless driving.

UTL – corporate social responsibility
So the current commemoration activities provide USPA with a wonderful opportunity to right its previous shameful omission, by remembering Festo as well as the four journalists. If USPA is not prepared to do this, then UTL and City Tyres need to put on their corporate social responsibility hats, and insist that it is a requirement of their sponsorship that five, not four, people are remembered. Otherwise, the words of Uganda Telecom Marketing Manager, Levi Nyakundi, during the sponsorship launch concerning "the company's social responsibilities to the *society*", would be meaningless. After all, society does not just consist of journalists.

Finally, it is all well and good for the scribes to paint zebra crossings in Lugazi, but would it not be more logical for the campaign to focus on what actually killed the 5 men (and a huge number of other Ugandans every year) i.e. overspeeding; overtaking on bends?

Kevin evicts *Big Brother Africa*
(2 September 2007)

I am pleased to announce that I have not watched a single episode of *Big Brother Africa*, nor do I intend to watch any.

Come on people, get a life! You, no doubt, have many challenges and problems to overcome in your lives, and you can use your time in far better ways than watching this TV rubbish.

I do not have DSTV at home since it is too expensive for my limited budget. The only time that I watch DSTV is when I go to a bar to see Premier League football. And now that GTV has thrashed DSTV 5-1 on rights for the only football league that most people are interested in, my viewing of DSTV will be close to zero.

From famine to bribery, from deforestation to floods and droughts, Africa is full of problems and challenges. In such a continental context, does it matter on *Big Brother Africa*:
- Who has the biggest whopper?
- Who has kissed who?
- Who has given who a hand job?
- Who has shaved their *Kandahar* in expectation of it receiving a whopper, whether big or small?

It is interesting how much of this wretched TV programme revolves around sex. Another of Africa's many problems is its HIV/AIDS pandemic. Might it be fair to conclude that *Big Brother Africa* has contributed to the further spread of HIV/AIDS both amongst the housemates and amongst the viewers?

Watching TV is a passive affair. Even when it comes to the English Premier League, it is far preferable to be out playing football oneself (or teaching a youngster how to trap, pass and dribble a ball) than watching the world's best on TV.

Last Tuesday, the World Athletics Championships were on TV. But I was not watching. Instead, I was coaching 2 young female athletes. With weights attached to their ankles and hands, they sprinted 30 times up a steep 40 metre tarmac hill. It was a truly beautiful evening, with a light breeze and the sun about to set. It was Uganda at its beautiful best. The fact that in June both girls became national senior champions (at 800m and 1500m) has brought me immense happiness and pride. Who needs to watch Bekele, Kiprop and Kluft (let alone *Big*

Brother Africa) on TV when one can experience life in its reality rather than "life" on a glass screen?

The girls are 20 and 21 years old. The 2008 Olympics in Beijing are a bit too soon for them. So we are targeting the 2012 Olympics in London. It is the start of an adventure far more exciting than anything you will see on *Big Brother Africa* or on any other TV crap.

Beware of ambiguous headlines
(28 April 2009)

There is one newspaper headline that always grabs my attention - "JUDITH (or SYLVIA or MARY etc.) HOOKS OLD *MUZUNGU*". I have to read the article that follows this headline, just in case it is about me. After all, if anybody greets me in Luganda with, *"Mukyala ali atya?"* (how is the wife), my reply is, *"Sirina mukyala, nnina byana kumi."* (I don't have a wife, I have 10 girlfriends). I would like to add to this reply "that is why I am always tired", but I don't know how to say "always" and "tired" in Luganda.

Headlines are important. They sell newspapers. A good headline can persuade the public to part with their money and buy the newspaper. Have a look at the headline on the front page of today's *Sunday Monitor*? Is it a good one? Did it grab your attention? If you had little money, would today's headline persuade you to spend Ug Sh 1200 on the *Sunday Monitor*, or would you feel that those shillings should be added to your savings for the wretched school fees due at the end of the current holidays?

It is therefore very important for newspaper editors to get headlines right. But they can get them wrong, most notably

when the headline is ambiguous (has two meanings), with the second meaning being very different, and sometimes very funnily different, from that intended. Here are some examples:
- **"Prostitutes appeal to Pope."** Does this mean that prostitutes, unhappy about having had their Munyonyo conference cancelled, have asked the Pope for assistance? Or does it mean that Pope Benedict finds prostitutes an attractive alternative to celibacy?
- **"Queen Mary having bottom scraped."** The editor wished to tell readers that the big British ship (ocean liner) called the *Queen Mary* was being cleaned by having rust and dirt removed from its bottom. But the headline could also mean that the British King's wife in the 1920's (Queen Mary) was having her bottom (bum) scraped/cleaned.
- **"Enraged cow injures Rakai farmer with panga."** The newspaper meant that the farmer was carrying a panga, and was hurt by an angry cow. But the headline could mean that it was the cow which was carrying the panga and injured the farmer with it.
- **"Two cars were reported stolen by the Kampala police yesterday."** Did the police do the reporting or the stealing?
- **"Ugandan virgin lands short of goal again."** This could mean that a young man from Jinja, who wanted to bonk before his 17th birthday, reached that day and still had not had sex. Alternatively, that the government had sold off insufficient unused land to potential investors.
- **"Kasese miners refuse to work after death."** Once you are dead, you are dead, and it is indeed difficult to work while in a coffin. But, there again, someone might have

got killed in the mine, resulting in the other miners going on strike.
- **"Two Ugandan ferries collide, one dies."** It would be hard to fit a ferry into a coffin. Alternatively, the collision just off Port Bell, might have killed a passenger.

And, finally, let me end with **"UPE dropouts cut in half."** Cutting, into two pieces, someone who leaves school before P7, would indeed be an incentive to remain in education.

Allegations, allegations and more allegations
(13 June 2008)

It is alleged that:
- Former army commander, General James Kazini, created "ghost" soldiers for financial gain.
- Pastor Christopher Lubega sent sexually explicit obscene emails to his daughter and other women.
- Major General Kale Kayihura (in March 2003) was held hostage for 6 hours by Congolese rebels.

As the above show, allegations come in all shapes and forms. They are so varied that one cannot give general advice on how to deal with them.

Have allegations been made against you? Were they true or false? What was your reaction? How did you deal with them – did you do something or nothing?

And, yes, *Roving Eye* would not be a human being if, at different stages of his life, he had not had to respond to allegations.

For example, a rather hurtful allegation was made by a *muzungu* lady who was reviewing the draft of my recently published book, *Ugandan Society Observed*. But to explain the allegation, I first have to explain one of the methods I sometimes use when writing a *Roving Eye* column.

I have a large number of Ugandan friends and contacts drawn from different areas and levels of society (e.g. lawyers, journalists, *boda-boda* men, newsvendors, shop assistants, businessmen and women, athletes, politicians, vegetable sellers etc.). When the subject seems right (e.g. "We Ugandans don't feel shame" (22 October 2006), "Lower Uganda's age of consent to 16 years" (16 March 2008), I will approach a few of them for their views on the subject. I then try weave some of their quotes into the article, perhaps together with my own views, which may be the same or different from those of the Ugandans I have interviewed.

So, what did the book reviewer write in her comments on the draft of my book, that so upset me? Did she allege that I was defiling schoolgirls? No, but for a journalist/writer the allegation was almost as bad as that. It was:

> "Long before Page 132, I had concluded that these quotes were a stylistic device by the author to support his own viewpoints."

I interpreted this as meaning that the people I had quoted were not real people and that I had made up the quotes. It was an allegation that hit at the very heart of my journalist integrity. *Roving Eye* was being accused of journalistic corruption!

So, how did I deal with this allegation? Fortunately, it was straightforward. The publisher of my book had previously been a journalist, who I had approached on several occasions for comments that I might use in a *Roving Eye* column. He was able to look at some articles in the book and be absolute 100% sure that the quote was real and genuine from a real and genuine person, because that person was................himself. He realised that the reviewer's allegation, like much of her grasp of Ugandan society, was nonsense.

Similarly, the following allegations made about *Roving Eye* are also untrue. That he:
- Had a homosexual affair with the Archbishop of Canterbury.
- Will stop supporting Fulham when they are relegated later this season from the Premier League.
- Almost had 3 car accidents while looking at beautiful babes when driving past Makerere University Business School (false – it was 6 accidents).

Roving Eye relaunch

(22 June 2008)

Today is the first day of the rest of my life. So it's time to "turn over a new leaf" by reloading, rebranding and altogether relaunching *Roving Eye* in today's historically momentous column. Let's ring in the changes.

Photo

Eagle-eyed readers will have already noticed, above, the new and up-to-date photo of myself. The previous photo was quite a few years old.

I receive emails from readers of all shapes and sizes (with both the emails and the readers being well described by "all shapes and sizes"). Very, very, very occasionally, I receive an email from a young lady reader offering to meet me in a lodge for considerably more than drinking sodas. So, I regret to inform her, as the new photo shows only too well, I am considerably older than she thinks I am. Indeed, had I accepted her invitation, it would have been less a case of cross-generational sex, and more a case of "Help the Aged".

Hipster jeans

But while the youth can be misguided, there is often much to learn from them. So from tomorrow, as part of the *Roving Eye* revolution, I am going to dress in a more youthful way.

I am neither born-again, nor a born-again bonker, but I do know that for some young women, it is fashionable to wear hipster jeans with a little of their panties/knickers/g-strings visible at the back. So, next time you see me on Kampala Road, I too will be wearing hipster jeans. Now, I am, like Colonel Gadaffi, a revolutionary. Therefore, in true revolutionary style, I will be showing not a little, but a lot of my underpants. They will be old underpants, as underpants, like revolutionaries, should never retire.

Bling

So there can be no doubt that I have "turned the corner" appearance-wise, I have discovered bling. The "crown jewels" of my bling is a large, gold medallion. It hangs from my neck, and because I now undo my shirt so I am unbuttoned to the belly button, the medallion glints in the sun as it sits above my stomach.

A "medallion man" typically has a hairy chest, but unfortunately I have no hairs on my chest. Sorry, that's a lie. As I look down on my not-so-broad, pigeon chest, I can see one hair sprouting, growing in "splendid isolation", between the chains of my medallion and nicely highlighted by them.

Mobile phone

I have left the biggest change in my reformed life to last. I have got to do something about my mobile phone. It is a dinosaur amongst phones. It is so old, that it only just about post-dates Speke (and I'm talking about the man, not the hotel).

There is a rather crude saying in England - "you are only as old as the women you feel." While this saying is unlikely to be used as a slogan in the current Ugandan campaign against cross-generational sex, it could be changed to, "you are only as old as the mobile phone you use".

My phone means my age is 103 years. It just about manages to splutter out a text message, and can do little more. In contrast, the latest mobile phones act as camera, video, radio, TV, computer and much else. And when researching this article, one of the world's most famous mobile phone companies told me that their next generation of phones would, among other things, be able to make tea and also test whether someone is pregnant. You heard it from me first, folks.

Roving Eye is pleased to join the revolutionaries who not only change the times but change with the times.

Your newspaper – the business page meets the sports page
(15 June 2008)

A typical national newspaper will have different sections e.g. foreign, politics, business, sports etc. Readers will often have favourite sections, looking at them before any other, or spending more time reading them.

As an athletics coach, with interest in football, I will generally spend some time on the sports pages. Also, I studied economics at university and am an anti-tobacco campaigner, so, however busy I am, I will always try take a brief look at the business section.

It follows that if *Roving Eye* is interested in the business and sports sections, he will also be interested in the connections between them.

So, let me throw "the cat among the pigeons" by arguing that the typical division in a newspaper between "business" and "sport" is an artificial one. Followers of Manchester United are of course greatly interested in the wonderful ball skills of Cristiano Ronaldo and what next season's first fixture is. But increasingly, these same fans need to know much about ownership, boardrooms, stock market listings, liquidity and merchandising. Indeed, whether Ronaldo will, or will not, be transferred to Real Madrid after Euro 2008 will depend substantially on issues more typically discussed in the business section.

There is another interesting link between the sports and business sections. In quality newspapers throughout the world more and more pages are devoted to sport. This reflects the need for the typically stressed business/manager reader to escape their office pressures, either by participating in sport themselves, or by putting mental distance between themselves and their work problems by immersing themselves in the sports pages.

To meet the needs of such readers, there are more and more heavyweight analytical articles. And less pure reportage such as "Team X beat Team Y 2-1, with the winning goal scored in the 83rd minute." For, who really cares a ****, apart from X and Y's supporters?

Instead, quality newspapers take an in-depth look at the wider links between sport and society. This can include not just sport and business/management, but sport and nutrition, sport and humour, sport and tragedy, sport and neocolonialism, indeed sport and "you name it."

One of Uganda's topmost newspaper editors once told me that typically his sports reporters could tell him how many times Barcelona had won the Spanish League, or the Arsenal vs Man U result 5 years ago. But that they would have great difficulty, or find impossible, writing an article about the wider links between sport and society described in the previous paragraph.

So, when the Cranes were beaten by Benin 4-1 last weekend, Journalist A might write a match report. Journalist B adds in another article blaming the defeat on particular members of FUFA. But what is lacking is a Journalist C arguing that selected senior FUFA officials need intensive management short-course training alongside business executives from MTN, Shell etc. specifying the particular management skills that need sharpening. Then, Journalist D's article shouts loudly "who cares" since football and all sport is just a lot of old nonsense compared to where the next set of school fees is coming from, or compared to your husband/wife having sex in a lodge with a lover.

It would indeed be wonderful to have seen these articles by Messrs/Ms A, B, C and D on the same day in the same newspaper's sports section following the Cranes' defeat in Benin. By asking larger questions, the quality newspaper attracts the more general reader to the sports pages, and not just the sports enthusiast/fanatic.

Following this look at the connections between the business and sports sections of newspapers, during Obote 3, *Roving Eye* will examine the links between the other newspaper sections.

Journalists in love with photos of themselves
(13 July 2008)

"Vienna was worth it!" screamed the *Saturday Vision*'s centrespread headline (July 5 2008). But was the article, written by sports journalist Fred Kaweesi, worth it? Well, yes and no.

Yes, because it was a well-written, interesting article about Kaweesi's experiences at the EURO 2008 football tournament.

No, because of the 9 photos that accompanied the article, 5 had in them, none other than............Fred Kaweesi.

Now, even if Fred Kaweesi was the most handsome man in the world and I was a sex-starved babe, would I really want to see him 5 times when reading about EURO 2008?

But to be fair to male model Kaweesi, the major fault lay not with him but with the *Saturday Vision* editor, whose response *should* have been, "Come on Fred, our readers already know what you look like from your mugshot. They want to know what Vienna looks like."

However, the world record for self-indulgent photography lies not with Kaweesi, but with another *Vision* sports journalist. He attended an international sports journalists' conference in the USA. If I remember correctly, his subsequent article in the *New Vision* was accompanied by around 7 photographs, with him appearing in all 7 of them! Why bother to invest in a photo album when you can get your newspaper to print your photographs for free?

So what is going on here? Why so many photos of self? Dalvin, 24, is the manager of a coffee shop, and he told me:

> "It's Africans. Major they want to show off. And Ugandans in particular. It is a big chance to be known. To be known as someone influential, you've got to appear as often as possible. And, some Ugandans will not believe he has been to Vienna, so that is why he has to appear several times on that page."

Moses, 23, works in a shop in a Kampala suburb. His initial opinion was very different from Dalvin's:

> "I don't have any negative opinion as to why this guy appears 5 times, as long as he pays for the whole page."

I then explained to Moses that far from Kaweesi paying the *Saturday Vision*, the opposite would be true i.e. the *Vision* would pay him – his salary – while the trip itself (to Vienna) was sponsored by *Supersport*. Moses replied:

> "Perhaps the *Saturday Vision* wanted to prove to people that it had real news from Vienna, and that it had a real journalist there."

> "But," said Dalvin, wanting the last word, "there only needed to be one photo of him in Vienna for the article to be meaningful."

Dalvin is, of course, right. And one could argue that even one photograph is not necessary. For example, David Mukholi, the editor of the *Sunday Vision*, visited Jerusalem recently, and wrote an article about the trip. It included – if my ageing memory is correct – not a single photograph of himself. And my conclusion would be that his journalistic standards are high, and that Kaweesi has some important lessons to learn from Mukholi when it comes to photographs.

And last, but definitely least, when a certain Kevin O'Connor covered the 2002 Commonwealth Games for the *Monitor*, apart from his mugshot, there were no photographs of Kevin O'Connor, despite him being a handsome, Richard Gere lookalike male model................

Red Pepper's Friday 13 superstitious nonsense
(29 March 2009)

Are Ugandans more superstitious than other peoples? I began to fear that the answer to this question might be "yes" when a Ugandan national newspaper (*Red Pepper*) devoted its front page to telling us that "the Angel of Death" would be visiting the Pearl of Africa on Friday 13 March. Its March 17 edition then tried to prove that the visit had actually taken place.

Road accidents

So what "proof" did *Pepper* provide? Its most ridiculous "evidence" concerned road accidents in the Kampala Extra Region - "Police spokesperson Judith Nabakooba said, according to the survey carried out, that there was a slight increase" in the number of road accidents and deaths compared with any other Friday.

It is true that Judith Nabakooba is an extremely beautiful woman, who can come to visit me, not just on Friday 13, but on any other day of the year. But given the huge number of terrible accidents that occur, often from 'overspeeding', on Uganda's frequently potholed roads, a "slight increase" in accidents, in one particular region, proves nothing.

Collapsing buildings

Similarly nonsensical is *Pepper* citing the collapse of Mirembe Shopping Centre in Nasser Road, Kampala. Our questionable engineering and architectural standards, unquestionable corruption, and (in Kampala) KCC's questionable regulation enforcement policies, mean that buildings are collapsing in Uganda all the time. So the fact that one collapsed on a Friday 13 means nothing, other than sadness and worry to the families of those killed and injured.

Fires

And so the article continued...there were fires on Friday 13 March. But one does not need to be a genius, nor hold a PhD in rocket science, but just be a reader of Ugandan newspapers or a viewer of the NTV news, to know that regretfully fires occur in Ugandan markets, schools etc. with disturbing regularity. And as the country possesses very few fire engines to extinguish killer flames, many deaths occur.

Prostitutes

Then, there was the "sexually-starved journalist" who was attacked by two prostitutes when he claimed he had no money to pay after using the services of one of them (i.e. *sirina ssente, njagala banja* – I don't have money, I'd like credit). My only comment about this supposed Friday 13 "proof" is .... I was not the journalist.

Conclusion

The belief that bad things happen on Friday 13 is superstitious nonsense. For as the internet encyclopedia *Wikipedia* points out, "Due to the large number of events that happen in the world, a similar list {of unhappy events compiled as occurring

Is O'Connor a "scumbag"?

(10 May 2009)

"Newspaper", "journalism", "free speech" – the definitions of what they mean are many, but at their heart will be the providing of an opinion. Some readers will agree, some will disagree, with that opinion. And from the latter group especially, some people will use the newspaper pages to offer articles or letters with a different opinion. It is by the reading of these alternative opinions that a reader forms/changes their own opinion/view.

Filthy scumbag

This process is a fairly straightforward one, and there should be no need to resort to personal abuse. However, regretfully abuse does happen, as reflected by the comments below of a certain Agnes, which she posted on the *Sunday Monitor*'s internet edition in response to the *Roving Eye* article, "Some truths about homosexuality" (April 26, 2009):

> "It's sad to hear a white man enjoying the Ugandan hospitality telling our young boys that homosexuality is part of growing up! I find this very disgusting and insulting. Why should we allow the likes of Kevin to corrupt the innocent minds of our young children with their homosexual tastes? For how long shall we continue undermining our values and allow such filthy people to freely infect our societies with trash! I think because of poverty and our curteous (sic) nature, we are taken advantage of by every scumbag that comes along."

In that *Roving Eye* column, my only "crime" was supporting the views of the outstanding senior Ugandan journalist, Bernard Tabaire, in his "When Christians condemn God's children during the Easter season" (*Saturday Monitor* April 11 2009). My article was reasoned and polite, and after pointing out that I was a heterosexual, I argued that many Ugandans needed to show more Christian "treat your neighbour as yourself" attitudes towards homosexuals.

Nevertheless, Agnes calls me "filthy" and a "scumbag", which is a highly abusive word, and means a terrible, despicable person.

White man

Agnes also feels the need to refer to me as "a white man", which is, of course, true. But the reference would surely leave Martin Luther King ("I have a dream that my four little children will one day live in a nation where they will not be judged by the colour of their skin but by the content of their character") turning in his grave.

Global Fund

If my polite, reasoned article requires Agnes to use the word "scumbag", one wonders what words of sufficient power would be left in her vocabulary to describe the several senior famous Ugandans who, according to the Ogoola Commission, "ate" the Global Fund, thereby killing many of their fellow citizens. That the Agnes's of this world appear to get more upset about homosexuality, than they do about corruption, surely says something about Ugandan society.

Phrases too loved by journalists
(10 January 2010)

A source who preferred anonymity, called Kevin O'Connor, said:

> "There are numerous phrases that get boringly repeated in Ugandan newspaper articles, such as 'a source who preferred anonymity'. A second overused phrase is 'due to unforeseen circumstances'."
>
> "Often", O'Connor insightfully continued, "the use of 'due to unforeseen circumstances' conceals the Ugandan tendency of not confronting issues. Thus, 'the opening of Kampala's Northern Bypass has been delayed due to unforeseen circumstances' might better read, 'the opening of Kampala's Northern Bypass has been delayed due to unforeseen circumstances, more commonly known as slowness and inefficiency.'"
>
> "A third phrase," O'Connor wittily observed, "is 'all roads lead to' as in, 'on Saturday morning all roads lead to Namboole Stadium where muscular athletics coach, Kevin O'Connor, will be found dressed only in a pair of running shorts, and with stomach protruding considerably further in front, than his non-existent bum does behind'."
>
> "All roads," a gushing O'Connor added, "certainly lead to my inbox at present. I receive more spam, more junk mail, than there are:
> - Newly created districts in Uganda.
> - Junk helicopters.
> - Dollars corruptly embezzled from the Global and GAVI Funds."

> "I especially resent receiving junk emails offering to increase the size of a part of my body that is big enough already, and I am not talking about my nose."
>
> "There are phrases" continued O'Connor, doing something that Ugandans generally avoid doing, i.e. criticising a dead person, "that were repeatedly used by a late sports journalist, and by 'late' I mean deceased rather than not arriving for meetings on time, though he did that as well."

And those phrases were, 'it is my submission that...' and 'it is my proposition that....' Now, if a journalist has their name at the top of an article, who can be doing the proposing other than that journalist? 'It is my proposition that' is unnecessary – the writer should have just got on and said whatever it was that he wanted to say, which was generally not very much.

But this journalist had a sickening extension of his stock phrase i.e. 'it is my humble submission that...' Now, journalists are many things, but humble is not one of them. They believe they have views and ideas that the rest of the world should know about. By definition, journalists are not humble.

O'Connor then took a deep breath, and, looking around him to see if anyone was listening, added:

> "*Roving Eye* has plenty of writing weaknesses of his own - some words unnecessarily repeated in the same sentence or paragraph; some standard phrases used again, again and again; unnecessary, redundant words that should be deleted; using every opportunity to draw attention to Fulham's victories over Manchester United."

Indeed, in something that is close to journalistic masturbation, I have even written articles in which I have only quoted myself. But it is my humble submission that I am not arrogant.

A "Kandahar" whopper

(25 April 2010)

The *Red Pepper* newspaper has a vocabulary all of its own. Below is stupid *muzungu*'s understanding of some of the words that regularly appear on its pages.

Whopper

When I was a kid, my Mum told me not to tell "whoppers" i.e. lies, or more exactly, big lies.

A few years ago the *Red Pepper* alleged that I had been paid 100,000 US dollars for organising a World No Tobacco Day march. The truth was that I had been paid 40,000 Ugandan shillings (about 20 dollars) as reimbursement of transport expenses, for attending 4 meetings at the Ministry of Health. In other words, the *Red Pepper* had told a "whopper".

Bootylicious

"Bootylicious" combines the words "booty" and "delicious". "Booty" means a prize plundered during war, or taken by force. So if pirates stole crates of chocolate bars and ate the chocolate all at once, their resulting big bums could be said to be "bootylicious".

Kandahar

But of all the words used by the esteemed *Red Pepper*, it is "kandahar" that is used the most often. On one occasion, the word "kandahar" appeared in four headlines on one page!

This obsession with "kandahar" is therefore worthy of detailed explanation by *Roving Eye*.

Let us consider the sentence, "You never forget the first time you enter kandahar." It is obvious what it means........

Kandahar is a city in southern Afghanistan. According to legend, ancient Kandahar was founded by Alexander the Great. Today, it is the commercial centre of Afghanistan. From all around, fruit, grain, tobacco, silk, cotton, and wool find their way into Kandahar. The city itself has numerous fruit processing and canning plants, and textile mills.

But modernity has not destroyed its historic architecture. Points of interest include the tomb of the first emir of Afghanistan, Ahmad Shah, as well as bazaars and mosques. One of these is the Mosque of the Cloak of the Prophet Mohammed, a most valued relic in the Islamic world. The sacred cloak is kept locked away, taken out only at times of great crisis.

Given its place in history and its wonderful architecture, we can understand why readers of the *Red Pepper* so often say, "You never forget the first time you enter kandahar."

Oh dear! *Roving Eye* has told a whopper! For as regular readers of *Red Pepper* will realise, their use of the word "kandahar" has an entirely different meaning i.e. vagina.

MPs swearing-in overkill

(29 May 2011)

"Grandeur as MPs swearing-in ends" the headline screamed. But it might as well have said "Fatness as MPs swearing-in ends" because photo after photo showed faces which were generally fatter than the average Ugandan's.

And I really do mean photo after photo. Because, just as with kids/parents and the PLE/O-level/A-level results, Ugandan newspapers really went into photographic overkill with the MPs swearing-in.

The state-owned *New Vision* won Gold Medal for exam photographic overkill, and it lived up to its reputation when it came to the MPs. Can you believe that one edition of the *New Vision* had 8 pages of photographs of MPs at the swearing-in ceremony?!

Now, once you have seen one photo of an MP's fat fingers clutching the Holy Bible, you have seen them all. One photo would have been enough, let alone one page, let alone 8 pages. And let's face it, the Holy Bible is a lot of old nonsense anyway. Recently, renowned scientist Stephen Hawking said, "There is no heaven or afterlife … it is a fairy story …" He could well have said that the Holy Bible is a "fairy story". Therefore an oath on it has very little meaning, whether the Bible is clutched in fat fingers or in thin fingers. Indeed, such an oath would have no more value whether it be sworn on "The Holy Book of Pornography" or on "Ugandan Society Observed", a classic book penned by that world-renowned author, Kevin O'Connor.

The overkill of newspaper exam photographs is almost certainly due to corruption, with journalists receiving "brown envelopes" from both parents and schools in order to ensure that a particular photo appears. I suspect that with the swearing-in overkill, we must look elsewhere, in the direction of *lazy journalism* – other than identifying the name and constituency of the MP, a page of swearing-in photographs requires very little work to produce. Similarly, we might point to *cheap* or *profitable journalism* since, who else, other than the photographer, has to be paid?

Fat fingers on fat bibles with thin content – that is my endearing memory of the swearing-in ceremony for Uganda's Ninth Parliament.

Dead but not dead!

(2015)

It was a typical *In Memoriam* page, full of gushing nonsense about Ugandans who appear to be saints, having done nothing negative in their lives, other than staring at us from mugshots that required a better photographer.

However, at the bottom of this *In Memoriam* page, in a national Sunday newspaper of 26 July 2015 (which I am pleased to announce to planet Earth was not the *Sunday Monitor*), there was something that made the whole boring page worth reading.

The headline in bold funereal black capital letters was, "CORRECTION". What followed made me laugh, and I hope it will at least make you smile:

> "Last week, in the article celebrating the life of Father Joseph Archetti, it was erroneously indicated that Dr Magrethe Junker was dead. Dr Magrethe Junker is not dead as stated in the article. We regret the error and the inconveniences caused."

Oh, my goodness! Dr Junker, co-founder of *Reach Out*, the Mbuya Parish HIV/AIDS Initiative, "we regret the error" of telling, especially through our internet edition, the whole world that you were dead, when in fact you were no more dead than Wayne Rooney. Though there have been times when Manchester United supporters have thought that their striker has been play acting dead in front of their opponents' goal.

And, yes, Dr Junker, we further regret "the inconveniences caused to you." Perhaps your friends and relatives had travelled long distances, many from *Bazunguland*, to attend your funeral, only to find that, Lazarus-like, you have risen from the dead. But, dear Doctor, it is important we look on the bright side, as in these times of a rapidly depreciating shilling, these overseas visitors would have provided a much needed boost to the country's balance of payments and helped shackle that shifty shifting shilling.

Dr Junker's experience of a media mortality mistake is similar to that experienced by the American humourist, novelist and writer, Samuel Langhorne Clemens (1835 – 1910), who is better known by his pen name, Mark Twain.

In 1897, there were reports that Mark Twain was dead. However, Twain's cousin, James Ross Clemens, was seriously ill in London, and it appears that some journalists confused him with Samuel Langhorne Clemens (Mark Twain). As a result, the following classic comment by Twain appeared in the *New York Journal* of 2 June 1897, "The report of my death was an exaggeration." Many years later, Twain changed the famous quote to, "Reports of my death have been greatly exaggerated."

Mark Twain was indeed a very funny man. But many of the quotes attributed to him while humourous, carry with them a degree of wisdom and truth. Thus:

> "There are basically two types of people. People who accomplish things, and people who claim to have accomplished things. The first group is less crowded."

This quote has similarities to another:

> "Whenever you find yourself on the side of the majority, it is time to pause and reflect."

And could a catchphrase of many politicians around the world be:

> "Get your facts first, then you can distort them as you please."

And if you find yourself in an unequal struggle, you could do well to remember:

> "It's not the size of the dog in the fight, it's the size of the fight in the dog."

But my favourite Twainism (if such a word exists) is:

> "It is better to keep your mouth closed and let people think you are a fool, than to open it and remove all doubt."

Well, Kevin, the journalist, may have opened his mouth in this article and shown himself to be a fool, but he is surely not as big a fool as the journalist who wrote that Dr Magrethe Junker was dead.

11

Poverty and inequality

Sporting inequality and cars
(25 February 2007)

Cars in a car park can say a lot about sport in Uganda. A few weeks ago, Kampala Athletics organised an 8 km road race at Kyambogo. On some rough ground, near the start, there were just two cars, mine and that of another athletics coach.

None of the 90 or so athletes who were competing owned a car. They had got to Kyambogo by jogging there, or by *matatu* or *boda-boda*. Athletes are generally young, and normally drawn from the lower rungs of society. They therefore lack financial resources to purchase a vehicle.

Golf
In contrast, the car park of a golf club will not only be full of cars, but they will often be expensive 4-wheel drive vehicles. It is not difficult to understand why belonging to the Kampala Golf Club is limited to a rich minority. Membership costs approximately Sh1m for the first year. Applicants must also be nominated by a member, seconded by another and be endorsed by 21 other members.

Obviously, it is no good being a member if you don't have the golf clubs (putters, driving woods and irons etc.), to play the game! Even if you buy a cheaper set of golf clubs, you will not have much change out of Sh1m.

And after the golf clubs, a golfer must still purchase suitable golfing clothing and footwear. Many golf clubs appear to attract more than their fair share of snobs, so it is reasonable to assume that "suitable golfing clothing" does not include T-shirt and jeans.

So someone who has the financial muscle to be a member of the Kampala Golf Club, owns a set of golf clubs and bought the wretched golfing clothing, will almost certainly own a car, and probably a posh one at that. Next time there is a golfing tournament, have a quick "peek" in the car park, and you will see what I mean.

The Index

The sociology of car parks at Uganda's sporting venues might lend itself to a research thesis. At its heart would be a simple statistic, the number of cars per participant/spectator.

Thus, at the Kyambogo road race mentioned above, say there were 92 runners, 6 officials and 2 athletics coaches. So there were 100 participants/spectators and just two cars i.e. one fifthtieth of a car for every participant/spectator.

I am not sure what one fifthtieth of a car is, perhaps a headlight, or a wheel or a seat belt.

Anyway, the *Roving Eye* Index of Sporting Car Parks (REISCP) would be 0.02.

While at the Kampala Golf Club, the figure would surely be almost one car per participant/spectator i.e. the REISCP might read 0.95.

It would be interesting to analyse all Ugandan sports in similar fashion. The basement of the REISCP league table would be boxing along with running. Cricket would be in mid-table.

Rugby
And where would rugby be? Well, given the fat men, supposed sportsmen, I have seen running behind their beer bellies on some Kampala rugby fields, then rugby would be towards the top of the table, not far below golf.

So, if you get to a sporting carpark, and because of the high REISCP, there is no room for your car, what should you do?

One option is to change sports and take up a real one like running. But then again, when it comes to the index of sporting prejudice, this columnist would surely win the league.

Brave Mukula bathed in cold water
(17 June 2007)

According to former Health Minister, Mike Mukula, a hardship he had to suffer in Luzira Prison was having to shower in cold water:

> "On my first night in prison," observed Mukula, "I dodged showering because the water was too cold for me, having been used to showering in heated water."
> (*Sunday Pepper*, June 10, 2007, p6).

No doubt to the nasal relief of other inmates, Mukula took courage in his hands, and yes, on Day Two, made the brave decision to shower in unheated water. Sorry Mike, for the sarcasm, but are you not getting a little bit out of touch with your fellow countrymen and women if bathing in unheated water is a daunting challenge?

For starters, Mike, what percentage of Ugandans are fortunate enough to own a shower? As David, 38, a shop attendant observed:

> "We're still a poor country, so it is hard for a Ugandan even to have a cold shower in their house. Most Ugandans get water from a stand pipe or well, and bathe in a bowl or basin."

Surely, though, from his A-class life of wealth and luxury, Mukula, would, for instance, notice all the kids carrying heavy yellow jerry cans. Not according to Mary, a 21-year-old athlete. She spat out, with venom, the following words:

> "The rich only care about themselves, so they have no idea how ordinary Ugandans live."

For example, there are bars in Kampala where a single cubicle doubles as a bathing area and a urinal. At times, there will be a member of staff bathing in it. At other times, there will be patrons urinating in it. More up market, there are those bars where the urinal cubicle is separate from the bathing cubicle, but where the urine must run through the bathing area to reach its ditch destination.

No-one expects Mike to share this type of bathing reality, but in a poor country, you can surely go too far in the other direction, and having gone too far, apparently still not feel any shame. In the now infamous *African Woman* magazine article, Mukula and his wife boastfully showed off their properties. Thus we learnt that their Kampala residence has eight showers, imported from Italy. And those showers have telephones, in-built radios, lights, mirrors and massage/steam facilities.

When you are in the elite, you generally look at your society as a finely graduated ladder, with you having reached the top through your own hard work and effort. But when you are impoverished, you tend to view the same society very much as "us" and "them".

If you have bathed in a urinal today, or are waiting in a long line with your jerry can to reach a standpipe in an IDP camp, there can be little doubt that you would regard 8-showers-in-his-family-house Mukula as one of "them", brave boy though he was for showering in unheated water in Luzira Prison!

Electrocuted by a hotel's prices and fence
(30 November 2008)

Kampala's *Golf Course Hotel* has the revolving *7 Hills* restaurant at the top of a 12-storey tower. Is it a tower of inequality reflective of the "haves" and "havenots" in Ugandan society? Or is it a towering investment whose benefits will eventually "trickle down" to the country's poor?

But before I start my 12-storey story, let me first get out my excuses. *Roving "sirina ssente, njagala banja"* (I don't have money, I want credit) *Eye* would not normally be found in such a classy joint. But I have a *muzungu* friend who has an expense account. And his occasional visits to Uganda allow me to sometimes eat in Kampala's most expensive restaurants.

On the way to the revolving restaurant, we made a small detour to the hotel's pleasant swimming pool. Right next to the pool, and separating the hotel from the golf course, is an electrified fence. Now, I know I gave up science at secondary school to study Latin, but the sight of an electrified fence next to a swimming pool started alarm bells ringing in my ears. So, a few days later, I asked my friend Lawrence, 24, who works as an assistant in a small shop in my local trading centre, for his views on the fence. He said:

> "That's just dangerous, 'coz it is easy for someone to get electrocuted because water increases voltage and attracts power. Only a drop of water can kill you."

I checked with *Sekanyolya*, the firm which manufactured the fence, and they said "not to worry" as the fence's electricity is only switched on at night. But, even so, boozed-up hotel guests have been known to take midnight swims, and goodness knows what would happen if they should then stumble, soaking wet, against the fence.

Our detour over, we took the lift up to the restaurant. It revolved once during our meal, and we enjoyed magnificent views – Kampala at night, with its lights flickering into the far distance, was a joy to behold.

Not such a joy were some of the prices, and I was glad that it was my friend's expense account, and not me, that was paying. Used to *Nile Special* at Ug Sh 1700 in a *duuka*, the *7 Hills'* price of Ug Sh 6000 made my head revolve, though that might possibly have been the restaurant revolving or the *Nile Special* causing my brain to turn in circles.

I asked Lawrence about this 6000 shilling price and he replied:

> "I don't have a fixed earning daily, but on average I would say I earn 5000 per day. So the price of beer there is more than my daily income. That place is just for big guys."

The previous week, I had attended a function at one of the *Golf Course Hotel*'s competitors – the *Serena Hotel*. I spoke to a waitress there, Laura (not real name) who said she was neither full-time, nor contract, but worked on a casual basis i.e. the *Serena* would call her in when they had a big event, and she earns Ug Sh 7000 per day.

In the unlikely event that Laura ever went to the *7 Hills* restaurant, and bought a *Nile Special*, then she, unlike Lawrence, would at least receive a balance from her daily wage.

And, of course, Lawrence and Laura are the lucky ones, for at least they have jobs. For the unemployed, the revolving *7 Hills* restaurant may as well exist on the planet Mars.

So, do investments like the *Golf Course Hotel* create jobs for the unemployed? Or do they merely add to the huge inequality between the rich and the poor in Uganda? *Roving Eye*'s jury is still out. Should they return a "not guilty" verdict then he looks forward to another free meal in the revolving restaurant. But if their verdict be "guilty", then it should be death by electric chair, or more appropriately by electric fence, for such investors.

1920s UK and 2009 Uganda – some similarities

(8 March 2009)

Although there are very many differences, there are also some interesting similarities, between the lives of poor British people in the early twentieth century, and many Ugandans today. Two similarities were looked at in a recent *Roving Eye* ("Legalise abortion in Uganda" 8 February 2009) i.e. the horrible realities of "backstreet" abortions when abortion has not been legalised; family size.

My mother (85) grew up in a slum in West London, and like my late father, was a manual worker. She (by phone from

London) and two Ugandan friends (Mike 32; John 24) provided the information for 3 more similarities.

Similarity 1 – *Obukunkumuka* and cracklings

A photo, taken in Mbale, showed a samosa seller with his trolley. Mike observed:

> "Those kids in the photo would be eating for free those very small pieces that have fallen down from the outside of the samosa to the bottom of the trolley. In Luganda, we call those small pieces *obukunkumuka*".

My mother, as a girl, would go to a fish and chip shop and ask:

> "Pennth {penny} of chips Wal {Walter} and some cracklings in it"

She was too poor to buy the fish. But, "cracklings" were the small pieces of batter coating that had fallen off the fish while being cooked i.e. similar to *obukunkumuka*. The crackling was free - a sort of *enyongeza*!

Similarity 2 – Pushing a wheel

John told me:

> "My parents were not rich. They didn't have the knowledge, let alone the money, to buy me toys. So one game we played was with disused car tyres. With 2 long sticks either side of the rubber tyre, we would push it along. There could be as many as 5 of us and we would start our race with, 'On your marks, set, go!'"

When I repeated John's comments to my Mum, she said:

> "Yes, there was something similar when I was a girl. I remember children rolling an old bicycle wheel with a stick. Also, you could get some wood in the form of a big round circle {a hoop} and push that instead."

Similarity 3 – Homemade cars

Since Mum was getting tired (and my airtime was running out), I did not ask her about the homemade cars of the two poor Ugandan rural boys shown in another photo. But I am sure that similar cars would have been found in her 1920's Britain. Mike said:

> "I had a car like the two in the photograph. I would get wires and tie them together with small cut pieces from the tube of a bicycle wheel. The wheels of our toy car were made from old *silipas*. But, Kevin, the boys in your photo are more clever than our generation – I can just about see that one car has even got springs as shock absorbers!"

Conclusion

My Mum had earlier said:

> "Children where my family lived would make toys out of all sorts of different things, and could amuse themselves with very little. It was not like most British kids today who are bought expensive toys and spend a lot of time on computers."

British kids of 2009 must never be allowed to forget the harsher realities of life of their many poorer ancestors. Similarly, rich Ugandan kids of 2009, found in international and other posh schools, and often seen buying toys in Kampala's Garden City and Shoprite/Game, need frequently to be reminded of the how the vast majority of Ugandan children amuse themselves when at play.

How much would you need to be paid to..........?

(12 July 2009)

After a hard training session at Kampala's Mandela National Stadium, I sometimes ask an exhausted runner, "How much would you need to be paid to do that again, right now?"

Well, if you had just finished 20 x 400m with 90 seconds recovery between each, your normal first answer would be, "No way! I could not do that again." But, if one keeps raising the imaginary reward (from $10 to $50 to $100 to $500......etc.) a price is eventually reached where the tired athlete is prepared (in theory) to do the training session again.

The lesson of this little story is that unless the task is outrageous (like jumping from the top of Workers' House), every man or woman has their price. And, generally, this price will be much lower in a poor developing country like Uganda than in a rich First World country.

Walk to Jinja

I tried the 'How much would you need to be paid' question on my friend Oscar, 24, a shop assistant in a Kampala trading centre.

> "So, Oscar" I asked, while trying to keep a straight face, "How much would you need to be paid to walk the 82kms from Kampala to Jinja?"
>
> "50,000 shillings," he immediately replied.
>
> "Wow!" I thought to myself, "I don't normally get out of bed for less than 50,000 shillings."

Lick a toilet seat

"OK Oscar" I exclaimed. "Here is a tougher question. How much would you need to be paid to lick the toilet seat in a public toilet?"

Oscar screwed his face up, and in a raised voice, almost shouted at me:

"I would not do it at any price!"

So I kept increasing the price, "500,000 Ugandan Shillings? 1 million? 5 million?..." Eventually I reached 20 million, and Oscar interrupted me with a forceful, "Ok I'll do it for 20 million shillings!"

I asked Oscar why he had changed his mind. He said:

"I've never held 20 million. I've only held 2 million in my life. I would first go for medical treatment after licking the toilet seat. I would think that could consume 1 million. That would leave me with 19 million. With that money of 19 million, I could invest it in buying some land out of town and building houses that I could rent out. The 19 million would also pay for my Bachelor's degree school fees at MUBS and perhaps allow me to go on to do a Master's degree."

Have sex with a pothole

I then suggested to Oscar that he ask me a, 'How much would you need to be paid' question. He thought for a few seconds and then said:

"Kevin. How much would you need to be paid to have sex with, I mean to bonk, a pothole in a public place?"

"Well, Oscar," I replied, "The money would be less important than ensuring that the pothole was an extremely deep one."

Who said that *Roving Eye* was a modest fella?

137 years to earn what Ronaldo gets in a day
(19 July 2009)

How long would it take a Ugandan waiter to earn what a top Premier League player earns in a day? I put this question to two Ugandans in my local trading centre in Kampala.

Issa, 32, is unemployed. His reply was brief and to the point. "One year," he exclaimed.

Jim, 36, runs a computer repair shop. However, on this beautifully sunny and warm yet windy Ugandan day, he could not locate the shop key. Instead of holding a soldering iron in his hands, he was sitting on a bench outside his closed shop, holding a bunch of keys which had the crucial one missing. Jim was hoping that his assistant, David, had the shop key. But David was keeping "African time" and had not arrived yet for work. So Jim had plenty of time for thinking, and it was indeed after some considerable thought that he eventually replied to my question. "Kevin, I would think it would take the waiter around 20 years" he said, while managing both to smile and yawn.

So, out came my calculator, and we tried to work out the answer. The first issue we tackled was what a typical Ugandan waiter or waitress earned per month. A waiter in my local bar had told me his monthly salary was Ug Sh 100,000. But Jim's response was, "Eh, Kevin, that is on the high side. They can earn anything from Ug Sh 50,000 to Ug Sh 100,000 in a month."

Anyway, for mathematical ease, and because we didn't want to embarrass our favourite football players too much, we decided to use the higher figure of Ug Sh 100,000 i.e. around Ug Sh 3,300 (£1) per day.

We had read that the top English Premier League player salaries were in the region of £100,000 per week i.e. £14000 per day. So it would take the waiter 14,000 days (i.e. 38 years) to earn the same as the footballer earned in one day. If the waiter was only on Ug Sh 50,000 per month it would take 76 years - and 137 years for this lower paid Ugandan waiter to earn the same as Cristiano Ronaldo (reported to be starting on £180,000 per week at Real Madrid) earns in one day.

Such incredible comparisons are part of the reason why Pele recently issued a warning, appropriately during a visit to Africa where European football has a huge following. He said that "soccer's image could be tainted for future generations if such large sums of money continued to change hands in the sport" (*Daily Monitor*, July 8 2009, p54).

He therefore called for footballers to be capped. By this, he did not mean that they should start wearing something on their heads during matches. But that FIFA should place an upper limit on their earnings.

Of economic and social inequality
(11 October 2009)

Inequality infects every aspect of life. That so many socialistic attempts to engineer equality have miserably failed means most of us accept that a fair degree of economic inequality is required to provide the rewards for business risk-taking and labour effort.

Economic and social inequality mix and match to complicate the picture. But a lot of social inequality is unneccesary, particularly when it takes the awful form of snobbery. In a Third World country such as Uganda, inequality gets stretched to its limits. At the rich end, we see individuals with mind-boggling ostentatious spending power that would turn heads even in the richer First World nations. At the poor end, of course, there is widespread, unremitting, grinding poverty.

Whether it is housing, transport, clothes, churches or whatever, there are hugely different rich and poor ends of the spectra. The same applies to gyms, but with one important caveat – most manual labourers do enough hard, physical work to mitigate the need to enter a gym, even in the unlikely event that their incomes permitted this choice of expenditure. That a side, there are upmarket gyms/health clubs for the rich and downmarket gyms for the not so rich.

The Kabira Country Club in Kampala falls into the former category. Invited there by a member friend, the guest entry fee was Ug Sh 15,000 – I nearly choked on my weak chin. Call me a privileged hypocrite if you like, but I felt distinctly ill at ease at this prestigious club. There were many "big stomachs." This is a good reason for attending a health club no doubt, but after living here for many years, it is difficult not to be affected by the fact that most Ugandans associate "big stomachs" with wealth and corruption.

And the *bazungu* diplomatic and aid community attend the Kabira Country Club in great numbers. Whose poverty they were eradicating, other than their own, on that Sunday, was difficult to say. Most expatriate donor personnel live a lifestyle in the Third World far more luxurious than when back in their own countries. The Club's gym, squash courts, swimming pool, obligatory jacuzzi and other facilities are all superb. But this is what you would expect, isn't it?

Such inequalities make me think of the words of the economist and historian, R.H.Tawney. He wrote that the individual differences in abilities and attitudes between people will always survive; but that their existence is not a reason for not seeking "to establish the largest possible measure of equality of environment and circumstance and opportunity. On the contrary, it's the reason for redoubling our efforts to establish it, in order to ensure that these diversities of gifts may come to fruition."

Tawney's wonderful words are worth pondering in the Kabira Country Club. I did not see much evidence of genuine Uganda sportsmen and women there. The club should consider working with the country's sports federations, so that its membership fee subsidises free entry to the gym of Ugandans who have a genuine chance of participating in the 2010 Commonwealth and 2012 Olympic Games.

A British dog causes surprise in Kampala!

(9 May 2010)

David and Mary were recently chatting in a Kampala bar about David's *kyeyo* experiences in the UK. He reeled off a long line of jobs he had done which included selling fish in a market.

> "But the one I liked the most", David concluded, "was taking someone's dog for a walk for a couple of hours, partly through lovely woods and forests. For that I was paid £50 each time, which is around 150,000 Ugandan shillings."

Well, Mary nearly fell off her chair with surprise, and her astonished reply was:

> "What?! 150,000 shillings for walking a dog for only two hours!"

And part of the shrill noise in Mary's voice was explained by the fact that the monthly salary for her Kampala job just happens to be exactly 150,000 shillings.

When I told the £50 dog-walking story to Fred, who manages a small shop in a Kampala suburb, he said:

> "I'm feeling bad that a person is paid £50 for taking a dog for a walk. Actually, many people here are paid 45,000 shillings per month, like people who work in the local-local restaurants. That means they are only paid 1500 per day. And they are working from 7 in the morning up to 10 at night."

At that point, Derek, who was listening to our conversation, interrupted:

> "Sometimes," he added with feeling, "it can be up to 11!"

> "That's 17 or 18 hours per day for 1500 shillings", Fred continued. So that person would have to work 3 or 4 months to earn the same amount as David earned taking that British dog for a walk!"

When such comparisons are made, other Ugandans doing *kyeyo* in the UK would be quick to point out that while wages are higher there, so are prices. For example, on a recent trip to London, buying a cup of tea cost me £1 (around 3000 shillings), while it only costs me 200 shillings near my home in Kampala. And a journey by underground train from my mother's house in a London suburb to the centre of town costs the equivalent of

15,000 shillings, while travelling by *matatu* from one Kampala suburb to the taxi park is 1000 shillings.

A more talented economist than I could provide all sort of analyses comparing British and Ugandan wages, prices, standards of living etc. Nevertheless, I will not forget for a long time, Mary almost falling off her chair when she learnt about that British dog being taken for a walk.

Jamwa – more guilty than of being fat?
(18 July 2010)

Mr David Chandi Jamwa, the former National Social Security Fund managing director, is extremely fat. In fact, he is so fat that one wonders whether his stomach would prevent him from being able to see his own erect penis. "Is it still there?" he might ask himself as he looks towards his feet.

Fatness is often associated with corruption in Uganda. The archetypical example being the fat traffic cop.

I asked some Ugandans whether Jamwa's fatness made them think he was guilty.

> "No!" Baddne, a 27-year-old IT administrator replied with feeling. "Being fat – he could just be using his salary to make him like that. But that he was in the USA playing casino! That one makes me conclude that he must have abused office."

Baddne showed his anger by adding:

> "Let government take everything he has. It should all be given back to NSSF. Don't leave him with even a T-shirt!"

Radreety, 21, a computer hardware technician, also thought that it was "not his size," but then provided a different explanation of Jamwa's alleged guilt:

> "It is his dress code that makes him look like a big spender. It makes you think that he would have used NSSF money buying bling bling."

Alvin, 27, a Manchester United supporter, was still reeling from the shock of learning from me that his team's second Premier League match of the coming season was away to the mighty Fulham. But he choked back his tears enough to be able to tell me:

> "I think because Jamwa is so fat he must be guilty. It is obvious that he stole the money of the Ugandan workers because he is greedy."

It is possible that Jamwa's obesity is due not to overeating but to a medical disorder. However, this did not appear to be the conclusion of most Ugandans I spoke to. Indeed, David, a 34-year-old small businessman, almost spat out the words – "He is so fat! Let him die of hunger in Luzira Prison!"

There is a famous expression, "You are what you eat." And should it be the case that David Chandi Jamwa spends a large part of his future life in Luzira Prison, then "You are what you eat" will have an added irony for the grossly overweight former NSSF MD, as "eat" in Uganda has a secondary meaning of obtaining money through corrupt means.

Akright should sack its ad agency
(12 September 2010)

There can be few advertising billboards that manage to insult most of Uganda's population in 12 words. But such is the billboard of Akright Projects Ltd, currently found besides many of our roads.

The 12 guilty words are, "A man is called a man only if he has a home." And pictured above this sentence on the billboard is a splendid mansion, the sort of expensive house you would expect to be owned by Mike Mukula – of Global Fund fame (or should that be infamy), whose trial is expected to take place during Obote 3.

The Akright billboard insults 2 key segments of Ugandans: women; the poor.

Women

So where do women fit into the statement, "A man is called a man only if he has a home"? Will the expensive house be jointly owned by the wife? What exactly will be her property and inheritance rights? And, you can bet one of Pastor Crespo Dollar's many dollars that almost all the work in the "man's home" will be performed by women – by the wife, or by the housegirl, or by both. And the domestic violence that occurs in the home will almost always be against women.

The poor

Most Ugandans don't own their own home, let alone an Akright Project luxury type of house. They rent *mizigo*. Thus, Jane and her two children pay Ug Sh 100k per month for the "privilege" of living in a 2-roomed Kampala *muzigo*. While, bachelor Bernard pays Ug Sh 40k per month for a one-roomed *muzigo* without electricity.

So, is Bernard not a "man", or is he only a man when Akright Projects says he can be classed as a man?

According to Joshua Onyait, Akright's marketing manager:

> "The two and three bedroom executive apartments under construction at Akright Kakungulu Satellite City, will be

spread to Namanve and Nansana estates at the launch-price of between sh 64m and sh 82m."

Now, a Kampala waitress working in a local restaurant/bar earns around Ug Sh 60k per month (plus food). So, even if she could save her whole salary, it would take her 1377 months (114 years and 9 months) to purchase the sh82m Akright house. And, unless she undergoes a sex change operation, she might not be permitted to buy her new home, anyway, as she is not "a man".

My advice to Akright Projects Ltd. is to give its advertising agency a red card.

Too poor to buy a newspaper
(6 March 2011)

"The Reader" is a marvellous novel. It was turned into the equally marvellous Oscar-winning film of the same name.

Moving into the plural, "The Readers", as today's cartoon shows, is a term that captures a wonderful aspect of my life in Uganda.

In a bygone era, 8am would find stressed-out me, with thousands of other equally stressed-out commuters, packed "like sardines" in trains, as we negotiated London's Victoria Station.

In Uganda, 8am generally finds a relaxed me reading the newspapers sitting on a bench in a Kampala trading centre, a few minutes walk from my home. But I am never reading alone!

I am in the fortunate position of being sufficiently financially well off to be able to buy the 3 national English language daily newspapers. As I read one newspaper, the other two never lie idle, but are avidly read by Ugandans, who come and sit next to me on the bench.

Such is the demand for reading the news, that I often find myself dividing each newspaper up, so more people can read. And, when I have finished skimming all 3 newspapers, I am encouraged to do my shopping, so the reading can continue for the maximum time, before I must return home with the journals.

Although I knew the answer to the question, I asked one regular reader, 27-year-old Serunkuma, sometimes a driver when he can find something to drive, why he did not buy his own newspaper, but always read mine. He replied:

> "First and foremost, the reason is that I can't afford it. They are expensive. I don't have money to buy."

I wonder how many expatriates and richer Ugandans are aware of this reality that many people here wish to read a newspaper but are too poor to buy one?

A newspaper is a valued commodity in Uganda, and when one is bought, it often then passes through many hands. A small example is that I regularly get people knocking at my gate asking for old newspapers because they want to read them.

That is why the sales of the two leading English newspapers in Uganda are small i.e. only around 30,000 each, but their actual readership is hugely higher.

Why are you not rich?

(2015)

In the recent national sample survey conducted by the *New Vision* newspaper (see final article in Chapter 9), poverty was ranked fourth of the issues that respondents most wanted presidential candidates to address. Among the uneducated, 22% say poverty is their biggest concern after water and sanitation, but drops to 11% among graduates.

In their interpretation of the survey's results (*New Vision*, August 6 2015), Taddeo Bwambale and David Lamu point out that:

> "Respondents in all the regions said sports betting companies were making many Ugandans poor and blamed government policies for the increased gambling activities."

This finding does not surprise me. In recent years, the number of sports betting outlets in my suburb of Kampala has mushroomed, as has the number of people (mainly young men) seen clutching betting slips. As they grasp their slips, they need also to grasp the basic fact that sports betting companies make a profit. So, by definition, there must be more losers than winners, and hence more poverty.

Bwambale and Lamu continue:

> "Corruption, as well as prostitution, drug and alcohol abuse, lack of income generation activities and low sensitisation on government policies, were perceived by respondents as perpetrators of poverty."

I asked a few Ugandans the simple question, "Why are you not rich?"

Ali, 27, is a *boda-boda* motorcyclist. He said:

> "I'm not a rich man. I'm just here. Because this *boda-boda* that I am driving, there is no money, even though I have been working as a *boda* for 5 years. I need another job, but these people {i.e. the rich} don't give us jobs."

When I put my question to unemployed Philip, 28, it required further elaboration. For his initial response was, "Rich, in terms of what? Skills? Expertise? Experience?"

I explained I meant in terms of money, and his response was:

> "I am not rich, but I am getting there. I may be unemployed but I am looking for work – I am networking. But also I am looking at having a personal business, probably in agriculture, growing cassava."

Justine, 25, sells second-hand dresses from a shop just 20 metres from my house. She remarked:

> "I am not poor. I am not rich. I am in the middle – the middle classes. What stops me getting richer is lack of enough capital for buying my stock. I can borrow from a bank or a SACCO but it is kind of risky. If I fail to pay

back, they can just take the security which is my land and house. The rate of interest is not that bad, but it is the fear of losing my security which is the problem."

Victor, 26, runs a small ICT company with his friend Deogracious, 19. Interestingly, the company is housed in a small garage, attached to a house, on the winding path which I use as the back way (safe from speeding cars) down to my local trading centre. The two young men rent the garage from the owner of the house.

Deogracious was optimistic:

> "We are heading there. We will expand the company to get more money. We will join up with the skills of other people, and put them to better use. Can you get for us a contract?"

> But he added, "There have been times in my life when I have been very poor. For example, around 2004 - 5, I was in the village and going to school without shoes."

Over to Victor, who observed:

> "Financially, I am not rich. But I am rich in ideas and skills. It is mainly because of the government that I am not rich. If only they could concentrate on development and on upgrading skills, rather than politics. An example is the Youth Development Fund, which the government set up and is administered by KCCA. It is supposed to help young companies and young people like ourselves. But that is just not the case, and in fact people at KCCA are extremely unhelpful."

> "There have been times," continued Victor, "when I have been extremely poor and down. At school, it was tough, and my parents struggled with fees, with books and with uniforms."

Let's leave the last words to Victor:

> "Rich people today," and the next word he uttered forcibly, "<u>inherit</u> their wealth. But for the rest of us there is no wealth to inherit, as our parents were poor."

12

Health and death

Grey hairs all over the Queen's land
(24 December 2006)

It is just before dawn as my Ethiopian Airlines plane starts its approach to London Airport. I look down to a mass of illuminated streets stretching to horizon – lights, lights and more lights.

The contrasts with Uganda continue inside the airport. In this one terminal, there are 11 baggage reclaim carousels. Entebbe Airport has just one carousel, though the number will increase with the approach of CHOGM.

The first time we go to a new place – or revisit a place we have not been for a long time – we notice a great deal.

In those first few minutes and hours, we see so much that is different from what we know.

I first came to Africa in 1975, and I still vividly remember the journey by car from Nigeria's Kano Airport to the centre of the city. I had not travelled out of Europe before, and I was astounded by what I saw.

Most obviously and immediately, everybody was black! There was hustle and bustle along the road, animals roaming around, and the women carrying goods on their heads, the different types of houses, and much, much else.

And we were only five minutes out of the airport terminal!

And it is not just the baggage carousels that I noticed when I returned to the UK.

The most stunning difference from Uganda is the age of people.

For, in Uganda, young people are everywhere. Uganda's youth are both its challenge and its beauty.

It is a challenge because, with almost 50% of people under 16 years, increasing per capita incomes and giving everyone an education, are tough objectives.

But Uganda's youth are also its beauty, because Ugandan young people are vibrant and generally smile despite their many problems.

When I get into a *matatu* in Kampala, it is not often that there are passengers older than me! But when I return to London I am staggered by the huge number of grey-haired people. Whether it is on the streets, or in shops, cinemas and hospitals of Britain - there are so many elderly people. Grey hairs are everywhere! And I find it deeply depressing.

It may be that because of my own grey hair, I am reminded of my mortality. For, as the proverb says, "Grey hairs are death's blossoms."

But I would like to think that my depression is due to the talk and issues in the developed world being so dominated by old people's concern.

Writer, Simon Raven, explains: "as you get older you become more boring and better behaved."

The life expectancy in Uganda is around 45 years, while in some First World countries it is 80 years and above. So, it is not surprising that after just a few hours in the plane between Entebbe and London, the demographic distance feels greater than the geographic distance.

It is a wonderful experience and privilege to travel to different countries, continents and cultures.

You see much that is strange and unfamiliar. But in those first few hours, drink much strong coffee to keep wide awake, for it is then that the sights are at their most startling.

Burn me when I die!
(31 December 2006)

My mother is 83 years old and we often joke together about her death. I doubt if Ugandan culture could make much sense of the following humour between British mother and son:
- "If you are going to die Mum, could you make it during the low season airfares from Uganda?"
- Or, if I am about to visit her in London for Christmas – "If you are going to 'pop your clogs' (die) Mum, then just after Christmas would be good time – what a bargain, two (Christmas and funeral) for the price of one air ticket!"

On death, my mother, like me, wishes to be cremated. In Uganda the custom in both Christian and Islamic traditions is burial.

When I talked about cremation to a Ugandan friend, she reacted with horror:

"What? You want to be burnt!"

Quite honestly, I find the immediacy of being cremated a much nicer prospect than being buried and slowly being eaten by worms and ants. And there is nothing more depressing than walking around cemeteries and seeing the graves of the long-forgotten dead, overgrown and neglected.

Isn't it typical of human beings' arrogance and self-importance that they feel they have to set up supposed permanent memorials to themselves in a graveyard, even though permanence, in reality, is temporary?

A function of most religions is to allow people to believe that there is something after death - that we are not just eaten by worms. That, for instance, we will meet our loved ones again in heaven (or possibly hell).

The rich and the privileged believe that, as in life, they deserve something bigger and better in death. Their funerals will be bigger, their gravestones will be better, and 12 months after their passing, we will have the "pleasure" of reading in the *Daily Monitor* and the *New Vision* those "In Loving Memory of" notices.

It is possible that bodies of the rich will attract a higher class of worms, for as the American writer, Dorothy Parker, wrote in *Epitaph for a Very Rich Man*, "He lies below, correct in cypress wood, and entertains the most exclusive worms."

Perhaps the utter pointlessness of worrying about how our bodies pass from the now to the hereafter was well captured by the Chinese philosopher, Chuang Tse:

> "Above ground I shall be food for kites (birds); below I shall be food for worms and ants. Why rob one to feed the other?"

Whereas epitaphs and "last words" normally capture human arrogance and self-certitude, they can also capture that human saving grace - humour.

I cannot say I have any admiration for royalty, whether it be Ugandan, British or wherever. But you have to have just a little bit of admiration for Britain's King George the Fifth, who in 1936, uttered one of history's most famous, "famous last words."

The King, when told on his deathbed by his doctor that he would soon be able to enjoy the health-giving air of Bognor, an English seaside town, he is allegedly, but famously, supposed to have replied: "Bugger Bognor!" Well, all I can add is, "Bugger Bbiina!" No gravestone please. And definitely no worms. Just burn me when you are ready, then scatter some of my ashes on the Namboole Stadium warm-up track and some at Fulham's Craven Cottage.

Making use of a digital weighing scale
(18 February 2007)

Oh, we journalists can be a cruel lot! Take, for example, the subject of fat women. Last week's *Roving Eye* featured a young woman runner, who grew so fat during her American sports scholarship, that she is now hardly recognisable as the beautiful athlete, with the perfectly proportioned body, who once graced our athletics tracks.

On the very same day, *Sunday Pepper* had a feature ("Bigger Is Bad: City Celebs who are Flab-ulous!!!"). It listed well-known females, accused of getting fat, or even obese. I am sure Angela Katatumba, Irene Namatovu, Karitas, Straka Mwezi and the many others were not pleased to see their names on the list, especially as, according to *Sunday Pepper*, guys fear dating fat girls because they are associated with laziness, slow thinking etc.

The *Sunday Pepper* did reserve maximum words and maximum nastiness for Straka when it observed that she seems to bulge on a daily basis and cannot maintain a relationship for a week because of her bulging body. Certainly, the transformation of Straka has been dramatic. Was it only in 2000 that I saw a young thin Straka emceeing a karaoke night at Kampala's DV8 Bar?

So, assuming Straka does wish to lose weight, what advice can I offer her?

Diet

Well, there is all the normal dietary wisdom of replacing some of the carbohydrates (rice, posho, potatoes, bread, chapattis etc.) with fruit and vegetables.

This may seem obvious advice, but it is not. For, I have seen fat women desperately trying to lose weight by doing morning aerobics at one of Kampala's most exclusive health clubs, and then immediately afterwards tucking into a huge calorie-filled breakfast. They take weight off, only to put it immediately back on again, and probably with a bonus too!

Digital scales

But, above all, I would advise Straka to purchase some digital weighing scales. The reason is that traditional weighing scales can be problematical when trying to lose weight through improved diet and increased exercise.

As you peer between your feet at the dial of the traditional scales, their distant and slightly moving figures often make it difficult to know whether your weight has decreased, increased or stayed the same. But modern digital scales give you your weight, in large exact numbers, to a tiny fraction of a kilo.

Motivational

So, if you weighed 80.5 kilos yesterday, but because of your diet/aerobic efforts weigh only 80.4 kilos this morning, the improvement is highly motivational and will encourage you to replace some of that posho with greens at lunchtime, and perhaps get to the aerobics session this evening. Such improvement breeds the desire for further improvement, but can result in strange behaviour to achieve it. Thus you may find yourself:

- Pushing extra hard when answering nature's "long call" in order to remove all unnecessary weight from the body before stepping on the scales.
- Taking off your wrist-watch before weighing, just in case that is the vital difference in making the numbers on the scale move in the desired downward direction.

So, Straka, invest in some digital weighing scales and that body of the year 2000 could be yours again.

Let me know if you are successful and I will send you my invoice!

Obituaries – lies and more lies

(4 March 2007)

The first verse of Philip Larkin's famous poem is:

> "They fuck you up, your Mum and Dad
> They may not mean to, but they do.
> They fill you with the faults they had
> And add some extra, just for you."

These are marvellous words, and so very, very true.

342   *Insights into Uganda*

Obituary page

While Larkin spoke the truth, it is strange that I was reminded of his poem by the typical untruth of an obituary/in memoriam page in a Ugandan newspaper.

Here is an example drawn from such a page:

> "Precious memories of a loving husband, father and grandfather.
>
> The gap you left behind will never be filled.
> Your hard work remains the family's treasure."

So, if this is the untruth, what is the truth?

Let's go through the "in memoriam", line by line.

Line 1

> "Precious memories of a loving husband, father and grandfather."

OK, but the most vivid memory you left behind was the shock on the face of Mummy (your "official wife") when your two *kyanas* arrived at your funeral, both sobbing as loud as Mummy, and bringing several kids with them. As monogamous Mummy recently tested positive for HIV/AIDS, she finally knows the reality of her "loving husband".

Line 2

"The gap you left behind will never be filled."

Given that, despite your attendance at church every Sunday, you left behind 15 children by three different women, it is reasonable to assume that "the gap you left behind" will be more than adequately filled.

Line 3

"Your hard work remains the family's treasure."

Agreed, you did work hard when you were in your office. But, it is also true, that every evening when you finished at the office, you went to your favourite bar, and then got home very late, often drunk. And furthermore, one of Mummy's "co-wives" is none other than a barmaid, at your favourite bar.

My father

Although this obituary/in memoriam was drawn from a Ugandan newspaper, the untruths are much the same, the world over. I have had wonderful parents, who gave me opportunities, especially educational opportunities, that they never had themselves. But when it came to writing the tribute to my father that was read at his funeral, I am aware that although I wrote predominantly truth, I did deliberately omit one or two not-so-very-good points in his character.

Uganda – more lies

Are Ugandan obituary/in memoriam newspaper pages more untruthful than say a British newspaper page equivalent?

The answer is "probably yes". The reason lies with Uganda's history. Before the coming of the Christian missionaries, Uganda was openly and truthfully polygamous. There were "co-wives", but each wife knew their place and position. But then the British, French and other missionaries arrived in Uganda, and encouraged Christian monogamy.

The result is that today, in Uganda, we have the worst of both worlds. We have people, especially men, who pretend to be monogamous (like on a Sunday), but who, in reality, are polygamous.

So, they live a lie. And then when it comes to their death, what do we get? We get another lie, this time on the obituary/in memoriam page of a Ugandan newspaper.

Would you shake hands with Jim Muhwezi?
(16 September 2007)

The National 20 kms Road Racing Championships took place last Sunday in Rukungiri. The Chief Guest was Jim Muhwezi of Global Fund and GAVI infamy.

My wife is a better driver than me, so while she was behind the wheel for the long, hot, 6-hour journey, my tough duties were limited to changing the music cassette in the player. In other words, I had a lot of time for thinking.

One thought that kept recurring in my mind was, "Should I shake hands with Jim Muhwezi?" My wife and I are usually the only *bazungu* present at such athletics events, so we do rather stand out like beacons. And I am a particularly bright beacon with its long grey hair on top. We often get pushed forward to meet V.I.Ps. In which case, should I, or should I not, shake hands with Jim Muhwezi?

David, a friend who had some involvement in the Ogoola Global Fund Commission told me earlier:

> "Now, come on Kevin, you are presumed innocent until proven guilty. And Muhwezi has not had his 'day' in court yet."

My reply was:

> "Now, **come on David**, even if only a percentage of the Ogoola Commission findings are true, then there are Ugandans who are dead today, who would have been alive, had it not been for Muhwezi's mismanagement and alleged corruption."

Waiswa, a 35-year-old Kampala small businessman, also took a pro-shaking Jim's hand line, but added a big dose of social snobbery. He said:

> "If it was just a local person, then I can refuse to shake hands. I would just ignore them. But if that someone is well-off, someone who is recognised {like Muhwezi} then you can't fail to shake hands."

A reason why David and Waiswa feel that they should shake Muhwezi's hand is to be found in Desmond Morris's *Peoplewatching – A Guide to Body Language*. He writes:

> "We seem to be incapable of beginning any kind of encounter without performing some type of salutation {greeting}. This is even true when we begin a letter to someone. We begin with 'Dear Mr Smith' and end 'Yours

> faithfully' ... even when Mr Smith is far from dear to us, and we have little faith in him.
>
> "Similarly, we shake hands with unwelcome guests and express regret at their departure, even though we are pleased to see the back of them."

However, an unwelcome guest is one matter, but life (which a well-managed Global Fund could have enabled) and death are surely a whole different matter.

So, what did I do in Rukungiri? Well, however my *Roving Eye* columns may come across, in the flesh I am actually an anxious man who generally prefers to stay in the background. Muhwezi flagged off the race, made his speech, and gave out the prizes. And despite me being well-known in Uganda, and being the coach of the runner who came second and almost won the woman's race, I stayed well and truly in the background. Muhwezi and my paths never crossed, so I did not have to make a decision about whether to shake his hand.

But if I learnt two things from my late father, they were running and morality. Bold gestures can be important in life, and a braver man than me would have sought out the opportunity, and refused to shake Muhwezi's hand. I apologise for being a coward.

Antiretroviral drug money "eaten"
(4 November 2007)

There are many non-corrupt Ugandans, but sometimes it does feel that corruption finds its way into almost every aspect of Ugandan society.

On a national level there is the current trial of three former health ministers and a presidential aide, accused of mismanaging immunisation funds.

But it is on a personal level, with supposed friends, that corruption can be the most wounding. I told Stephen's story in "Ugandans and zero sons & daughters" in Chapter 2, but let me repeat it here. Ten years ago, Stephen, who my wife and I had treated like a son, tested positive for HIV. At that time, the price of antiretroviral drugs was hugely expensive and far beyond our own financial means. So we asked our relatives and friends to make monthly standing order payments into our bank account to fund Stephen's treatment. After accompanying him on his initial visits to Mildmay Hospital, we then gave him the money every month so he could buy the drugs there himself.

Sometime later, Stephen told us that his company was sending him to Djibouti for a four months training course. Our first thought was "what about your drugs?" So we gave him the money to buy four months worth of drugs.

Many months later, Stephen had not got back in touch with us. We contacted Mildmay and to our horror, we learnt that for an almost two year period, he had not been there to buy the drugs. He had simply been "eating" the money contributed by our friends and relatives. There had also been no training course in Djibouti – it was a clever piece of fraud to extract the maximum money from us.

Last weekend, I was reminded of the ubiquitous (everywhere) nature of corruption when watching the Cooper (FIFA Referee) Test at Mandela National Stadium. One of the fitness tests involves running 150 metres repetitions on the athletics track starting from the crown of the bend.

Over the years, I have seen these tests about six times. The large majority of referees complete the test fairly. But there is always a minority who, as they get tired, cut the bend. They therefore run a shorter distance i.e. pass the fitness test by crooked means.

For God's sake, these are the men and women that we are entrusting with upholding the rules and regulations of football. But, then again, according to the Ogoola Commission, the Global Fund also had its rules and regulations broken. Whether it be cheating referees or it be the misuse of funds, corruption is corruption.

Budget should increase tobacco taxes
(1 June 2008)

Yesterday was 31 May. "So what?" you may say. Well, 31 May is a most important date as it is the World Health Organisation's, *World No Tobacco Day*. This marvellous festival of health traditionally allows the *Roving Eye* column to take a look at the tobacco issue.

Anti-tobacco case
The anti-tobacco arguments are well-known, but to summarise: tobacco is the NUMBER 1 preventable cause of death in the world. Tobacco smoke contains more than 4000 chemicals, at least 50 of which cause cancer. Tobacco kills almost five million people worldwide each year. If current trends continue, it is projected to kill 10 million people a year by 2020, with 70% of those deaths occurring in developing countries such as Uganda. Tobacco also takes an enormous toll on health care costs, lost productivity, not to mention the pain and suffering inflicted upon smokers, passive smokers and their families. *And,*

it is more painful to die of cancer in Uganda, as most hospitals and clinics do not have the sophisticated pain-relieving drugs that are readily available in rich countries.

These are pretty powerful arguments, but if you need any more persuasion, listen to Vice President Gilbert Bukenya who, during a 2007 tour of West Nile, stated that tobacco growing should be abandoned in favour of other cash crops, as tobacco farming had made the people poorer i.e. tobacco increases poverty.

So, what to do? Well, the good news is that Uganda signed, then ratified (June 2007) the World Health Organisation's Framework Convention on Tobacco Control, the world's first global public health treaty. Its implementation will mean that Ugandans will become more aware of the dangers of smoking, for example, through large, powerful warnings on cigarette packets, which will replace the current tiny weak ones.

Tobacco taxes

The tobacco industry normally tries to defend itself in Uganda by pointing out that it is a "tax cow". Thus, in 2006/7, the Ugandan government generated Ug Sh 49.59 billion in tobacco taxes.

But, this is where it really becomes interesting. So, dear reader, without any intended rudeness on my part, please could I ask you to read the following sentence twice?

- Increasing tax on cigarettes will both increase Ugandan tax revenue *and* reduce Ugandan deaths and sickness.

This sentence is worth reading twice, just to take on board that it captures a wonderful win-win policy option i.e. both the Ministry of Finance and the Ministry of Health should argue for an increase in tax on tobacco in Uganda's 2008 budget, which Dr Ezra Suruma will finalise after his return from Japan on June 4.

In a memorandum delivered to the Minister of Finance on May 2 2008, three "Tobacco or Health" activists (Dr Margaret Mungherera, Mr Phillip Karugaba and this columnist) concluded that a 20% increase in tobacco excise duty would increase Ugandan tax revenue by over Ug Sh 5 billion per year. Just think how many schools, hospitals and clinics could be built with 5 billion shillings (not to mention Ugandan lives saved and suffering reduced).

The reason why such a tax increase would increase tax revenue is because the demand for cigarettes – to use the language of economics – is *inelastic* i.e. if the price of cigarettes increases by a certain percentage, the quantity consumed will reduce, but by a smaller percentage. This reality is explained by the fact that the nicotine component of tobacco is addictive – it is indeed tough to quit smoking, even when its cost increases.

Ugandans suffer and die from malaria, from HIV/AIDS and from much else. But there is no need for Ugandans to suffer and die from tobacco-related diseases. The most simple and effective way to stop this unnecessary suffering is to increase taxes on tobacco, thereby also increasing government revenue. Let's hope the Minister of Finance, Dr Ezra Suruma, is listening to this genuine, heartfelt plea.

When you should use the "F-word"

(3 August 2008)

Roving Eye will shock readers by today using the "F-word" - in his very first paragraph and on a holy Sunday as well. So let's ignore those religious thought police in their towers of hypocrisy. Courage, Kevin, courage. Here we go then; no turning back now --- "*Fitness*".

So I've said it, and although I have spat an "F-word" in your direction, let me start by gently explaining that this "F-word" does not refer to fitness to hold public office. Though, that many hold office, but few are fit to do so, is an observation that has stimulated many journalistic articles and editorials.

In the areas of sport and exercise, fitness can be understood in different ways.

There is the extreme fitness of Haile Gebrsalassie and Maria Mutola, which we "mere mortals" find difficult to comprehend, let alone copy.

For us ordinary human beings, we should not take as our point of reference genetically favoured, single-minded fanatics, sometimes called world class athletes.

We need to ask more gentle questions of ourselves, like: "Can I do a little bit of exercise without getting out of breath?"

When the answer is "no," this is often linked to a second "F-word" .... "*Fatness*".

If you are overweight, then it may not worry you. After all, much African culture looks at fatness more tolerantly than in First World countries. Many Ugandans view fatness in terms of success, of having made it in life, and then make a related link to corruption.

But varying degrees of obesity (extreme fatness) carry varying degrees of health risks.

Examining diet and alcoholic (especially beer) intake can provide keys to losing weight. As can increasing the amount of exercise taken.

But as with all such New Year-type resolutions: How to keep going? How to remain motivated?

The first tip is to record progress. Seeing improvement in written down, objective terms, is itself a source of motivation, especially to those wedded to a mindset of performance/achievement levels by their education and by their bosses.

It is very easy to measure your weight (in kgs or lbs) at regular intervals. Measuring your fitness is trickier. But simple fitness tests done at home (why pay to join an expensive gym?) are OK e.g. the number of situps in a minute; or pressups or squat thrusts per minute.

A minute can be a surprisingly long time, so if you are unfit, you can use 10, 15 or 30 seconds, to begin with, before moving on to a minute. And if you are very unfit, a medical checkup is advised before you try improve your fitness.

A second tip can powerfully increase your motivation to keep going: exchange your weight and fitness test levels with a friend. In the past, I have exchanged them with a senior journalist and a computer expert, by emailing them a progress chart, at fortnightly intervals. They sent theirs to me.

As the two weeks drew to a close, I found myself desperately peering at the weighing scales, fitting in some extra walking/jogging, and – heaven forbid – even drinking less beer. I am now temporarily teetotal, and one beneficiary of not drinking alcohol (other than my wife and potential "arguees") are the weighing scales.

It may all sound a little comical, but it works. And the reasons are straightforward. We humans are generally competitive souls who like to succeed. We want the approval of our peers and superiors, and we don't like to lose face, even when it is failing to lose a fat, bloated face!

You may never become a Haile Gebrsalassie or a catwalk model, but if you are overweight, and don't like it, then use one F-word (Fitness) to get rid of another F-word (Fatness).

The man who saved my life
(12 October 2008)

"This man saved my life" is a phrase I have never used before in this column. But, today, it is a truthful and genuine observation.

So, about whom am I referring? Let me start by saying that I am not referring to Pastor Benny Hinn, nor any other of those so-called healers, whose only genuine saving is into their bank saving accounts.

The man who saved my life was Dr Peter Sherpakova, senior consultant neurosurgeon at Mulago National Referral Hospital. It was with great sadness that I have just learnt from a newspaper that Dr Peter passed away in the Ukraine on 1 September 2008.

Let me tell you the story. It was early 2003 and, by this time in my life, I had lived for so long in the Third World that I walked anywhere, at any time, without fear. Nothing bad had ever happened to me, so why should it happen on a January 2003 evening? It was a month later that a Ugandan lawyer friend told me, "You must have been mad, Kevin. A *muzungu*, walking near Kampala's Old Taxi Park, at night, carrying a briefcase!"

Whether the thug, like so many in Uganda at present, was carrying an iron bar, I have no idea, because I don't remember anything about the attack. But I was very seriously mugged.

While I had previously received many massive blows to my ego, this was the first massive blow to my head.

Now, I have to admit that, despite loving Uganda, it would not be my first choice of country in which to undergo brain surgery. Let's face it, corruption is so bad here, that you might never see your brain again.

But my wife was told at Kampala's International Hospital that I had a badly fractured skull and a large blood clot on the brain and, if I was not operated on immediately, I would die.

It was Dr Peter who, that night, performed the operation. The world only missed one *Roving Eye* column, for within 10 days, I was back at my keyboard. Friends have told me that I made a complete and total recovery, which I think is true, because my jokes are just as bad as they always were!

And if you think I am ugly, you should have seen me when my long hair was shaved off for the operation. Grown men and women used to look at me, and then run away in the opposite direction, screaming and shouting.

So, unlike those fake healers who, from time to time, make appearances at Namboole Stadium crusades, Dr Peter, you were a genuine healer. You used your medical knowledge and science to save the life of many people, including one humble journalist, who no longer walks near the Old Taxi Park (nor even the New Taxi Park) at night carrying a briefcase.

Dr Peter, I was not at Namungoona Orthodox Church on Friday to celebrate your life. Nor will I do so at any church or crusade. But I would like to thank you, a practitioner of rational medical science, for saving my life.

Unseasonal thoughts on death
(28 December 2008)

Three days ago, Christians around the world celebrated the birth of Jesus Christ. It is worth pointing out that there are many people of other religions, or of no religion, who do not believe that Jesus Christ ever existed. Or, that if someone called Jesus Christ did exist on planet Earth around 2000 years ago, he was a remarkable human being, possibly the Nelson Mandela of his time, but that he was not the son of God.

Death

Whatever the truth of these matters, it is a birth that was foremost in people's minds last Thursday. So *Roving Eye*, with typical lack of seasonality, will not consider the subject of birth, but the subject of death, and especially the obituaries and death announcements, that appear in newspapers.

When I lived in the UK, my understanding of "obituary" was an account of someone's life, normally of a famous person, that appeared in a newspaper shortly after they died. It would be written by journalists and would attempt to be *balanced* i.e. as well as covering good points, the obituary would also describe that person's weaknesses/shortcomings/faults.

Death announcements

Such *balance* poses challenges in Uganda, given the strong African cultural tradition of not speaking negatively about the dead. Furthermore, what are described as "obituaries" in Ugandan newspapers are more akin to death announcements. They are adverts, often with a photograph of the deceased, which announce the death, or commemorate the anniversary of the death. The adverts are paid for by the family, and in line with cultural traditions, only contain positive comments about the deceased.

My impression is that such death announcements form a bigger part of a Ugandan newspaper than, say, a British newspaper. If this is correct, then, there are several possible explanations.

Firstly, life expectancy is around twice as long in the UK than in Uganda. Therefore, there will be more deaths in Uganda and hence more death announcements. However, one must also take into account the lower per capita income in a poor Third World country like Uganda, which means less resources are available to fund such newspaper adverts.

Death's importance

Secondly, does the marking of a death have a bigger role in African culture than elsewhere? There are traditions like the lighting of fires, sitting with the body overnight, looking at the face of the deceased through a glass panel in the coffin, last funeral rites etc. – none of which took place when my father died in London a few years ago.

The first funeral service I attended in Uganda, was of a driver at the office I then worked in. One memory of that church service was the sobbing and wailing of one particular Ugandan lady – so loud that it seemed she might "raise the roof" of the cathedral. It was some time before I was to hear such loud sobbing and wailing again – it was from Manchester United fans after Fulham went to Old Trafford a couple of years ago and beat Man U.

"Play acting"

But to return to being serious, back at the office after the funeral, a number of the lady's younger Ugandan colleagues told me that they thought her noise in the church had been completely "over the top" and that she had been "play acting".

Recently, I asked my friend Patricia, a 43-year-old Ugandan professional working in the education sector, about some of the behaviour patterns surrounding death in Uganda. She said:

> "It's our tradition. It is what people have learnt from their parents. For example, the wailing at a funeral. Some people wail because they are genuinely sad. Others because they think it is the right thing to do."

Patricia, who has lived all her life in Uganda, apart from 3 years when she worked in both USA and UK, continued:

> "Yes, some people do play act. For instance, when my sister died, there were some people wailing who did not even know her. This sort of behaviour is acceptable because it is part of our Ugandan culture, but in Europe, for example, it would be regarded as unacceptable exhibitionism. And it is noticeable these days, in more elite Ugandan families, there is less wailing, and more quiet, dignified crying."

Conclusion

Cultures change and people come and go on life's stage. Whether souls rest in eternal peace, or whether there is nothing after death, just the eating of buried bodies by ants and worms, is, of course, not for me to say, but for readers to adjudge according to their own belief systems.

Could tobacco play a part in Uganda's population control?

(1 March 2009)

A tobacco control workshop I recently attended in Ghana put the following question in my mind – could the Ugandan government use cigarette smoking as part of a population control policy?

The country's economic growth is impressive. However, because Uganda's population is growing too quickly, the result has been lower, than otherwise, increases in income per head. This begs the question as to whether tobacco could have an important role to play in Uganda's population control.

Death rate 1 – Killing yourself

Tobacco smoke contains more than 4000 chemicals, at least 50 of which cause cancer. Around 1.3 billion people smoke worldwide – half of them will die of a tobacco-related disease before their 50th birthday.

The tobacco industry argues that it is people's choice whether to smoke or not. In reality, there is no choice, since tobacco contains addictive substances, such as nicotine, which drag the smoker towards wanting another cigarette after another cigarette. They therefore find it difficult, often impossible, to quit smoking and instead use money on cigarettes they could otherwise have spent on items like food, clothes and education.

The more Ugandans there are who smoke, the more Ugandans there will be who die - thereby increasing the country's death rate and reducing its population growth rate.

Death rate 2 – Killing others
But these extra deaths do not end with the smokers themselves. The smoke they blow out is inhaled by non-smokers (including babies and children) and can kill them. "Second-hand" smoke, therefore, further increases the death rate and reduces population growth.

Birth rate 1 - Impotency
It has been proved that tobacco use can cause erectile dysfunction (impotency). Cigarette packs should carry a warning, "Smoking can seriously damage your penis". Male smokers who suffer in this way will have fewer or no children, thereby reducing both the birth rate and the population growth rate.

Birth rate 2 - Kissing
In the mating process between human beings, kissing is generally found at an early stage, with sexual intercourse and the production of children, coming at a later stage.

Now it has been said that when a non-smoker kisses a smoker, it is rather like kissing or licking an ashtray i.e. the taste is disgusting.

Thus, the more Ugandans who smoke, the more they will put off potential sexual partners, thereby introducing delays into the mating process, and reducing the country's birth and population growth rates.

Conclusion
Dear reader, the above makes some serious points. But, in case you have not realised *Roving Eye*'s sarcastic humour, tobacco should definitely **_NOT_** be considered as a means of reducing Uganda's population growth rate.

The dangers of alcohol

(20 September 2009)

The British Medical Association has just demanded that the UK's government ban all alcohol advertising.

Alcoholism and related alcohol problems are as bad, if not worse, in the UK than they have even been. A recent survey has shown a worrying amount of boozing by 12 to 16 year olds.

This is all bad news for Uganda. For it emphasises that if a rich country like the UK - with all its greater resources and higher educational standards - cannot solve its alcohol problems, it is impossible for a poor country, such as Uganda, to do so.

Therefore, from the angle of Uganda as a country or a society, the future on alcoholism looks bleak, even hopeless. Furthermore, Uganda has the additional problem of crude cheap alcohol, produced in its villages and towns, which the rich countries do not have.

But for individual Ugandans who are addicted to alcohol, there is hope. For instance, there is a worldwide organisation called *Alcoholics Anonymous* (normally just referred to as "AA") which has meetings at different centres around Uganda and in Kampala. One group meets for one hour at Christ the King Church in Kampala, every Tuesday and Friday at 1pm.

And should you be a "big man" or "big woman", don't worry that you might be recognised at a meeting, as confidentiality is one of the rules of AA.

Around the world, AA has solved many people's alcohol problems, including those of many Ugandans.

Let me now nail two alcohol lies. Firstly, that alcohol companies pay a large amount of tax revenue to the government, so aren't they wonderful! However, what readers should also recognise is:

- The health costs incurred by the government of treating the damage to Ugandans' bodies and minds caused by excessive boozing.
- The damage to individual's work and to their family life (especially domestic violence against women) caused by alcohol.
- The deaths and injuries caused by drink/driving.
- Increasing HIV/AIDS and unwanted pregnancies in Uganda, since the decision to have sex, including unprotected sex, often takes place after drinking booze.

The second lie is the warning that appears on alcohol adverts i.e. "Not to be bought/consumed by people under 18". In my opinion, this is all part of the marketing policy of multinational booze firms to increase their sales. The typical young teenager wants to break rules, rebel, be naughty, experience adulthood before they should etc. So, when a 15-year-old sees "Not to be bought/consumed by people under 18", they are more likely, not less likely, to put extra effort into getting booze, thereby increasing the sales and profits of alcohol companies.

If you have an alcohol problem don't despair. Try to get in touch with one of the various organisations in Uganda that can help you, such as AA. Please, click on the following link for further information https://recoveryministries.wordpress.com/ministries-2/aa-support-group/aa-meetings-uganda/

It could be the start be of new and better chapter in your life. And, given that so many Ugandans are poor, imagine the benefits of the money that is not now wasted on alcohol, being instead spent on food, clothes and school fees.

There is a way out of the alcohol trap.

Pet insurance – whatever next

(15 November 2009)

The London recreation ground was bathed in glorious autumn sunshine. The most notable part of my view, other than the tall majestic trees surrounding the park, was the large number of pet dogs being exercised by their owners.

The *Roving Eye* column has commented before on the hugely different attitudes towards pets in developing countries like Uganda compared to affluent countries. For example:

> "A pet in a rich country, typically a dog or cat, is kept for no other purpose than company and friendship. It will be well fed, normally on meat twice per day, and will sometimes be overweight. So for most Ugandans – struggling to meet human family needs such as school fees, medical expenses etc. and enjoying meat just on big occasions – it is not sensible to own a pet, and indeed any animal which does not have an obvious purpose."

And moving from socio-economics to culture, a Ugandan once told me"

> "The idea that a dog is dirty is ingrained in the African mind… and in Luganda, if you want to insult somebody, you just tell them, '*Oli ng'embwa*' ('you are like a dog')."

So, I know a little about how Ugandans view animals, but I realise there is much I don't know and which will surprise me. But when it comes to animals and pets in London, my town of birth, surely not much will surprise me. Oh, foolish me! Stupid

Kevin gets it wrong again. For, on a recent visit to London, I was stunned to stumble across – and this is not a joke – pet insurance. I did not know such insurance existed on this planet. But as I found brochures in supermarkets and in the post office advertising pet insurance, I assume that this type of insurance must be common in Britain and other developed countries.

One brochure began:

> "Injury or illness can happen all too easily to any pet... give them the best professional care and attention... so you can relax in the safe knowledge that should anything happen to your pets, all you have to worry about is getting them better.....by just paying a few pounds a month."

So if, for instance, an insured dog experienced one of the following, then, on average, the insurance company could pay the owner the approximate figure in brackets:

Fractured leg (£1,200); road traffic accident (£700); heart disease (£600): spinal problems (£900): lameness (£700).

Given that most Ugandans do not even have health insurance for themselves or their families, they would surely find pet insurance an unbelievable concept.

Where will it all end, you may ask? Well, an airline has recently been established in the USA catering exclusively for pets! Now, I trust that a typical London dog-owner will regard this, like me, as a bizarre news item, and that "it could only happen in America". But I was totally ignorant on pet insurance, so when it comes to the future of pet airlines, don't use me as your expert consultant, but only as your bottom-of-the-class dunce!

Do you pick your nose?

(7 February 2010)

An early childhood memory is of my mother telling me loudly, "Don't pick your nose!"

Of course, one can pick one's nose both on its outside and on its inside, but she was definitely referring to inside picking!

And what was a young Kevin exploring for inside his nose? I was looking for what is referred to in English slang as a 'bogey', (sometimes spelt 'bogy') – a small piece of dried, or drying, nasal mucus.

Naughty children can do rather unpleasant things with bogeys e.g. attaching them to objects, like the underside of a chair, in order to hide them from parents or teachers. They have even been known to flick bogeys, missile-like, at other children.

Adults, generally, don't pick their noses in this way. But they may do so unknowingly, without thinking. I plead guilty to occasionally finding my finger inside my nostril! And, very, very, very occasionally (I hope) the guilty finger has even been inside the guilty nose in a public place!

In a Kampala trading centre, I spoke to two Ugandans about bogeys and noses. Gerald, a 24-year-old shop assistant said:

> "In Luganda we would say *okusokola enyindo* for nose picking. If I wanted to say 'stop picking your nose' to a child, I would say *'lekera'wo okusokola enyindo.'* For your word 'bogey', we would use *obukakampa*. There is a similar word in Luganda *ekikakampa* which is the hard skin of a wound that has not cured yet. *Obu* means small and *eki* means large."

"From your description, Gerald," I observed, "the English word for *ekikakampa* is scab."

Leonard, 27, runs a small cosmetic shop, and after listening to Gerald and myself, said:

"In Buganda culture, we regard picking the nose as bad manners. For example, I can't talk to someone when I am doing this".

Leonard put his finger inside his nostril to show what he meant – no doubt relaxed by the fact that I had done the same when explaining the subject.

Then, as his final comment on nose picking, Leonard said with emphasis and feeling, "It's backward!"

Gerald added:

"It's considered unclean. For instance when you are going to share something, or shake hands with somebody. After all, our world is a world of sharing. However, I do find myself sometimes picking my nose, but not in public."

However, Gerald's last comment is not entirely correct. Our conversation about the subject had started when he was picking his nose at the entrance to his shop i.e. definitely in a public place with many bystanders.

But it is not only Gerald and *Roving Eye* who sometimes unknowingly pick their noses in public. On the internet, there are websites where you can allegedly "Watch (the British Prime Minister) Gordon Brown pick his nose and eat bogeys in Parliament live."

So, it would seem that we all sometimes pick our noses. But it is best to avoid doing so on live TV!

All good wishes to Mr Gureme

(3 October 2010)

F.D.R. Gureme, or should that be Mzee F.D.R. Gureme, has never been my favourite Ugandan journalist. And I say that in full knowledge that I live in a culture where the elderly are rarely criticised.

The reason for my dislike of his articles is that they are so often about .... himself, with so many words devoted to describing his "achievements" during his 84 years. When Mr Gureme starts to write, then conceit has no bounds.

Even in a recent interview with Arthur Baguma ("The pros and cons of turning 84 years old", *The New Vision*, 17 September 2010) Gureme could not refrain from telling readers that he had been "an extraordinarily brilliant child".

I once wrote an article entitled, "To ink or not to ink", about the advantages and disadvantages of dyeing one's hair. I know from Mr Gureme's article in response that he is an "inker" (he would be that type of man, wouldn't he?) and therefore can be added to the list of prominent Ugandan males (Kabaka Ronald Mutebi, Prof. Apollo Nsibambi, Mayanja Nkangi, Mulwanyamuli Semwogerere, Muganwa Kajura, Mathias Nsubuga) who, according to *Red Pepper* (23 September 2010, p 23), are "inkers".

But while Gureme may "ink" and be immodest and altogether "full of himself", I felt genuine sorrow and sadness when I read the Baguma interview. For Gureme describes his past "sharp retentive memory", but now says:

> "My memory is leaving me....amnesia has taken its toll....
> What I do not understand is that I remember things my

grandmother used to tell me, but easily forget things of yesterday."

These are the classic symptoms of Alzheimer's disease, something that my 87-year-old mother also suffers from. Two of her sisters had Alzheimer's so, it may be genetically common in my family. My nephew and I sometimes joke when we can't remember something – "Is it the early onset of Alzheimer's!?" But, although there are now drugs available that slow down its progression, Alzheimer's disease is no joke. It is sad to see the memory of an elderly person deteriorate, and Alzheimer's is well-captured in the cinema by films like "Iris" (about novelist Iris Murdoch), "Away From Her" and "The Notebook".

All good wishes to Mr Gureme as he fights memory loss.

Shortages and corruption in the health sector
(2015)

The final article in Chapter 9 showed that in the national sample survey conducted by the *New Vision* in June 2015, health was ranked top of the list of areas that respondents wished presidential candidates to address.

The health issues were ranked as follows (percentages are rounded to the nearest digit): drug shortages within health centres/ambulance shortages (53%); few health centres/long distances to them (16%); few health workers (15%); rude health practitioners (12%); none (6%); poor maternity services (5%); high cost (5%); corruption (5%); malaria (4%); no hospitals (3%); unlicensed/unqualified health practitioners (3%); poor sanitation within the community (2%); poor salaries (1%); don't know (1%); chronic illnesses (HIV, TB, diabetes) (1%); lack of toilets/latrines (1%); poor sanitation within health centres

(1%); expired drugs (0.5%); family planning (0.2%); illegal drugs (0.2%); poor health insurance (0.2%); poor sanitation related diseases (diarrhoea) (0.2%); high rate of abortion (0.1%); refused to answer (0.1%).

While a shortage of drugs and ambulances was top of the list with 53%, this average disguises some pronounced regional variations. Such shortages were described as their biggest health problem by 75% of respondents in the northeast and 65% in West Nile.

I decided to visit my local *dduuka* in a Kampala suburb to discuss the survey results and related health issues.

Its owner Jackie, 45, agreed that "drugs are not there in health centres, especially village ones."

Jackie went on forcibly to highlight a problem she had recently encountered:

> "The most typical challenge I face is that doctors are very slow. They are not active. For example, last week, I went to a government hospital in Rubaga. And they delayed. I went there very early in the morning and they did not see me until after lunch. We were there without food. The doctors said they were in a meeting. But there were many patients."

Drinking at the *dduuka* were Mark and Brian. Mark is 25 years old and has just finished a Bachelor's degree in Business Computing at the Makerere University Business School (MUBS), but is currently unemployed. He remarked:

> "The biggest health problem in Uganda is HIV. The youth lack sex education. So they can infect each other."

Mark was staggered to learn that HIV was only ranked 15th in the *New Vision's* health survey, mentioned by only 1% of respondents, especially as this percentage also included TB and diabetes.

Brian, 22, is studying for a Diploma in Computer Science at MUBS. He observed:

> "I believe corruption is the biggest problem in the health sector, which is a mess. The Ministry of Health deploys doctors and nurses to government hospitals. Therefore their names are on the payroll. They collect their salaries, but in reality are doing private work."

> "I know a hospital in Arua," continued Brian, "where the doctor just appears for 2 or 3 days at the end of the month before he disappears for his private work. The Ministry of Health has been informed of this but takes no action. I suspect he is conniving with someone at the Ministry."

Mark then neatly brought together two of the issues (shortages and corruption) considered in this article. I would like to say that he spat out the following words with anger, but instead it was with a wry, "what can you expect", smile. He said:

> "The reasons why there are no drugs is because of corruption. The government gives the drugs to the hospitals and health centres, but they are taken away and used in private practice. Even in Mulago, you can be diagnosed, but you have to go outside and buy them, and you are often directed towards the Mulago doctor's own private clinic. Or, if you want to get the drugs within Mulago, you have to pay someone extra money to get them."

My discussions at the *dduuka* put some flesh (or should that be rotting flesh) on the *New Vision* health survey, and left me deeply depressed.

13

Katogo (mixture)

Hurdles in telling humour

(14 January 2007)

There are not many *Bazungu* who have won prizes in Uganda FM radio competitions, but I am one of them. When I had to collect a prize from Dembe FM, the disc jockey, "Bina Baby", interviewed me on air.

During the interview, I cracked a joke and Robinah said: "Kevin, you should be a comedian!"

I was struck by that comment as humour is very, very important to me. I look around myself and I see many self-important, pompous human beings. Sometimes they are rich and privileged. Sometimes they are royal or religious. But always they need to be deflated with the pin of humour.

On another level, poverty means that many Ugandans have tough lives. If I can make a poor Ugandan smile, it gives me a boost, and I hope it gives them a little boost in dealing with their daily, and many, challenges. If life's cards had been dealt differently, it could have been me, and not them, who were poor. So, none of us should forget the saying, "There, but for the grace of God, go I."

But in attempting to make people laugh in Uganda, I do face one big hurdle. For, of all things, it is humour that has the greatest problems in crossing cultures.

My British upbringing means that my jokes are heavy in sarcasm and cynicism. Therefore they are often not understood in Uganda, where statements are generally interpreted by their literal meaning.

But a joke that creates laughter is a source of pleasure. For example, here is a joke that, two years ago, made the *boda-boda* men, down at my local trading centre, laugh.

Its basis was the Carling Cup Final (Liverpool vs Chelsea) which resulted in the following type of headline in Ugandan newspapers over the weekend of the match: *United, Arsenal to close gap*.

In other words, as the then league leaders, Chelsea, had no Premier League match, it gave Manchester United and Arsenal a wonderful opportunity to close the big points gap between them and Chelsea.

So, I told the *boda-boda* men, who know I am a Fulham supporter, that:

> "As Chelsea are playing in the Carling Final, it gives Man U, Arsenal and Fulham a great chance to close the gap on Chelsea."

Well, the *boda-boda* men laughed long and loud! For the gap between Chelsea and Fulham was, at that time, a mere 39 points! My joke had worked!

Telling a joke in my pidgin Luganda, is a bigger challenge, since not only must the humour cross cultures, but the listener needs firstly to realise that I am indeed speaking Luganda, and secondly understand Luganda words spoken in a heavy London accent.

And sometimes, therefore, the joke is not understood, and the resulting lack of laughter means that I remember the words of the nineteenth century novelist, George Eliot:

> "A different taste in jokes is a great strain on the affections."

But it was the French novelist, Colette, who said:

> "Total absence of humour renders life impossible."

So, when the joke is successful, it is marvellously rewarding to hear the air filled with the wonderful music of human laughter.

In trouble for speaking out
(22 April 2007)

Over the years, *Roving Eye* has put forward a variety of controversial views. For example:
- The genocidal contribution of the Catholic Church to the HIV/AIDS epidemic owing to its anti-condoms dogma.
- The immediate legalisation of abortion in Uganda.
- The boastful demonstration of wealth by Mike and Gladys Mukula to *African Woman* magazine about their Kampala residence.
- That the "W" in George W. Bush must stand for *Wanker* (slang for someone who masturbates) and his pea-brained obsession with Iraq will provide a presidential legacy of enduring shame.
- That Mr S. Kadokech, a supporter of female genital mutilation (FGM), needed to be castrated in order to

experience sex without orgasm, one of the many horrible results of FGM for women.

Unpleasant email

The articles always end with my email address as I enjoy receiving feedback from readers.

The most unpleasant email I have ever received from a reader, stopped just short of suggesting that I should be executed. The fate she proposed was that, amongst other things:
- Ugandans should rise up against imperialists (supposedly like me).
- I should be deported.

Interestingly, her hatred of all things *Roving Eye* was not caused by a column on any of the controversial topics described above.

The *gomesi* and sumo-wrestling

So, what had brought her abusive opprobrium down on my pointed head with, even by *muzungu* standards, its extremely large, nose ……..It was that I had dared to admit, in a previous article, that I found the *gomesi* an unattractive and unflattering garment. And then, with a touch of typical *Roving Eye* humour, I had added that a fat Ugandan woman wearing a *gomesi*, with its *ekitambala* (sash) perched on her stomach, bore a distinct resemblance to a Japanese sumo-wrestler.

Culture

Well, that reader certainly attacked me with all the power and force of a sumo-wrestler, but unfortunately, she had failed to understand my article. For, it was only minimally about the *gomesi*. Its subject was how our attitudes (and our likes and dislikes) are very much shaped by the country/culture we grow up in. Thus, had I been born in Luwero, and not in London, 54 years ago, and had spent my whole life in Uganda, then almost certainly I would today find the *gomesi* a beautiful costume.

Young Ugandans

The article also pointed out that some Ugandans, particularly younger ones, shared my dislike of the *gomesi*.

Thus, Mary, a 23-year-old business studies student, told me:

> "I hate them (*gomesi*). They are hot, and the *kikoyi* make them especially uncomfortable to wear. I had to wear a *gomesi* to a *kwanjula* recently. But I took it off immediately after the ceremony. I only wore it to be respectful to the older family members. But if it had been up to me, I would have left the awful thing at home."

There are many aspects of the traditions and culture of Uganda that I love and admire. But the *gomesi* is definitely not one of them. I just hope that the lady who sent me the email does not have the strength of a sumo-wrestler. As, if I meet her on a Kampala street, she might unleash a few painful slaps in my direction.

To comb or not to comb – that is the question
(6 May 2007)

Combing one's hair. A straightforward subject you may think. But living in Uganda has shown me that it is a subject open to some interesting cross-cultural differences.

During my previous life in the UK, I would have combed my hair in public hundreds, possibly thousands, of times. It is a normal thing to do there. But a few years ago, in Kampala, I had just got out of my car, and because the wind had disturbed my hair while driving, I began combing it. The Ugandan companion who I was moving with, told me sharply:

> "Kevin, don't do that! We, Ugandans, don't comb our hair in public places."

This was news to me, and a surprise. So, I asked three Ugandan friends for an explanation.

"Ash" and "lice"
David is a 22-year-old barman who told me:

> "Many years ago, before the coming of the electric razor, Ugandans used to cut or shave their hair less often. It was therefore longer, and some people would have 'ash' {dandruff} and even lice in their hair. It was thus thought very wrong to comb hair in public, because these things might fall on food or people. Such an attitude towards combing has remained until today, even though the electric razor means that most people's scalp and hair are very clean."

Hygiene
Mzee "Name Withheld" runs a small grocery shop in a Kampala trading centre. He observed:

> "Culture doesn't allow us to comb in public. Hygienically, hairs are supposed to be left in saloons or gazetted areas."

At the mention of 'gazetted areas,' I asked:

> "Mzee, do you mean I can comb my hair in Mabira Forest, 'coz that is a gazetted area, or at least it is at the moment?"

> "No! That is not what I mean, Kevin," replied Mzee. "What I mean by gazetted area is, for example, an open space in the village where a barber works. But if I combed my hair in my shop it could easily fall into the sacks of beans, rice and flour."

Ladies' toilet

Finally, I turned to Violet, a 26-year-old marketing manager. She observed:

> "As an African, combing hair is considered a bathroom or bedroom issue, as part of dressing up. Even at work, I will still go to the 'Ladies', considering there's a mirror, and make up my hair."

So, there you have it. The comb in my pocket will have to be strictly out of bounds as I negotiate public places in Kampala and elsewhere in Uganda.

And now, as the classic British comedy show of the 1970s, 'Monty Python' had as its catchphrase, "for something completely different."

Bishop Tumuhairwe

Last Tuesday's *Red Pepper* (p6) ran a most serious story about Bishop Nathan Tumuhairwe who had been arrested for allegedly beating up his wife. However, the newspaper gave the story some unintended humour with its headline: "BISHOP ARRESTED FOR BEATING WIFE INTO COMMA."

I asked myself whether it would have been any less serious had he beaten his wife into a 'question mark' or a 'semi-colon'? Was this a case of unintended *punch*uation? At least, as I write, the Bishop's wife's life had not been brought to a 'full stop'. Perhaps, *Red Pepper*'s Managing Director will order that the future use of the word 'comma' in its headlines should be put into a 'coma', along with the combing of hair in public places.

Bus passengers must be more outspoken
(9 September 2007)

This article concludes with 5 questions to *Gateway Bus Service Ltd*. The following words were written by my wife, Sue:

"On Monday 27th August, shortly after midday, I was driving from Kampala to Jinja when I was involved in an incident that could have proved fatal. I was waiting to overtake the car in front, but could not, as there was much oncoming traffic. Another vehicle was travelling behind me. Suddenly, and seemingly from nowhere, a *Gateway* bus (reg. UAG 152J) came thundering past us at high speed, horn blaring loudly, and heading straight towards the oncoming traffic. It passed so close to our vehicles, that all three of us were forced off the road. The oncoming cars also had to get out of the path of this menacing monster. A head-on collision was narrowly avoided.

"Coming to a halt near a ditch I was thoroughly shaken, as was the driver of the car in front of me. As I drove past, he was still sitting at the wheel, staring ahead, as if the realisation of how close he had come to death was just dawning.

The bus driver's rudeness
"A few kilometres ahead, I noticed that this same bus had stopped to pick up passengers that had been off-loaded from another coach. But buses rarely leave Kampala with empty seats. So, UAG 152J was presumably already full, begging the question – why were more passengers being allowed to board? Was bad driving now being followed by corruption?

"Incensed at what had happened earlier, I decided to take a stand. I pulled over, got out of the car and went to confront the bus driver who was now overseeing the loading of passengers.

When I told him how close he had come to causing a fatal accident by his reckless overtaking, his response was to shout, "Since when has overtaking three vehicles been illegal?" This angered me further and I asked for his name, as I intended reporting him to the *Gateway* management. He replied, 'I'm called F**king'. Eventually, realising I was deadly serious he reluctantly gave me a name (but whether it was his real one, I have no idea).

The bus passengers

"I turned to go and could hear him laughing. However, before leaving the scene, I boarded the bus and made an impassioned plea to the startled passengers: they should not allow bus drivers to behave so recklessly; innocent people are dying on Ugandan roads everyday because of such dangerous driving and that one day they themselves might become victims of some fatal bus accident. And with that, I left.

"Further ahead, and within a short distance of each other, were the scenes of two earlier accidents, one involving an overturned petrol tanker, the other a trailer that had plunged off the road. I hoped the passengers of the *Gateway* bus saw these accidents as they hurtled past, and pondered on my earlier words."

Ugandan passivity

My wife's account raises many issues, one of which is the attitude of the passengers of bus UAG 152J. Ugandans are renowned for their friendliness. But a component of this is often a certain passivity, or as one senior Ugandan journalist once put it to me, "An unwillingness to confront issues". But in this one area of life at least – road safety – Ugandans need to be less friendly, less passive, and be prepared to be forcibly outspoken.

As individuals, or in a group, they must order their bus drivers to slow down/drive more carefully. Or, in *matatu* taxis, such as in Kampala, where the fare is paid at the journey destination, they should threaten the driver with non-payment unless he immediately improves his driving.

5 questions for *Gateway*

So, here are my questions to *Gateway Bus Service Ltd*:
1. What disciplinary action do you intend to take against the driver of UAG 152J?
2. Is UAG 152J fitted with a speed governor?
3. Are all your buses fitted with speed governors?
4. Are they regularly maintained?
5. Can they be tampered with by drivers to enable speeding?

The Monitor's Letters' Page awaits *Gateway*'s response.

Author's Note

Gateway suspended the driver as a result of this article.

Kevin meets a seer

(30 September 2007)

There has been much in recent newspapers about seers (prophets) e.g. "The seer's prophecy unfolds as Uganda, Rwanda heads to DRC" (*Daily Monitor*, September 8 2007) by Timothy Kalyegira. In an earlier article, Kalyegira had "quoted the seer as predicting that Uganda and Rwanda would once again fight as they did in Congo in 1999."

So, it was timely that on a recent visit to my local trading centre that not only should I "see" a seer, but that I should also receive a detailed set of prophecies.

I recognised him as a seer as I could just spot the grey hair of wisdom peeping below his inked black hair. And his only requirement of me was that I should buy him a bottle of *Nile Special* before each prophecy. So, we settled down in a bar, and the future began to unfold.

> "I foresee," said the seer, "that Pastor Martin Ssempa's newspaper articles will be just as nonsensical in 2008 as they were in 2007."

I deliberated on this astonishing insight, as I bought the seer his second *Nile Special*. As for me, I was only going to drink soda, as if I was to fully appreciate the seer's wise words, my brain must not be affected by booze.

> "I prophesise," continued the seer, "that there will be no *Big Brother Africa* evictions in 2008 as there will no *Big Brother Africa* TV programme."

Then, the prophecies began to flow as fast as the *Nile Special*:

- "In 2008, Kevin's hair will remain as long and as white, and his nose as large."
- "There will be more and bigger potholes in Kampala."
- "The Cranes will not win the Africa Cup of Nations."
- "Many 'Are you ready for CHOGM' posters will not have been taken down, along with one remaining poster from Pastor Peter Ssematimba's failed Kampala mayoral campaign."

I bought the seventh bottle of *Nile Special*, and as I sat down at our table, the seer staggered back from the toilet. He said:

> "This must be my (burp) last beer, otherwise I will *susu* in my trousers."

> "O wise one," I replied, "please make your final prophecy a big and important one."

So, the seer thought long and hard and then his eyes, as red as Manchester United's shirts, looked equally long and hard at me. What followed was an inspirational moment that I will remember until my dying day:

> "I predict" said the seer, "that in 2008, Fulham will win the European Champions League."

As my team is currently lying 4th from bottom of the English Premier League, so it indeed takes a human being with very special powers to foresee such an outcome.

I helped the seer stumble out of the bar and on to a *boda-boda*. Fortunately, I have his mobile phone number. So if you, Timothy Kalyegira, or anybody else wishes to make use of his powers of prophecy, then please email me at the address below. I have agreed to act as the seer's agent and will only be charging a 15% commission per prophecy.

Gadaffi renames Uganda

(30 March 2008)

Tomorrow is the last day of March, and March 2008 will surely be remembered in Uganda for Col. Muammar Gadaffi's visit. Indeed, our newspapers/radio/TV could tell us about little else, and for lovers of alliteration (i.e. using several words together that begin with the same letter or sound) let me say that we definitely did have "Muammar Manic March Media Madness".

And, in the unlikely event that we might forget his visit, we have namings/renamings to provide permanent reminders. Of course, there is the *Gadaffi National Mosque*. But a Kampala street has been renamed after the Libyan leader, and according to *The New Vision* (March 25, p3) "the Government has erected a giant monument at Buganga, Nkozi to honour Libya's {1980's} support to the liberation war". Perhaps the monument should be extended to include the many Libyan soldiers who were killed in 1979 while trying to prop up the murderous Idi Amin regime, but memories can be both short and selective when required.

With so much naming and renaming taking place in honour of Gadaffi, let's identify some additional possibilities.

Roving Eye's first suggestion is *Gadaffi Dark & Lovely Hair Dye*. My hair started going white in my late thirties. I cannot accept that at the ripe old age of 66 years, the Libyan leader has totally black hair. Yes, I allege that Muammar Gadaffi is an *inker* (as opposed to an *Inca*, who used to live in South America).

Secondly, the Libyan security men gave "bloody noses" to their Ugandan counterparts, the Presidential Guard Brigade (PGB), at the mosque opening. According to *Red Pepper* (March 25, p4), during a scuffle, "the PGB were beaten hands down by the well-equipped and technically better drilled Libyan guards." So, move over PGB and *Saracen*, the *Gadaffi Alarm Protection Services* (GAPS) will indeed fill gaps in Ugandan security. Though an alternative name is *Gadaffi Alert Guards* (GAG) since a gag is no doubt useful should the security men come up against anybody who does not agree that revolutionary leaders should rule for ever.

Thirdly, the construction of the *Gadaffi National Mosque* dismantled Fort Lugard, replacing it with something that is not even a replica. In his March 25 letter to the *Daily Monitor*, Ellady Mutambi (Executive Director, Historic Buildings Conservation

Trust) wrote that when the Libyan contractors relocated the old building "the original structure was changed by using other materials, yet it was supposed to be a replica". When religion meets history, in this example at least, religion won, so let's rename Fort Lugard as *Fort Gadaffi*.

For the fourth and final naming/renaming, I turn to *Microsoft Encarta* which states that "in 1977, Gadaffi instituted the so-called *jamahiriyah* (Arabic, "state of the masses")" in Libya. Now, it was the Queen Marie Antoinette who, not long before the 1789 French Revolution, famously displayed her ignorance of her subjects' poverty. On being told that the poor had no bread, she is alleged to have replied, "Let them eat cake". *Roving Eye* will now display his ignorance of the masses by declaring "Let them eat jam", indeed "Let them eat *Jamahiriyah Jam*".

Resignation – not the Ugandan way
(4 May 2008)

There have been calls for the Minister of Education, Ms Geraldine Namirembe Bitamazire, to resign over the Budo Junior School fire tragedy. Bitamazire resign? You must be joking! Or, as tennis player John McEnroe would have put it, "You cannot be serious!"

I have no idea how much blame should be attributed to Ms Bitamazire for the fires at Budo and other schools. But what I do know is that resignation is not part of the political culture, or perhaps just not part of the culture, in Uganda.

The *Roving Eye* column previously analysed this issue ("We Ugandans don't feel shame" *Sunday Monitor* October 22, 2006) when considering why Messrs Muhwezi, Mukula and

Kamugisha did not resign over the Global Fund scandal, but waited to be pushed (i.e. sacked).

In contrast, in many countries and socio-political cultures, it is often the case that a government minister will resign when a very serious shortcoming is unearthed in their ministry. It is considered by themselves, by their peers, and by society at large, to be *the honourable thing to do*.

An insight into why the Bitamazires of this world are not resigning folk was provided by an interview she gave to the *Monitor* in August 2003. Much of what she said was interesting. But one sentence really stood out. Concerning her 46 years working in the education sector, Ms Bitamazire was asked: "What is your biggest disappointment?" She replied:

"I wouldn't really point at any disappointment right now."

In other words, I have not done anything I now regret......... Or, put another way, I have not made any mistakes. So, someone with this mindset is hardly likely to resign, are they?

Yet, with the possible exception of the Messiah, and the Fulham goalkeeper, everybody makes mistakes, everybody has disappointments.

And Bitamazire is not alone in whitewashing her past. The producer/interviewer of a popular Ugandan TV programme told me that when she asks interviewees, especially the 'big men', "what are your regrets" or "what one thing in your life do you wish you had done differently", the replies are generally very short, with minimal information provided.

But when she asked me the same questions, she could not stop me talking! My list of regrets and disappointments was longer than the belt holding up a corrupt traffic policeman's trousers.

So, why are so many prominent Ugandans not prepared to talk openly about their disappointments and failures?

> "It is just the way that we Ugandans have been brought up," Michael, a 40-year-old publisher told me. "For even in the home, a father, for instance, will not want his wife and children to know his failures."

While, John, a lawyer, added:

> "In our culture, we do not like talking publicly about losses and disappointments. For example, if we have problems, we just say we have problems, without going into further detail about them."

All politicians talk too much. And of politicians, ministers talk the most. But of the very many words that come out of Ugandan ministers' mouths, the two that will not be there are, "I resign".

Getting on top of your problems
(26 October 2008)

You and I, indeed every human being on Earth, have problems of varying sizes. Today's column considers how a simple mental prioritisation of past and present problems, can help reduce your worry and stress.

Cliff Sempijja, 25, lives in a Kampala suburb and by using 3 of his problems as examples, today's column will draw more general conclusions, some of which may be relevant to you.

Problem 1 – The chicken
Cliff is an unpaid social worker/church leader, which might lead on to him becoming a pastor. The main source of family income is his mother's roadside vegetable stall, and Cliff

regularly helps her out selling potatoes, tomatoes, onions, *mukene* (silver fish) etc.

Last weekend, I was driving past and I noticed that their stall had been left unattended. Perched in the middle of the stall was a very fat chicken, enjoying an early Christmas lunch in October. It was voraciously eating from the stall, or more correctly gorging itself as if "there was no tomorrow". So, later in the week, I asked Cliff whether the chicken was theirs. He replied:

> "No, Kevin, the chicken was certainly not ours! We have a problem with the next shop. Their chickens keep on coming around. And I tell you it has really become a big issue 'coz they eat and destroy things. We don't want to hit them 'coz the owner will become so angry with us."

Cliff served a woman buying *obumonde obuzungu* (Irish potatoes) - she would surely have bought *lumonde* (sweet potatoes) had I not been standing there! Cliff then continued his story:

> "We have told our neighbouring shop-owner several times about this problem, but she only assures us how she will give us chicken parts when she cooks and prepares them for Christmas. But this does not solve anything as by the time Christmas comes about, we would have lost a lot of things such as *mukene*. Then, there is hygiene - the chickens leave watery droppings around our stall, which can even make my customers run away. I hate those chickens."

Problem 2 – Tuition fees

Cliff and I moved on to discuss another of his problems. This requires few words, as it is a problem shared by very many Ugandans – tuition fees. He took a deep breath and said:

> "I finished my A-levels {Biology, Chemistry and Agriculture} two years ago. My dream was to go to university and become a doctor. But I couldn't afford the tuition fees for campus."

Now, "every picture tells a story" and Cliff's worried face told the obvious story that the tuition fees were a much bigger problem for him than his neighbours' chickens.

Problem 3 – Drinking acid

We then considered one of Cliff's past problems. He continued:

> "When I was 14, something terrible happened in my life. My young brothers had been playing and they put a large amount of white acid powder from old batteries into a cup. I came home, thought it was sugar in the cup, poured tea into it and then drank it all. It burnt my stomach big time. I nearly lost my life. Fortunately, my big brother, who knows something about medical things, was there and got me to drink large amounts of water. A lot of life came back and I got better."

Cliff's story struck a chord with me, for as readers of a recent *Roving Eye* ("The man who saved my life", 12 October 2008, in Chapter 12) will know, I also came close to death in January 2003.

Conclusion

Cliff and I concluded that while the chicken problem and the tuition fee problem were problems, they were of much less importance than the biggest problem Cliff had experienced in his life – drinking battery acid. For, if his big brother had not been present, Cliff may have died, and he would not in October 2008 be talking to me outside his mother's vegetable stall. And similarly, if my brain surgery in a Kampala hospital had been unsuccessful, I would not be standing there talking to Cliff.

By prioritising past and present problems in our mind we can reduce the anxiety/worry/stress of whatever problem today brings us.

In similar vein, it is sometimes worth thinking how much worse things can be. You may have many problems this week, but you could have been in that terrible road accident that killed 30 people at Lugazi, or under those walls which collapsed at the NSSF building construction site.

I know these mental methods are rather simplistic. But they have sometimes helped me. And they may help Cliff. And they might help you.

How I pity corporate managers of 2009
(15 March 2009)

Despite experiencing "burnout" in 1996, I still realise that managerial life was relatively easy then, compared to 2009, due to additional challenges faced by managers today, resulting from informational technology developments.

1996
Even as a British Council senior manager, in March 1996, on my desk at work, there was only:
- One landline telephone, with my secretary filtering all phone calls.
- One intray (OK, it did sometimes resemble Mount Everest, given the huge number of files in it).

Two other March 1996 key points:
- We did not have email – only fax and telex.
- I had never used a mobile phone.

2009

In contrast, 2009 managers have information hitting their brains from intrays, landlines, mobile phones and email. Furthermore, high-powered, high-flyers use strange things called blackberries.

As a low-powered, low-flyer, living in a modest Kampala suburb, until recently I thought a blackberry was a fruit that grew on bushes. Blackberries, in the information technology sense, enable the very dubious pleasure, while sitting on the toilet at 6am in the morning, of not only receiving phone calls, but also emails.

Of all these technological developments, I am glad that the mobile phone did not exist in my pre-1996 management career. I could spend several weeks holiday travelling around Uganda, and while I might still have work in my brain, nobody from the office could contact me by phone, so it was easier to relax.

I raised these issues with 3 Ugandan managers, heading companies and organisations of different sizes.

While playing golf

John, 33, is a successful Ugandan businessman, who is the MD of a company employing 12 people. He lives in the up-market Kampala suburb of Bugolobi. He said:

> "It happens all the time. One moment I am relaxing playing golf. Then, I answer my mobile phone and immediately it turns into a stressful moment – I stop thinking golf and I start thinking about whatever is the latest crisis at work."

Fun in Jinja interrupted

Sheila, 35, is a small businesswoman who employs 4 people in her Kampala shop. She told me:

> "One time I was having fun in Jinja with my husband and kids. An important client phoned and wanted me to come back to Kampala and solve her particular personal problem. My thoughts went away from Jinja and back to my shop."

No interest in wedding and no sleep

Dorothy, 45, heads an important Ugandan professional association and is also chief executive of a private business. She said:

> "I was having a nice long weekend, 3 hours drive outside Kampala. I was attending a wedding. I got this phone call on my mobile and was told that there was a meeting I should be chairing in Kampala! It had completely slipped my mind!"

> "I was absolutely helpless," Dorothy continued, "I lost interest in the wedding. I felt like a fool, very disappointed with myself and extremely stressed. I did not sleep a wink that night."

Conclusion

On a recent BBC World Service Radio programme, Neil Tennant (lead singer of the pop group *The Pet Shop Boys*) observed:

> "New technology has a tremendous momentum" (i.e. moving forward at an extremely rapid speed) "and this momentum invades people's privacy."

How right you are, Mr Tennant.

Children, church and carnage
(31 May 2009)

Uganda's road carnage (slaughter/deaths) has rightly generated many newspaper articles. Today's *Roving Eye* provocatively continues the discussion, based on his observations in one Kampala trading centre.

Vehicles turning right at its T-junction, frequently do so on the wrong side of the road's central divide. This is to avoid the congestion caused by a taxi stage in the other lane. The congestion is usually brief, so if the reckless drivers instead used the correct lane, their journey would only be delayed by around 10 seconds.

I asked two workers at the trading centre for their views on these drivers' dangerous behaviour.

Primary school

A visibly angry David, the owner of a video library, loudly exclaimed:

> "They know they are breaking the law when they come round the corner in the wrong lane. When I cross the road, I only look the way they are supposed to be coming from, so they can easily kill me. I am 34 years old, so imagine how much more dangerous it is for a child."

David's comment about children is very relevant, as opposite the T-Junction, is a primary school. Now, it has frequently been thrust down my throat by readers responding to previous *Roving Eye* articles, that African culture regards children as "a blessing". But does this only apply to one's own children? Or, to other people's children as well?

Nearly every driver approaching that T-junction will know that it is next to a primary school, with many children crossing the roads at different times of the day. Dead children, killed by reckless drivers are, presumably, not a blessing, but a tragedy.

Church

Not caring about killing other people's children is an extreme form of selfishness that links to the comments of David's assistant, Larry, 24, a part-time business studies student. He observed:

> "Those drivers are impatient. They only think of themselves. They do not think of others."

Larry's words rang in my ears more loudly than the bells of the church which is also right next to the T-junction.

Inside that church people, at least in theory, are taught not to "only think of themselves", but to think of others i.e. to treat their neighbours as themselves.

Questions

So, I leave you with two questions:
- To what extent are the horribly huge number of deaths and injuries on Ugandan roads due to factors found in many developing countries e.g. poor vehicle condition, potholes, poor (or no) driving instruction, drivers with no licences etc. etc. ?
- And to what extent are those deaths and injuries just due to unchristian selfishness?

It is indeed easier to ask questions than to answer them.

A small lie told in Kampala

(14 June 2009)

I normally start my day by skimming through the Ugandan newspapers, while sitting on a wooden bench outside a small shop in a Kampala trading centre. One morning, I was surprised to find that the bench was not there. The two teenage shop assistants told me it had been stolen.

I later described this theft to Luke, 25, a Ugandan friend. I added that the thief would surely sell the bench to make money. Luke replied:

> "Kevin, I don't think the thief would sell the bench. It is more likely that he was going for funeral rites (*olumbe*). It is our tradition, that we put a fire (*kyoto*) outside the house of the deceased. In Kampala, it is hard to get firewood, so there is a lot of stealing by mourners, of wooden things like benches and tables."

Later that week, Edward, 45, the shop-owner, was present and laughed loudly when I asked about the stolen bench. He said:

> "The bench has **not** been stolen. Let me explain. A thief came at night and broke into the shop from the room behind. He stole many items. The next day, we moved the bench from outside the shop to the room behind. We did this because idlers, some of whose identities we do not know, sat on the bench during the day. We think that some look at our products with a view to later stealing them. But I had told my shop assistants that the bench should be brought out from the room for *good* customers like you."

"Phew!" I jokingly thought to myself, "isn't it wonderful that a strange-looking, long-haired, sunglass-wearing, eccentric, ageing, hippy, with virtually no bum or chin and an exceedingly long nose, should still be regarded as a *good* customer."

"Why my shop assistants did not bring the bench outside for you," Edward continued, "is that they did not know enough English to give you a full explanation about the robbery. So, they found it easier to tell you that the bench had been stolen, and therefore gave you a stool to sit on."

I draw two conclusions from the above.

Firstly, as the bench had not been stolen, the shop assistants had told a small lie. I can understand a language-based reason as I do appreciate some of the shop assistants' situation in reverse i.e. I can only speak horribly pronounced kindergarten Luganda. But as soon as I have to go beyond anything more difficult than *akasana kaaka nnyo* (the sun is shining), I have to speak in English. However, I do hope I would not tell a lie.

Secondly, although I have lived in Uganda since 1994, and am aware of *olumbe* and *kyoto*, I knew nothing about the stealing of wooden items by some mourners. In other words, even if I live until I am 185 years, there will still be much about Ugandan society and culture that I do not know or understand.

The importance of the 50th anniversary
(22 November 2009)

Next Saturday is a hugely important 50th anniversary. But before that global event is revealed as a world exclusive in today's *Sunday Monitor*, let us look at other examples of 50th anniversaries.

October 9, 2012 will be a massive 50th anniversary for Uganda, as it will be half a century since the country gained its independence from the colonial power. I wonder how it will be marked? How the marvellous memory of the birth of Uganda as an independent nation will be celebrated?

From time to time, we see photographs in our newspapers of elderly Ugandan couples celebrating their 50th wedding anniversaries. Around the world, the 50th wedding anniversary is normally referred to as golden, the 25th anniversary as silver, and for the small number of couples that make it to 60 years of marriage, it is their diamond anniversary.

Given Uganda's low life expectancy, it would be interesting to know what percentage of Ugandan couples actually make it through to their golden anniversary i.e. are still alive and together after 50 years of marriage. For such couples who do stand this challenging test of time, their special anniversary is indeed worthy of celebration.

All sorts of 50th anniversaries come and go. Other 2009 50th anniversaries include: the birth of Motown Records; the Antarctic Treaty; the first successful space flight by a living being (monkeys called Able and Miss Baker); the hovercraft; the recyclable aluminum beer can and the Barbie doll.

I was in Britain recently when the 50th anniversary of its first motorway (the M1 between London and Birmingham) was celebrated. Despite there being countless items on TV and radio, it was an anniversary that barely registered in my brain.

So what is the important 50th anniversary taking place next Saturday, and which has definitely registered in my brain?!

Let me start by telling you what it is not:
- For readers who think that I am older than I am, let me confirm that Saturday November 28, 2009 is not my golden wedding anniversary. I have known my wife a long time, but not that long!

- And for readers who think I am younger than I am, especially any beautiful ladies, I regret to inform you that I am sufficiently aged to have been in primary school way back in 1959.

So what is this 50th anniversary that wills be celebrated next Saturday, from America to China, from the world's biggest cities to its smallest villages and on which day our newspapers will be especially thick to accommodate all the extra feature articles, advertising and advertorials? It is this:

- On Saturday November 28, 1959, *Roving Eye* attended his very first football match at Fulham's Craven Cottage.

As a small seven-year-old, he was held up by his father to see over the heads of the standing crowd. Fulham beat Burnley 1-0, Jimmy Hill scored the goal, and 50 years on, I can still vividly remember the ball hitting the back of the net.

There can therefore be few bigger dates in world history as Saturday November 28, 1959, and that is why humankind attaches such importance to next Saturday's 50th anniversary.

O'Connor and hand movements
(28 March 2010)

It's got to be 'O'. Sorry, it's got to be O'Connor. And as O'Connor walked into his local trading centre in Kampala recently, he came upon a collision between a *kamunye* (*matatu* taxi) and a lorry. Fortunately, it was a minor accident – nobody had been hurt and the police were already present.

Now, *Roving Eye* found something extremely interesting about this scene. Well, he would, wouldn't he? His catchphrase is, after all, "For the observer of human behaviour, every scene has its interest" – a phrase that he has repeated in his column more times than two famous Premier League footballers have had sex since marriage with women that weren't their wives i.e. an awful lot of times.

What was interesting were not the vehicles, now blocking the road, preventing traffic from passing and thereby ironically stopping even more accidents from happening on Uganda's dangerous roads. What was interesting were the 50 or so Ugandans standing around the vehicles, in animated conversation with each other.

I say "Ugandans", but more correctly I should say "Ugandan men". For, in local trading centres all around this country, the people who have got nothing better to do than partake in idle chatter are almost always men.

I swear on the Bible (which, for an atheist, does not mean very much, does it?) that almost all these excited men were gesticulating in the same way i.e. they were throwing their arms/hands down from an upward position to down by their sides.

Although there are all sorts of different body language around the world, I have rarely seen this double arm gesture elsewhere. When I asked Daniel, a 24-year-old shop assistant, about it, he said:

> "It's a sign of expression. It's like emphasising. For example, if I said, 'Kevin has knocked someone', then I might throw my arms down by my side. Another example is if my girlfriend offered me a packet of condoms when I wanted live sex. I would throw my arms down by my side as I said, 'I don't want them, damn it!'"

How appropriate that "it's got to be O'Connor" ends his column on condoms. My nickname is not Kevin O'Condom for nothing.

Learning something new

(25 July 2010)

Sixteen years after setting foot on Ugandan soil for the first time, there is still so much about its culture and society that I don't understand and which require an explanation from a Ugandan to destroy my ignorance.

This can apply to big things or to relatively small things in life. An example of the latter is provided by my car journeys along a murram road near my home. For no apparent reason, there are small rocks scattered along a section of it.

I find myself weaving between the rocks as I drive, rather like a skier doing slalom on a snow slope. Sometimes, I have to stop and wait while oncoming cars also negotiate the rocks. On one occasion, when I thought a rock was small enough to pass beneath my car, it got stuck, and the vehicle would not move forward. Anxiety rushed through my brain, and I feared I would have to call a mechanic to solve the problem. But fortunately, by reversing the car, I was able to move free of the rock.

So, why are the rocks there? I knew the road was being prepared for tarmacking, so perhaps the rocks were in some way connected with that? But that explanation didn't seem to make any sense.

It was not until I spoke to Sarah, a 45-year-old financial specialist, who must also negotiate the same road by car, that light was thrown on the issue.

With little rain recently, murram roads have grown dusty. But this road is especially dusty because of the long, long gap between the flattening of the murram and the arrival of the tarmac. Sarah explained that speeding vehicles are throwing up a huge amount of dust, which covers the houses next to the road. Some of their inhabitants had, therefore, put the rocks on the road to slow down the traffic, thereby reducing the dust.

Indeed, previously, I had often seen vehicles speeding on this road, especially large four-wheel drives, going up the hill to the more luxurious houses at its top.

So, Sarah had added a little bit of knowledge to my understanding of Uganda. But my road to understanding Uganda has many rocks and potholes of its own. And it is a road so long that it has a destination at its end that I will never reach in my own lifetime even if I live to Obote 3 or to Uganda winning the World Cup.

Construction ignorance

(21 November 2010)

As the *Roving Eye* column has pointed out more times than new districts have been created in Uganda, it is important in life to know what you don't know. Thus, when it comes to building and construction, I am fully aware of my ignorance.

After all, after 3 years at secondary school, when a new curriculum forced me to choose between giving up chemistry or giving up Latin, I continued with Latin.

Thus, I can tell you that the word "science" comes from the Latin *scire* meaning "to know". While "construction" has its root in the Latin *struere* meaning "to build".

But when faced with a pile of bricks, after demonstrating my knowledge of Latin, I would have no idea what to do with the said pile. And as for the construction resulting from the bricks, I would not know whether it was built like a pack of cards or like a brick shit-house.

Let's put my appalling ignorance on the back-burner for a few moments, while we consider Uganda's building boom. It has certainly transformed the Kampala suburb I have lived in for fourteen years. Walk along a road one year, and hardly recognise its surroundings when you pass along it the next year.

I have put this construction boom down to Uganda's striking economic growth rate and rising income of its middle classes. But a *Sunday Monitor* reader provided a different explanation in an email:

> "Have you never wondered what fuels the country's eternal housing boom and why the rate of new cars accelerates all the time, while cars and houses (and loans) are without doubt hugely expensive in relation to even the best local salaries?"

His answer to these questions was <u>corruption</u>.

Finally, let me tell you about a certain landlady. She knows a lot about auditing, but considerably less about construction. So, while lines and cracks may be acceptable under my eyes as 60 years looms worryingly on the horizon, they are not acceptable in the walls of the various jerry-built houses that the landlady owns.

You can accuse me of having feet of clay if you like, but I would rather have feet of clay than foundations of clay. So, I would rent rather than build a house and, by the way, give me Latin any time!

Five, not four, jokers in a pack

(12 December 2010)

In response to the question, "What is your favourite joke?" Kevin replied:

> "Don't criticise masturbation. It is sex with the person you love (i.e. yourself)."

However, when he told this joke to 4 Ugandans (Francis 24, IT; Raymond,31, student of mental health at Butabika Hospital; Peter, 35, and Lawrence, 24, both electricians), despite their excellent spoken English, not only did they not laugh, but they did not understand the joke until Kevin explained it slowly and methodically to them.

However, this did provide the opportunity for Kevin to ask each of them to tell their own favourite joke.

Handsome Lawrence's joke also involved that most wonderful commodity, sex:

> "A female student once lost the keys to the school store. The Acholi headteacher wanted to punish her. He locked her in his office with him, and said, 'You either give me the keys or lie down for six strokes.' But, unfortunately, because of his thick Acholi accent, his pronunciation of 'keys' sounded like 'kiss', and 'six' just like 'sex'!"

Francis's joke was short:

> "A husband complains to his wife, 'You never buy me anything!' The wife replied, 'When you die I will buy you a *kanzu* to bury you in.'"

Peter came up with a joke he had already told me last year. It involves a "stupid" girl, her knickers and climbing a tree. I did not find it funny in 2009, and it was no funnier in 2010.

Last, but not least, came Raymond. Regretfully, the *Monitor* insists that *Sunday Life* is a family magazine, whatever that might mean. I have told its editor that if the magazine wishes to focus so much on kids, perhaps *Monitor Publications Limited* should move into publishing primary school books? Anyway, what this censorious policy means is that I cannot tell you Raymond's joke because it would be regarded as unsuitable for a "family" audience. Let me just tell you, dear readers, that the joke involves oranges, berries, pineapples and men's bums. And if you contact me at the address below, I would be pleased to email you the full, uncensored version of Raymond's joke.

Nabbed by the traffic cops
(23 January 2011)

My goodness, *mukyala* was angry. In the 30 years since their first date, her husband had rarely seen her so full of rage.

Yet, an hour before, as she had set off along the Entebbe Road, to collect me from Banana Village near Garuga, she was perfectly calm. So, what had happened to convert her mood from a placid puddle of calmness into raging rapids of venom?

Well, she had been nabbed by the traffic cops just before Kajjansi for driving at 60kph in a 50kph zone. She would have to pay a Ug Sh 100,000 fine at Diamond Trust Bank, then return to Kajjansi Police Station to collect her confiscated driving permit.

Now, it is reassuring to see an increasing number of traffic policemen on Uganda's dangerous roads. Though, whoever chose their white uniforms must surely have shares in *Omo* and *Nomi*. But, my wife was angered for 2 reasons.

Firstly, she did not see the 50 km speed limit road sign. In countries such as the UK, road signs are generally single, lonely fellas, which one cannot fail to spot as they look forward to a life of bachelordom. In contrast, Ugandan road signs are polygamous, surrounding themselves with *byana* (girlfriends) i.e. other signs and notices for schools, clinics, supermarkets etc. In this forest of sexual freedom and procreation, it is very easy not to see the roadside *mzee*, as he struts his stuff amongst so many admirers.

Secondly, as a friend in Entebbe was later to tell us, "everyone knows that there are cops with speed guns at Kajjansi." Everyone, except my wife, that is. Indeed, so well known is their presence, that when my wife returned to Kajjansi to collect her permit, the officer in charge told her that only 4 motorists had been "done" on that day for speeding. Thus, when the typical driver approaches Kajjansi they slow down, and then madly accelerate as soon as they get past the traffic cops. There sadly remains, therefore, much dangerous fast driving on the Entebbe Road.

The problem for the cops is that while there is a forest of polygamous signs, there are very few maximum speed limit ones, and thus very few places where the police can stand with speed guns.

So, what are the lessons of all this? Firstly, if you are a sign on the Entebbe Road, use a condom, because there are enough of you already. Secondly, that the police, as a matter of urgency, must get more maximum speed limit signs in place, so they can vary the location of their speed guns on a daily basis.

Spam, spam and spam

(10 April 2011)

In a recent column, *Roving Eye* observed, "I like my coffee like my women – hot, sweet and black."

So, it was with considerable excitement that I read an email from Edna Peters Garang.

It started with, "Hello Dear," which was, in itself, enough to get my underpants bulging. But the next sentences made me feel that this could be a good morning for pocketing:

> "I am 22 years of age and from Sudan....I want friendship with you that shows mutual understanding, trust and love. My interests include making friends, internet surfing and swimming."

I thought that Edna and I might not only surf the internet together, but also surf each other's bodies.

On the same day, I received an email from Mr Samuel Kofi (Branch Manager, International Commercial Bank, Kumasi, Ghana) who wished to transfer twelve million seven hundred and fifty thousand (12,750,000) dollars into my personal bank account, of which I would be allowed to keep 35%. Armed with a calculator, I worked out that my share would be 4,462,500 dollars i.e. almost as much as my monthly salary from the *Sunday Monitor*.

So, Edna wanted to transfer love, Samuel wanted to transfer money, and it still wasn't even midday. Oh, what a wonderful continent Africa is!

What both these emails have in common is that they are spam i.e. unsolicited and indiscriminate bulk messages. I learnt from a website that Samuel's email is an example of:

"the so-called '419' (advance fee) scam. It is a type of fraud dominated by criminals from Nigeria and other countries in Africa. Victims of the scam are promised a large amount of money, such as a lottery prize, inheritance, money sitting in some bank account etc. Victims never receive this non-existent fortune but are tricked into sending their money to the criminals, who remain anonymous. They hide their real identity and location by using fake names and fake postal addresses as well as communicating via anonymous free email accounts and mobile phones."

And, Edna, if I am wrong, and your email is genuine and not spam, then you can contact me at the email address below. After all, what man would not wish to tinker with a Dinka?

Why I fear driving

(7 November 2015)

I do not like driving and I especially do not like driving on Ugandan roads. I have developed a fear of driving, which Christine Katende in her excellent article (*Daily Monitor* July 9 2015) calls "driving phobia."

This fear has many causes, the most obvious of which is the huge number of horrific road accidents that we read about daily in our newspapers. A recent example was when 3 people were killed (including an NTV journalist and *Miss Tourism Northern Uganda 2014*) on the Kampala-Masaka highway. Their *Toyota Prado* had nine occupants (instead of the maximum of six) and its driver was told, as they were late for the *Miss Tourism* beauty pageant for western Uganda in Mbarara, to drive more quickly. According to one news report, the result was that the driver "lost control of the vehicle and it swerved off the road and plunged into a swamp." All road deaths are unpleasant, but there is something particularly horrible when thinking about the unnecessary loss of a beautiful young woman, and her no doubt mangled body being retrieved from the crash scene.

Accident causes
The cause of the above accident, and so many others, was speeding, or to use a Ugandanism, "overspeeding". Ugandan pedestrians generally walk in slow, languid fashion. But put them behind the steering wheel of a car or lorry and many (especially the men) will convert – and I don't mean become "born-agains" –to being vehicular monsters, with foot glued to depressed accelerator.

Another source of accidents is overtaking, especially overtaking on bends or when there is a continuous yellow dividing line which prohibits overtaking. Though I think many drivers don't know the meaning of the line, or if they do, ignore it.

Our *matatu* driver friends display many faults on the road. But the one that particularly irritates me is their non-use of the right hand side mirror. They pull out irrespective of whether another vehicle is just about to pass them.

Bina Baby
It was reassuring to learn from Katende's article that many other people share, with me, a fear of driving. One is Dembe FM's Bina Baby (Robinah Mbabazi). Robinah comes across as a confident person, but she is most certainly not when behind that dreaded steering wheel. She says:

> "Although I invested in driving lessons, the fear of driving has not disappeared...... I still cannot overtake or drive in

the middle of the road because I am afraid I might be crashed by the car behind me."

Kevin Baby and Bina Baby must be twins, and if it was not for our differing bum sizes, we would surely be identical twins. I, too:
- Do not drive at night.
- Automatically think I have made a mistake when I hear another driver hoot.
- Find it difficult to park in allocated spaces – I certainly cannot reverse into one, and need a space, almost as long as the Owen Falls Bridge, when driving forward into one.

Lucky Dube and my wife

A method I use to reduce my anxiety behind the wheel is to play CDs of the late, great Lucky Dube. I find his music and voice reassuring and soothing. It is true he died in a car, but it was not in a road accident – he was killed in a carjack in Johannesburg on 18 October 2007.

But the best solution to my fear of driving is not to drive at all! My wife is a much better driver than me, so she does all the driving. This reality leads to two further points.

Firstly, a close Ugandan female friend told us that:

> "A Ugandan man would never say 'My wife is a much better driver than me.'" So, Ugandan husbands, is this true?

Secondly, what then is my role in our car, other than sitting in the passenger seat in shades, unsuccessfully trying to look handsome? Well, it's back to Bina Baby and myself being twins – in the car I am a DJ who selects CD tracks to play, or flicks between FM music stations to avoid all adverts. What a tough life I have!

Glossary

Bazungu: white people (sing. *muzungu*)
Boda-boda: bicycle/motorcycle taxi
Dduuka: small shop
Enfuddu: tortoise
Ekidukaano: diarrhoea
Ekimansulo: striptease
Enyongeza: a bit extra
Kaamulali: The *Red Pepper* (newspaper)
Katogo: a traditional dish, defined as a mixture of ingredients, or stew
Kaveera: polythene bag
Kikoyi: traditional garment worn under a *gomesi*
Kwanjula: ceremony where a prospective bridegroom is formally introduced to and accepted by his fiancée's family
Kyana: colloquial for girlfriend/mistress (pl. *byana*)
Kyeyo: manual work overseas
Long call: defecate
Maaso awo: stop ahead there – used by *matatu* commuters so the drivers can stop
Mandela National Stadium (in Kampala): more commonly referred to as Namboole Stadium
Matatu: 14-passenger commuter taxi
Mukene: tiny silvery fish (similar in appearance to whitebait)
Mukyala: wife or lady

Murram road: reddish earthen road
Muzigo: one/two roomed rented accommodation (pl. *mizigo*)
Mzee: elderly person, generally male – word of Swahili origin but commonly used throughout eastern Africa
Olugambo: gossip
Pupu: faeces
Savedee: born again Christian
Sigiri: charcoal stove
Susu: urinate (also "short call")
Taata: father
Wofuna parking: park where you can – interchangeably used instead of *maaso awo*

Currency exchange rates are those pertaining at the date of publication of an article.

In 2015, the Ugandan Shilling was rapidly depreciating. In December 2015: £1 = Ug Sh 5180; US$1 = Ug Sh 3374